CAMBRIDGE LIBRARY COLLECTION

Books of enduring scholarly value

British and Irish History, Nineteenth Century

This series comprises contemporary or near-contemporary accounts of the political, economic and social history of the British Isles during the nineteenth century. It includes material on international diplomacy and trade, labour relations and the women's movement, developments in education and social welfare, religious emancipation, the justice system, and special events including the Great Exhibition of 1851.

The Christian and Civic Economy of Large Towns

This three-volume study by the Scottish churchman and social reformer Thomas Chalmers (1780–1847) is a revealing work of Christian morality as applied to urban economic theory. Having moved to Glasgow in 1815, Chalmers was given a free hand in 1819 for an experiment in urban ministry at the new parish of St John's in the poorest district of the city. His reforms improved education and reduced the need for institutional poor relief by dividing the area into manageable 'proportions' that were closely looked after by parish elders and deacons, reviving a traditional community spirit and promoting self-help. Volume 3, published in 1826, was written after Chalmers left St John's to become Chair of Moral Philosophy at St Andrew's. It focuses on the relationship between labour, wages and poor relief, discussing how labouring classes should not depend upon welfare and wages to relieve want, but rather practise self-help to reform their condition from below.

Cambridge University Press has long been a pioneer in the reissuing of out-of-print titles from its own backlist, producing digital reprints of books that are still sought after by scholars and students but could not be reprinted economically using traditional technology. The Cambridge Library Collection extends this activity to a wider range of books which are still of importance to researchers and professionals, either for the source material they contain, or as landmarks in the history of their academic discipline.

Drawing from the world-renowned collections in the Cambridge University Library and other partner libraries, and guided by the advice of experts in each subject area, Cambridge University Press is using state-of-the-art scanning machines in its own Printing House to capture the content of each book selected for inclusion. The files are processed to give a consistently clear, crisp image, and the books finished to the high quality standard for which the Press is recognised around the world. The latest print-on-demand technology ensures that the books will remain available indefinitely, and that orders for single or multiple copies can quickly be supplied.

The Cambridge Library Collection brings back to life books of enduring scholarly value (including out-of-copyright works originally issued by other publishers) across a wide range of disciplines in the humanities and social sciences and in science and technology.

The Christian
and Civic Economy
of Large Towns

VOLUME 3

THOMAS CHALMERS

CAMBRIDGE UNIVERSITY PRESS

Cambridge, New York, Melbourne, Madrid, Cape Town,
Singapore, São Paolo, Delhi, Mexico City

Published in the United States of America by Cambridge University Press, New York

www.cambridge.org
Information on this title: www.cambridge.org/9781108062374

© in this compilation Cambridge University Press 2013

This edition first published 1826
This digitally printed version 2013

ISBN 978-1-108-06237-4 Paperback

THE

CHRISTIAN

AND

CIVIC ECONOMY

OF

LARGE TOWNS.

BY

THOMAS CHALMERS, D.D.

PROFESSOR OF MORAL PHILOSOPHY IN THE UNIVERSITY OF ST. ANDREWS.

VOL. III.

———

Glasgow:

PRINTED FOR WILLIAM COLLINS;

WILLIAM WHYTE & CO. AND WILLIAM OLIPHANT, EDINBURGH;

R. M. TIMS, AND WM. CURRY, JUN. & CO. DUBLIN;

AND G. B. WHITTAKER, LONDON.

1826.

CONTENTS.

—

CHAP. XVII.

PREFACE.

NEARLY three years have now elapsed since the publication of the Second Volume of this Work, during which time, circumstances have occurred, that have induced its Author somewhat to change the plan of the concluding Volume, and that have had the effect, furthermore, to retard, and he fears also, to enfeeble the execution of it. What he more particularly alludes to, is the recent history of those popular combinations, which have taken place all over the country, for a rise of wages. The truth is, that he had scarcely begun to investigate the connection between a poor-rate, and the price of labour, when the latter of these two elements, although in a different connection, became the subject of a most interesting practical treatment by Parliament on the one hand, and by the population on the other. He has long regarded it as one of the most mischievous effects of the English pauperism, that it depresses the wages of labour, and that, beneath the rate of its own compensations; and, of course, as one of the chief blessings to society that would follow in the train of its abolition, that we should forthwith behold a better paid, as well as a better principled class of workmen than before. He has ever been on the side of a more liberal remuneration for industry. But when the people took this cause into their own hands, and proceeded to enforce it in their own peculiar way, he could not but regret, that a cause so worthy of the highest efforts, both of philanthropy and patriotism, should have been dishonoured by the outrage and the violence wherewith it was associated. He has not, therefore, stepped out of his course, in order to treat of combinations. The subject has been thrown across his path, and he must have turned aside if he had shunned the encounter with it. The workmen of England, have aggravated, by their own misconduct, the prejudices of the more affluent orders against the cause of their advancement in society. And it might serve to appease these prejudices of the wealthy, as well as to tranquillize the feelings, and to elevate the habits of the poor, if, instead of that way of turbulence which they have tried and found so ineffectual, they could be made to understand that more excellent way, upon which, without noise, or uproar, or rebellion, they might raise the comfort and the sufficiency of their own condition, and at length attain to a permanently higher status in the commonwealth.

In his management of this question, the Author feels that he has laid himself open to two charges, which form nearly the opposite extremes of each other.   The first is, that he has most unnecessarily expanded that part of his demonstration, which rests on the most obvious, and generally admitted principles of political economy; and thus subjected all his intelligent readers to the annoyance of a most wearisome reiteration, and that, too, with nothing better than the merest truisms of the science.   All which he can plead in mitigation, is, that on every argument which stands related either to the virtue or comfort of the people at large, he would fain address himself to the popular under-standing.   He believes, that by a very direct and intelligible process, even our merest peasantry might be conducted from such notions as are the most elementary, to such lessons, as if practically observed by them, would both elevate and secure their economic condition in society.   Any truth which is pregnant with such important application as this, cannot be too clearly expounded, or too closely approximated to the capacities of the yet uninitiated and unlearned.   And should he be so fortunate as to gain the assent of the plebeian community, to those positions in which their wel-fare is mainly concerned, he will most gladly forego the sympathy of those philosophers, who can only breathe with delight among those heights of a loftier speculation, where the very obscurity in which they have enwrapt themselves, has served the two-fold purpose of mystifying their doctrine, and of magnifying their fame.

But the second charge that we apprehend is far

more serious. It is not enough that the lower classes should be instructed in the way of their economic amelioration. There is a certain prevalent imagination among the higher classes, that the cheapness of British labour lies at the very foundation of our country's prosperity and strength. Now, in advocating the cause of a higher remuneration for industry, we have to combat this imagination. We have to turn from the plebeians to the patricians of our commonwealth; and in so doing, it will be said that we have made a transition from such puerilities as no student of political science needs to be told of, to such paradoxes as no student of political science can possibly admit. This applies more especially to all that we have said of the nearly instant resuscitation of capital; and of the limits, whether natural or artificial, to the extension of foreign trade. We regret not to have delivered ourselves more fully upon these two subjects, and particularly on the latter of them. Independently altogether of the truth or falsehood of our principles, it will be said, and with good reason, that if they be in any way fitted to startle or to perplex by their novelty, they should not be offered to the first notice of readers in a subsidiary capacity, or be employed to aid the solution of a great practical question, while themselves so questionable. We are sensible, that a separate and general treatise would, at their first introduction to the view of the public, have been a better place for them.

In adopting our present course, we have been obliged to relinquish the consideration of those institutions, or public charities, which are related either to crime or to disease; such as prisons and penitentiaries, along with asylums, infirmaries, and various other receptacles for that involuntary suffering, which is apart from general indigence. We are the more reconciled, however, to this omission, that in a former volume of this work,* we have stated that great principle which applies to the latter institutions, and which we could only have expounded at greater length, had we resumed the subject. In regard to the former institutions, we have to remark, that the whole system both of ecclesiastical and of economic polity which we have ventured to recommend, has a direct bearing upon crime, in so far as regards the prevention of it; and that, without depreciating the worth of that philanthropy which has selected for its object the right management of prisons, we hold this to be of very inferior moment to the right management of parishes. We deem it of more importance that the one subject shall be perfected, than that the other shall be entered upon; and that the present volume is more in harmony with the two former, because, instead of being an appendix on the right treatment of the outcast few, it is a continued pleading in behalf of those methods which the Author conceives to be most effectual for enlight-

* See Vol. II. p. 218, &c.

B

ening the minds, and elevating the general condition, of the multitude.

There is one benefit that has resulted from this delay in the publication of the third volume. During the Author's suspension of his argument, experience, a far better schoolmaster than he, has been at work, and giving a few more of its lessons, to which he defers, as greatly more valuable than any reasonings of his own. The condition of that experimental parish which he left in Glasgow upwards of two years ago, is, in regard to its pauperism, far more flourishing than ever. It is well that he ceased to have the conduct of that experiment, and that it passed into other hands. The truth is, that by every month of his continuance in that city, the delusion was becoming more inveterate; that while the prosperity of the operation could not be denied, still it was a prosperity which hung altogether upon the exertions and the influence of the individual who had introduced it. That spell, he trusts, is now conclusively broken; and most glad he is to understand, that the now proclaimed experience of his successor in office, has spread a more just and more extensive conviction upon this subject, than he could have achieved himself by the labours of a whole incumbency.*
On this subject we again challenge the whole host of sceptics or of enemies to the scheme,

* We are glad to learn that Mr. M'Farlan is on the eve of publishing the results of his experience, while minister of St. John's Parish, Glasgow.

if they can substantiate one instance of jugglery in
the practical administration of it. Its success has
not been the result either of any collision, or of
any extraordinary combination of circumstances,
that could with difficulty be realized in other parishes. It is a scheme which seeks for itself no
more than toleration; and depends for its prosperous result, not on that strenuous management
among the office-bearers of a parish, which is rare,
but on a natural operation among the families of a
parish, which is universal,—an operation depending upon certain laws which are co-extensive with
the species, and stable as the constitution of humanity.

And here he must advert to the failure of that
attempt, which was recently made in Parliament
for the extension of this scheme to the country at
large. Mr. Kennedy, its author, evinced himself
to have an enlightened acquaintance with the parochial management of the question; a management, truly, in which all the natural and essential
principles of the problem are involved. The process defined by his bill, is the very process by which
a parish can be most safely and surely conducted
back again from a compulsory to a gratuitous system of pauperism. Yet it met with a general, and,
for the time, an effective opposition in Scotland,
—an opposition which might have been altogether
saved, had the proposal been not for an imperative, but for a permissive law. The distinction
between these two methods has been unfolded at

some length, in a former chapter of this work, on the parliamentary treatment of the question of pauperism. There could have been no such array of resistance called forth by the enactment of a leave to any parishes that would, as by the enactment of a law, binding on all parishes, whether they would or would not. To force an innovation upon the land, is a very different measure from making that innovation free to all those districts of the land where a sufficient concurrence shall be obtained in its favour, and where a voluntary application shall be made for it on the part of the local and existing authorities. In the one way, there must be the reaction of a simultaneous and wide-spread hostility. In the other way, there is no provocative offered to the adverse feeling of the many, by a mere offer of liberty to the few who are not adverse. Had even only two or three of the border parishes of Scotland entered the retracing process under the shelter of a permissive law, this were a sufficient germ for the spread and final prevalence of the gratuitous system of charity throughout all our borders. The success of a few outset parishes would at length ensure the imitation of all the rest. The process would be strictly a tentative one. That change which, if compulsory and instantaneous, would be felt and dreaded all over the land, like the violence of any sweeping whirlwind, would, under such a permissive operation, go quietly forward from parish to parish, by a series of firm, because by a se-

ries of experimental stepping-stones. The old
Scottish system, for it is utterly wrong to call it a
new system, would recover place and confidence,
just as it demonstrated its own efficacy in those
parishes that had resumed it, under an act guarded
and modified in the only way which could make
such an act at all tolerable. At every step of its
progress, we are persuaded that it would stand
more erect than before, in the pride and confidence
of its vindicated honours; while all the brightness
which it gathered on its path, would be, not from
the meteoric light of theory, but the light of a
sound, and sure, and sober experience. And it is
not till, in the blaze of this experimental light, the
truth had become so manifest as to overpower the
convictions of all; not perhaps then, till after the
lapse of one or two generations, should we expect
those greater cities of our land to adopt in the
permissive, that which they had rejected in the
imperative form, or to open their gates for that
system as a friend, the appearance of which, in the
guise of an invader, had so promptly and so powerfully alarmed them.

It is thus that the soundest cause might sustain
a temporary mischief, from circumstances for which
it is not in any way responsible. And here we
might advert to that discredit and derision which
were incurred, in consequence of a glaring inaccuracy in the editing or printing of a former number
of the Edinburgh Review. The Author of this
volume contributed the whole of the first article in

the 58th number of that work, on the causes and cure of pauperism, and the *first half* of the very short article which concludes that number. Its remaining half was appended to it, but not by him, nor was he at all aware of it till after the publication. It is in this appended part that there occurs a most provoking misstatement of the number of paupers in England, by which it is estimated at ten times greater an amount than it ought to be. This might have passed for a typographical error, had it only occurred once, as the statement was first made in figures, and could have been easily accounted for by the omission of a cypher. But then, in the next paragraph, it is again blazoned forth, not in figures, but in ordinary language; and proved most annoying to the Author at the time, from the grotesque character which it was fitted to stamp on the whole speculation wherewith it was associated. He did no more, however, than intimate the error to the celebrated editor of the journal, and publish a correction of it in one of the Glasgow newspapers.* It has since been commented upon with great severity in many pamphlets, and many periodicals. The slip is so

---

* The insertion appeared in the Glasgow Herald of Friday, May 1st, 1818, under the head or title of " Edinburgh Review;" and the following is that part of the insertion which relates to the error in question:—
" Another extravagant error has been admitted into pages 500 and 501, on the same subject; where, for $9\frac{1}{4}$ paupers in each 10 of the population, it should have been printed $9\frac{1}{4}$ in each 100; and for nine tenths, it should have been nine hundredth parts."

very monstrous a one, that it might appear ridiculous to make it the subject of any grave explanation. But, of all men, it is most incumbent on the advocate of a controverted or obnoxious principle, to observe the most scrupulous accuracy in the facts and details of his argument; for his smallest inadvertency might furnish a triumph to the adversaries of a good cause, or give a colour to their most wicked and malignant imputations.

THE

CHRISTIAN AND CIVIC ECONOMY

OF

LARGE TOWNS.

CHAP. XVII.

ON THE WAGES OF LABOUR.

THE difficulties of removing such a great national evil as pauperism, are of two classes, which are wholly distinct the one from the other; and it would clear away much of its darkness and perplexity from the question, were these difficulties kept by the inquirer as separate in thought, as they are separate in reality. The first difficulties are those which are presented by the economic condition of the lower orders. They are such difficulties as have their seat among the circumstances and necessities of the people. It is the imagination of many, that to do away a legal provision for indigence, would be to abandon a large population to a destitution and distress that were most revolting to humanity ; and in as far as this imagination is true, it offers a most formidable difficulty, and one, indeed, which should foreclose the question altogether. The population ought not to be so abandoned; and if, in virtue of the abolition of pauperism, they shall become worse either in comfort or character than before, then this abolition ceases to be desirable. We happen to think, that no such consequences would ensue, and that, on the supplies of public charity being withdrawn, there would not only be much less of actual want in the country, but that this want would be sure to find relief, and in a way greatly more consistent both with the comfort and virtue of families. In other words, we happen to think, that the first difficulties have no real or substantive existence whatever—that if any portion of the British territory were submitted, in a right way, to the trial,* they would, one and all of them, vanish before the touch of experience—and therefore, that, by a series of distinct and successive operations on each of the portions, the whole of our land might at length be made to emerge from this sore evil. In as far as the needs and habits of the population are concerned, we hold the problem to be manageable, and most easily manageable; and, such being our conviction, we have long deemed it a worthy object of our most strenuous endeavours to prove

---

* For the method of conducting such a trial, in any parish, see the 16th chapter—and for the method of obtaining permission for the trial, see the 15th chapter of this work.

it so by argument, or, what is still better, to evince it so by actual exhibition.

But, one cannot be long engaged in the prosecution of such a task, without coming into contact with other difficulties which are wholly distinct from the former, and which may be termed the factitious, or political difficulties of the question. Even though there should be, as we believe, no essential or natural difficulties at all, yet the difficulties of this second class are enough, in themselves, to retard the progress of light and of sound doctrine upon the subject, and far more to retard the accomplishment of any sound practical reformation. It is a very possible thing, both that certain views should be just and well-founded; and yet that those whose co-operation is indispensable to give effect to these views, should be very long of giving their consent to them. One might feel no difficulty in ridding any specified district of its pauperism, after that he has been permitted to take his own way, and pursue his own measures, with its families—while, at the same time, he may feel the uttermost difficulty in gaining the permission. They who have the constitutional right, either to arrest his proceedings, or to allow of them, must first be satisfied; and whether from honest conviction, or from the tenacity of a wedded adherence to old and existing methods, they may stand in the way of all innovation. Ere he come into contact with the human nature of the question among the poor themselves, he may have far greater obstacles against him in the law of the question, and in the obstinate prejudice or wilfulness of those men with whom the right is vested of adjudging or administering for the poor. We should like the reader's clear apprehension, of the utter difference and dissimilarity which there is between these two sets of difficulties. The place of encounter with the one is in the parish, and among the applicants for relief from the parish. The place of encounter with the other may be in the vestry, where men have assembled to act upon the law; or in the quarter sessions, where men have assembled to pronounce upon, and to enforce the law; or, finally, within the walls of Parliament, where the proposal is submitted to repeal or to rectify the law. It may be true, that there is a system of utmost facility, which, if adopted, shall be of omnipotent effect to expel pauperism from a parish, and with less of want and wretchedness among its families than before; and also true, that there shall be a weary struggle with the incredulity and perverse misconceptions of influential men, ere the system shall be suffered to have a trial. It might so be, that there is a method, which, after that it is established, shall be found of easy and effective operation amongst the poor, but which, before that it is established, shall have to encounter many years of formidable resistance amongst the present guides and governors of the poor. And this is enough to make the problem of Pauperism a difficult problem. But still it is of importance precisely to see where the difficulty lies —and not to confound the natural difficulties which are inherent in the subject of management, with the political difficulties by which the way of the philanthropist is beset, when he comes into collision with the prejudices or partialities of those who at present have the right or the power of management.

At the same time, it ought to be remembered, that if the natural difficulties of the problem be indeed so very light and conquerable, its political difficulties must, of necessity, subside, and at length vanish altogether. It is the imagination, in fact, of the greatness of its essential difficulties, that mainly gives rise to the opposition of our influential men, or to what is still more hopeless than their active opposition, the listlessness and apathy of their despair. Could we succeed in proving, that there is really nothing in the condition of the lower orders which presents an insuperable barrier to the abolition of pauperism, the barrier of prejudice and dislike, on the part of the higher orders, to any radical change, must finally give way. Truth may be withstood long, but it cannot be withstood eternally. The provisions of Law will at length be made to accord with the principles of Nature; and whatever shall be found by experience, in the human nature of the question, to be most wholesome for the people, the law of the question must, in time, be

moulded into a conformity therewith. The voice
of wisdom will ascend from the Parish to the Parliament; and the light which is struck out among
the details and verifications of but an humble
district in the land, will ultimately force all those
inveteracies that now barricade the hall of Legislation.

Let me now give one or two specimens of the
way in which both sound opinion, and sound policy, may be baffled, and, for a time, arrested;
and that, in virtue of certain impediments, to
which even the most enlightened views on the
question of Pauperism stand peculiarly exposed.

There is first, then, an incredulity which is sure
to be immediately lighted up, on the mention of
so great an achievement, as the deliverance of a
whole empire from its legal and compulsory Pauperism. The very hopelessness of a result so
mighty and marvellous, induces a heedlessness of
every explanation that can be offered regarding it.
The thing looks so utterly impracticable, as to
carry, in the mere announcement of it, its own
refutation. The apparent romance and unlikeli-
hood of the whole speculation, beget a certain
arch incredulity on the part of the hearer; and
this is the most unfortunate posture that can well
be imagined, for the entertainment of any demonstration in its favour. And there is really so
much of empiricism in the world—the public ear
has been so repeatedly assailed by the crudity,
and the nostrum, and the splendid imagination,

of successive adventurers—so manifold have been the promising theories which have passed, one after another, before the view of British society, and then passed away into utter abortiveness, that truly we cannot wonder, if the general infidelity be now so strong, as to have settled down into the attitude, not merely of determined unbelief, but of downright listlessness. This is the kind of outset that we have to encounter, at the very opening of our proposals on the subject of Pauperism; and the more surely, because of the magnitude of that change after which we aspire. It is this magnitude which stamps an aspect of extravagance and wildness on the whole speculation; insomuch, that the only treatment that is held meet for it, by many, is a rejection as summary and contemptuous as if it were one of the visions of Utopia.

Now, to meet this impression, and to overcome the incredulity which is founded upon it, it can be urged, that though suddenly a very great achievement may be impracticable, yet that gradually it may not be so—that a way may be devised of breaking it into distinct and successive steps, each of which is most easily practicable—that though the proposed transition is far too gigantic to be accomplished at once, yet that piece-meal, and by inches, the whole of it may be described in time, with no other than every-day instruments, and no other help than that of ordinary men—that though the mischief cannot be exterminated by a blow, it may by a process: And so, the whole of our demand is not for a sublime power that shall inflict the one, but for a sober-minded patience, that shall wait the result of the other. This is the very nature of our proposal for the extinction of pauperism. We have no mystic charm to propose, that shall work an instant extermination. We would go over the ground, not by flights, but by footsteps—insomuch, that the deliverance of a single parish is not completed but by the disappearance of its whole existing generation of paupers; and the deliverance of the whole empire is not completed, but by this separate operation being repeated upon each, till it has overtaken all the parishes. We are not aware of one impracticable link or stepping-stone in the whole of that consecutive series, by which, at length, the evil, in its last vestiges, may be utterly swept away; and what we should like to press into this service, is not the enthusiasm that will impel to a lofty and magnificent daring after some enterprise which is great, but the assiduity that will work its way through a course or succession of littles, and, without any straining or impetuosity whatever, will wait for the termination of it.

But no sooner do we get rid of one antipathy, than we are instantly met by another. The very men who have no credit for what is great, may have no value for what is gradual. When, to get the better of their incredulity about the efficacy of our process, we tell them how slow it is, then we have just as hard an encounter as before with their indifference. There is the substitution of one mental prejudice or perversity for another; and in making our escape from the first, we run into a conflict with the second. In the first instance, there is the same unbelief in the possibility of all pauperism being done away, as they would have in a magical performance; and in the second instance, whatever is to be done in the way of reformation, has no charm for them, unless it can be done with a rapidity that would be altogether magical. We do not see how it is possible to suit the taste of such people with any acceptable speculation on the subject of pauperism—sceptical as they are of any relief being practicable, and, at the same time, impatient as they are for that relief being immediate. We cannot devise for them a scheme that shall at once be moderate enough in its aim to suit the narrowness of their apprehensions, and at the same time speedy enough in its operation to suit the extravagance of their wishes. When they hear the promise of a total deliverance, they spurn it away from them as romantic. When the romance is mitigated, by the proposal that the deliverance shall be very gradual, they spurn it away from them as tardy. It is not more beyond the limits of human strength to do what is great in a great time, than to do what is small in a small time; but they will not allow these elements to be properly sorted together. They first quarrel with the greatness of the achievement, as the thing which makes it to be hopeless; and then they quarrel with the greatness of the time which is required for doing it, as the thing which makes it to be worthless. After all, these are the more egregiously romantic, who would have nothing to be done, unless it can be brought about with the quickness of legerdemain; and theirs is the imagination which, of all others, outruns the soberness both of arithmetic and experience. It is not uncommon that the same individual should feel distrust in the possibility of some given accomplishment, because of a greatness that threw over it an air of the marvellous, and, at the same time, an utter disregard for the accomplishment at all, unless it could be done with a velocity which would indeed make it marvellous. This incredulity on the one hand, and impatience on the other, are frequently attributes of the same mind, although as frequently, perhaps, each is realized separately on two distinct classes; and it is between those who are hopeless, and those who are precipitate, that it is so difficult to extricate a nation from the evils of a wrong domestic economy.

And yet, if a method be proposed, by which relief from a great existing pressure might be made to commence immediately, although it cannot be completed immediately, this surely should be held as not altogether unworthy of regard. Though not wholly lightened in a year of some

grievous burden, yet if a process can be devised
by which it shall be made lighter next year than
it is at present, and gradually lighter each successive year, until it has melted finally away, this
surely ought not to be treated with indifference,
because of the many impetuous spirits, who will
be satisfied with nothing short of a deliverance
that shall both be total and immediate. The man
who is heavily in debt, will be thankful of deliverance, even though it should be only by successive
instalments. And it is thus, that we would have
the cure and the clearing away of pauperism to
proceed. The relief commences immediately,
but it must proceed by instalments. There may
be the lapse of a whole generation ere it is con-
summated. We do not propose to lift the en-
chanter's wand, for the purpose of an instant dissipation. The evil must be dissipated gradually.
We do think that great things may be done, but
we demand time for the doing of them. We do
not ask that any gigantic strength should be put
forth, but only that a sober and very practicable
business should be persevered in.

There are various methods, and these gradual
ones too, by which it is proposed to attack this
hydra of pauperism, and, if possible, by inches
to destroy it. For the full exposition of our own
method, we must refer to former chapters of this
work ; and we now enter on the consideration of
another method which still engrosses a good deal
the attention of our public and parliamentary

men. It is to be observed, that indigence may arise from two sources—either from inability for work, or from the inadequacy of its wages. The original pauperism of England, it is said, was restricted to those who were poor from impotency; and it is regarded by many as an abuse or corruption of it, that it should ever have been extended to able-bodied labourers, in order to make up for any deficiency in their wages. Now, the great aim at present is, to repress pauperism within its original limits, by putting an end altogether to this latter application of the poor's fund,—thus separating between the distress which age and impotency bring upon the labouring classes, and the distress which is occasionally brought upon them by the fluctuations in the price of labour. There are some who would be satisfied with the lopping off of this last excrescence from the system of poor-laws in England; while others contemplate the possibility, and admit the desirableness of an ulterior reformation. We think that there is a gradual process for the extermination of the system in both its branches, which is alike applicable, and from the very outset of it, to each of them. Yet this does not supersede the importance of discussing, separately and at some length, the effects of a poor rate when applied in aid of defective wages. We feel, however, that this will require a few preliminary explanations.*

---

* We are quite sensible that several of the principles advanced in the course of our discussions, are abundantly obvious to all who are in any way

The first thing to be attended to, is the way in which the price of any article brought to market is affected by the variations of its supply on the one hand, and of the demand for it on the other. The holders of sugar, for example, after having reserved what they need for their own use, bring the whole surplus to market, where they dispose of it in return for those other things which they do need. It must be quite obvious, that if there be more of this sugar exposed than there is a demand for, the great force of the competition will be among the sellers, to get it off their hands. Each will try to outstrip the others, by holding out a greater inducement for purchasers to buy from him—and this he can only do by holding it out to them on cheaper terms. It is thus that each tries to undersell the rest—or, in other words, the great supply of any article of exchange is always sure to bring down the price of it.

On the other hand, let the same article have been sparingly brought into the market, insomuch that, among the buyers, there is a demand for it to a greater extent than it is to be had. The force

---

conversant with the first elements of political science. It may be thought, that, on this account, they should be immediately assumed as the basis of an ulterior argument; but that it is an idle detention of the reader to argue over again to him those positions or doctrines wherewith he is fully satisfied already. But we can never help the feeling, that on this subject we are addressing practical, as well as studious and speculative men; and that, though at the hazard of other-satiating the latter by a redundant explicitness, we can scarcely err against the former either by an excess of simplicity or of copiousness.

of the competition now changes place. It is among the purchasers, instead of the sellers. Each will try to outstrip his neighbours, by holding out a larger inducement to the holders of a commodity now rare, and, therefore, in more urgent request, than usual. This he can only do by offering a greater price for it. It is thus that each tries to overbid the other—or, in other words, the small supply of any article of exchange is always sure to bring up the price of it.

The price, then, of a commodity, falls with the increase of the supply, and rises with the diminution of it; a law of political economy, which is expressed still more shortly thus—that the price of every article of commerce is inversely in proportion to its supply.

But it is conceivable, that there might be no variation whatever in the supply—that, from one week to another, the same quantity of sugar, or corn, or any other commodity, may be brought to market, and yet, for all this, may there be a great weekly variation in the price of them. The truth is, that not only may the holders of an article have not always the same quantity on hand for sale, but the buyers may not always have the same need of it. There may be a fluctuation in the demand for an article, as well as in the supply of it; and it is quite evident that the price just rises and falls with the demand, instead of rising and falling inversely to it. Hence the more extended aphorism in political economy, that the price of any commodity is directly in proportion to the demand, and inversely in proportion to the supply—a doctrine that is somewhat more loosely and generally expressed, by saying, that the price of an article depends on the proportion which the demand and the supply bear to each other.

There is nought in the interposition of money to affect this process. Its office is merely to facilitate the exchange of commodities. But the proportion of their quantities in the exchange is just the same, when made to pass through such an intermedium, as when brought closely and directly into barter. The venders of so much corn may, with the price of it, buy so much sugar. It is not convenient to bring both these articles, or perhaps either of them, in bulk and body, to the scene of the negotiation; and so the money that is received for the one is given for the other. This, however, does not affect the proportion between the number of quarters of the one commodity, which, in the then state of the market, is held as equivalent to the number of hundred-weights of the other commodity. This depends on the two elements of demand and supply alone; and is the same as if the expedient of money for carrying into effect the contracts of merchandise, had never been devised.

The mere intervention, then, of money, will not perplex the reader out of a right estimation upon this subject. He has only to remember, that either by adding to the supply of any article, or lessening the demand for it, the price of it is diminished; and that either by lessening the supply, or adding to the demand, the price of it is increased.

Now there are certain articles, that, in this respect, are far more tremulous than others, or that more readily vibrate in price, and with a much wider range too of fluctuation. All are aware of the fluctuations of the corn market; and how, in consequence, the heart, and often the frenzy, of deep and desperate adventure, are associated with the temptations and the losses of such a trade. The truth is, that, generally speaking, the necessaries of life are far more powerfully affected in the price of them by a variation in their quantity, than are the luxuries of life. Let the crop of grain be deficient by one-third in its usual amount, or rather, let the supply of grain in the market, whether from the home produce or by importation, be curtailed to the same extent,—and this will create a much greater addition than of one-third to the price of it. It is not an unlikely prediction, that its cost would be more than doubled by the shortcoming of one-third or one-fourth in the supply. Not so with an article of luxury, and more especially if something else can be purchased for it in the way of substitution. For example, let such be the failure of West India produce, on any particular year, that rum is deficient by one-third from its usual supply. There will be a consequent rise in the price of it, but nothing at all like the rise which an equal deficiency would create in the price of grain.

Such is the fact; and there can be no difficulty in apprehending the cause of it. Men can more easily suffer the deprivation or the diminution of a luxury; and when its price offers to rise extravagantly, they can limit their demand for it. I can commute the use of rum, for the use of another and a cheaper substitute; or, failing this, I can restrain my consumption, or abandon it altogether. Its scarcity will enhance its cost on the one hand; but this, on the other hand, can be met or counteracted, to any extent, by a slackening of the demand. The point of equilibrium between the sellers and the buyers of rum will be shifted; and its price will become higher than before, but not so high as it would have been, had rum been an indispensable of human comfort, and therefore given all the more of urgency to the applications of purchasers. This is not the case with rum; but it is so with grain. The mass of our families could not, without distress or great inconvenience, limit their use of it to two-thirds of their wonted consumption. Each will press forward to obtain a larger share of the general stock than his neighbour; and it is just this earnest competition among the buyers, that raises the price of necessaries greatly beyond the proportion by which the supply of them is deficient. Men can live without luxuries; and will be content to put up with a smaller allowance of them for a season, rather than pay that price to which they would be elevated by a demand as intense as all must have for the neces-

saries of existence. Men cannot live without necessaries, and will not be so content to put up with
a reduced allowance of them, as they would of the
mere comforts or expensive gratifications of luxury.
It is thus that the same proportional lack in each
class of commodities gives rise to such a difference
of effect in augmenting the price of each of them;
and it is just the more earnest demand, in the one
case than in the other, that explains the difference.

A failure in the general supply of esculents to
the extent of one-half, would more than quadruple
the price of the first necessaries of life, and would
fall with very aggravated pressure on the lower orders. A failure to the same extent in all the vine-
yards of the world, would most assuredly not raise
the price of wine to any thing near this proportion.
Rather than pay four times the wonted price for
Burgundy, there would be a general descent, on
the part of its consumers in high life, to claret, or
from that to port, or from that to the home-
made wines of our own country, or from that
to its spirituous, or from that to its fermented
liquors. And the facility of thus substituting
one indulgence for another, is not the only refuge against an enormous charge upon these articles. There is also the facility of limiting the
amount of the indulgence, or of withdrawing from
it altogether—a refuge that is not so open to the
population under a famine of the first necessaries
of existence. There is much of shifting and of
substitution certainly among families, when such a

calamity visits them—as from animal to vegetable
food, from flour to meal, from meal to potatoes.
But, on the supposition of a general short-coming
in the yearly produce of the land, the price of each
of these articles rises successively with the run of
purchasers towards them. On the one hand, the
eagerness of demand after all the varieties of food,
will enhance the price of all, and greatly beyond
the proportion of the deficiency in the supply of
them; and, on the other hand, this enhanced price
is necessary so to restrain the consumption of the
families, as to make the deficient stock of provisions stand out till the coming of the next harvest.
It is thus, by the way, that a population survive so
well those years of famine, when the prices, perhaps, are tripled.   This does not argue, as is obvious from the explanations which we have now
given, that they must therefore be three times worse
fed than usual. The food of the country may only,
for aught we know, have been lessened by a fourth
part of its usual supply; or, in other words, the
families may, at an average, be served with three-
fourths of their usual subsistence, at the very time
that the cost of it is three times greater than usual.
And to make out this larger payment, they have
just for a year to retrench in other articles—altogether, it is likely, to give up the use of comforts,
and to limit themselves more largely in the second,
than they can possibly do in the first necessaries of
life—to forego, perhaps, many of the little season-
ings wherewith they wont to impart a relish to their
coarse and humble fare, to husband more strictly

their fuel, and be satisfied for a while with vestments more threadbare, and even more tattered, than what, in better times, they would choose to appear in. It is thus that, even although the first necessaries of life should be tripled in price for a season, and although the pecuniary income of the labouring classes should not at all be increased, yet they are found to weather the hardships of such a visitation. The food is still served out to them at a much larger proportion than the cost of it would, in the first instance, appear to indicate. And, in the second instance, they are enabled to purchase at this cost; because, and more especially, if they be a well-habitted and a well-conditioned peasantry, with a pretty high standard of enjoyment in ordinary years, they have the more that they can save and retrench upon in a year of severe scarcity. They can disengage much of that revenue which before went to the purchase of dress, and of various luxuries that might, for a season, be dispensed with —and so have the more to expend on the materials of subsistence. It is this which explains how roughly a population can bear to be handled, both by adverse seasons, and by the vicissitudes of trade —and how, after all, there is a stability about a people's means which will keep its ground against many shocks, and amidst many fluctuations. It is a mystery and a marvel to many an observer, how the seemingly frail and precarious interest of the labouring classes should, after all, have the stamina of such endurance, as to weather the most fearful reverses both of commerce and of the seasons; and

that, somehow or other, you find, after an interval
of gloomy suffering and still gloomier fears, that
the families do emerge again into the same state of
sufficiency as before. We know not a fitter study
for the philanthropist, than the workings of that
mechanism by which a process so gratifying is
caused, or in which he will find greater reason to
admire the exquisite skill of those various adapta-
tions, that must be referred to the providence of
Him who framed society, and suited so wisely to
each other the elements whereof it is composed.

There is nought which appears more variable
than the operation of those elements by which the
annual supply of the national subsistence is regulated. How unlike in character is one season to
another; and between the extremes of dryness and
moisture, how exceedingly different may be the
amount of that produce on which the sustenance
of man essentially depends! Even after that the
promise of abundance is well nigh realized, the
hurricane of a single day passing over the yet un-
cut but ripened corn, or the rain of a few weeks,
to drench and macerate the sheaves that lie piled
together on the harvest-field, were enough to destroy the food of millions. We are aware of a compensation, in the varieties of soil and exposure, so
that the weather which is adverse to one part of
the country might be favourable to another; besides, that the mischief of a desolating tempest in
autumn must only be partial, from the harvest of
the plains and uplands falling upon different months.

Still, with all these balancing causes, the produce
of different years is very far from being equalized;
and its fluctuations would come charged with still
more of distress and destitution to families, were
there not a counterpoise to the laws of Nature, in
what may be termed the laws of Political Economy.

The price of human food does not immediately
depend on the quantity of it that is produced, but
on the quantity of it that is brought to market;
and it is well, that in every year of scarcity, there
should be instant causes put into operation for increasing the latter quantity to the uttermost, so as
to repair, as much as possible, the deficiencies
of the former. It is well, that even a small
short-coming in the crop should be so surely followed by a great advance of prices; for this has
instantly the effect of putting the families of the
land upon that shortness of allowance, which shall
cause the supply, limited as it is, to serve throughout the year. But, besides the wholesome restraint which is thus imposed on the general consumption of families, there is encouragement
given, by this dearness, to abridge the consumption upon farms, and, by certain shifts in their
management, to make out the greatest possible
surplus, for the object of sale, and of supply to
the population at large. With a high price, the
farmer feels it a more urgent interest, to carry as
much of his produce to market as he can; and,
for this purpose, he will retrench to the uttermost

at home. And he has much in his power. More particularly, he can and does retrench considerably upon the feed of his cattle; and, in as far as this wont to consist of potatoes or grain, there must an important addition be gained in this way to the supplies of the market. One must often have been struck with the comparative cheapness of animal food, in a year of scarcity. This is because of the greater slaughter of cattle which takes place in such a year, to save the heavy expense of maintaining them; and which, besides affording a direct accession to the sustenance of man, lightens still more the farm consumption, and disengages for sale a still greater amount of the necessaries of life. We do not say, but that the farm suffers a derangement by this change of regimen, from which it might take years to recover fully. But the evil becomes more tolerable by being spread. The horrors of extreme scarcity are prevented. The adversity is weathered, at its furthest point. The country emerges from the visitation, and without, in all probability, the starvation of one individual; and all, because from the operation of the causes that we have now explained, the supply of the market is made to oscillate within smaller limits than the crop—insomuch, that, though the latter should be deficient by one-third of the whole, the former might not be deficient by one-fifth or one-sixth of what is yielded usually.

This effect is greatly increased, by the suspending of distillation in years of scarcity. And after all, should the supplies be yet very short, and the prices therefore far more than proportionally high, this will naturally, and of itself, bring on the importation of grain from foreign parts. If such be the variety of weather and soil, even within the limits of a country, as in some measure to balance the scarcity which is experienced in one set of farms, by the comparative abundance of another set, this will apply with much greater force to a whole continent, or to the world at large. If a small deficiency in the home supply of grain induce a higher price than with other articles of commerce, this is just a provision for a securer and readier filling up of the deficiency, by a movement from abroad—a thing of far greater importance with the necessaries, than with the mere comforts or luxuries of life. That law of wider and more tremulous oscillation in the price of corn, which we have attempted to expound, is in itself a security for a more equal distribution of it over the globe by man, in those seasons when Nature has been partial—so as to diffuse the more certainly, and the more immediately, through the earth, that which has been dropped upon it unequally from heaven. It is well, that greater efficacy should thus be given to that corrective force, by which the yearly supplies of food are spread over the world with greater uniformity than they at first descend upon it; and, however much it may be thought to aggravate a people's hardships, that a slight failure in their home supply should create such a rise in the cost of necessaries, yet certainly it makes the impulse all the more powerful, by which corn flows in, from lands of plenty, to a land of famine. But what we have long esteemed the most beautiful part of this operation, is the instant advantage which a large importation from abroad gives to our export manufacturers at home. There is a limit in the rate of exchange to the exportation of articles from any country; but up to this limit, there is a class of labourers employed in the preparation of these articles. Now, the effect of an augmented importation upon the exchange is such as to enlarge this limit—so that our export traders can then sell with a larger profit, and carry out a greater amount of goods than before, and thus enlist a more numerous population in the service of preparing them. An increased importation always gives an impulse to exportation, so as to make employment spring up in one quarter, at the very time that it disappears in another. Or rather, at the very time when the demand for a particular commodity is slackened at home, it is stimulated abroad. We have already adverted to the way in which families shift their expenditure in a year of scarcity, diverting a far greater proportion of it than usual, to the first necessaries of life, and withdrawing it proportionally from the comforts, and even second necessaries of life. Cloth may be regarded as one of the

second necessaries; and it were woful indeed, if,
on the precise year when food was dearest, the
numerous workmen engaged in this branch of industry should find that employment was scarcest.
But in very proportion as they are abandoned by
customers at home, do they find a compensation
in the more quickened demand of customers from
abroad. It is in these various ways, that a country
is found to survive so well its hardest and heaviest
visitations; and even under a triple price for the
first articles of subsistence, it has been known to
emerge into prosperity again, without an authentic instance of starvation throughout all its families.

The better to illustrate the principles of our
immediate argument, we may here state a case
which looks at first to be an anomaly, and yet is
capable of being resolved in a way that is quite
consistent with the view which we have laboured
to impress. Our general doctrine is, that the
price of a commodity oscillates with the quantity
of it which is brought to market; but that the
oscillations are much larger with a necessary, than
with a luxury of life. Now, there is an apparent
exception to this, in the case of the more rare and
valuable spiceries. There is a well-known practice among the monopolists of these, which obtained so far back as centuries ago, when, to enhance their price, they destroyed a large proportion of their cargoes, at every time that there
was danger of an overplus being brought to mar-

ket. And they found their account in this. Or, in other words, an article that is more entitled to the denomination of a luxury, than the one we have already specified,—certainly far more a luxury than rum, as confined, in the use of it, to a very peculiar class, the affluent in society,—may bear a greater resemblance to corn, than to rum, in the magnitude of those oscillations which the price of it undergoes. Take, for example, the three commodities of grain, and sugar, and nutmeg. Let the supply of each fail, by one-third of its wonted quantity. With such a deficiency, the price of grain may be doubled, or perhaps trebled ; the sugar will rise in price, too, but not to any thing like the extent of the former ; while the nutmeg, which is certainly more of a luxury than sugar, in as far as it is of rarer indulgence, and restricted, in the use of it, to a far more select class of society, which in this respect, therefore, stands at a wider distance from the grain than the sugar does, will come much nearer to it, in respect of the oscillation that its price undergoes. It too may double or treble its price, on suffering the deficiency of a third part in its supply.

Now, the account of the matter is simply this. Sugar, though a luxury, is yet used in such quantity, that it forms a very heavy article of family expenditure. The offer to double its price, on the same deficiency that would double the price of grain, behoved instantly to be met by a severe retrenchment and economy, on the part of the great majority of its consumers. With grain, it is an object to economise; but, from being a necessary, it is not easy to do so beyond a certain extent. So that there is in that article, an intense demand, and, consequently, a high price. With sugar, it is also an object to economise; and, from being a luxury, it is possible to do so to any extent. Hence a slackening of the demand with it, which will keep down its price more than in the case of grain. With nutmeg, which is the veriest of all luxuries, it is still more possible to economise, than even with sugar; but then it is no object. There is not sixpence a year consumed of it for each family in Great Britain; and perhaps not one family that spends more than a guinea on this article alone. Let the price then be doubled or trebled; this will have no perceptible effect on the demand; and the price will far rather be paid, than that the wonted indulgence should in any degree be foregone. The aged gentlewoman, to whose taste the nutmeg flavour is an improvement upon the tea, will not be driven from her dear aromatic, by such a doubling or trebling of its price, as might incur to her the additional expense of perhaps a halfpenny in the month. The same holds true of cloves, and cinnamon, and Cayenne pepper, and all the precious spiceries of the East; and it is thus, that while, in the general, the price of necessaries differs so widely from that of luxuries, in regard to the extent of oscillation, there is a remarkable approximation in this matter, between the very commonest of these necessaries, and the very rarest of these luxuries.

Wages form the price of labour; and this price, like that of every other commodity, is determined by the proportion which obtains between the supply of it in the market, and the effective demand for it. Should the supply be diminished, or the demand increase, the price rises. Should the supply be increased, or the demand slacken, the price falls. But there are certain commodities that undergo a much greater fluctuation of price than others, though there should only be the same change with each of them in this proportion between the demand and the supply. Take, for example, the two articles of wheat and rum. A government contract for wheat, to the extent of one-twentieth part of its whole stock in the country, would increase its price far more than a similar contract for a twentieth part of all the rum. One bad harvest that caused a deficiency in the crop to the same extent, would raise the price of this grain in a much higher proportion, than the spirit would be raised by a deficiency of the same magnitude from a bad season in the West Indies. The cause of this difference is very obvious; yet, from its application to our present subject, it must be still a little expatiated on.

Wheat is a necessary of life. Rum is not. I can want spirits. I cannot want bread. Neither can I so conveniently reduce my consumption of the latter article as of the former. And I will, therefore, pay a greater price to overcome the greater inconvenience. This holds particularly true of the great mass of families in a population. Bread is the staple article of their subsistence; and, generally speaking, one can less bear a retrenchment upon his usual allowance of food, than a retrenchment upon his usual indulgence in a luxury. Should the price of rum offer to rise beyond a certain amount, I can abstain from the purchase of it: I can shift my demand to another kind of spirits, or I can give up the use of them altogether. In reference to grain, I have no such control over my determinations. I can neither want it altogether, nor can I, without considerable suffering, make any great abatement in my demand for it. With a luxury of life, the sellers are more dependent on the taste and whim of the purchasers. With a necessary of life, the sellers have the purchasers in their power. It is thus that a rise in the price of spirits, consequent on a deficient supply, might so far limit the consumption, as to prevent it from rising extravagantly. But when grain is deficient in quantity, each has a far more urgent demand for his wonted supply of that article, and will make greater sacrifices to obtain it. There is a far more intense competition in the one case than in the other—insomuch, that a very small deficiency in the harvest will produce a greater rise of price on the one article, than a similar deficiency in the im-

ports will produce upon the other article. It is
thus that grain, in respect of price, is among the
most tremulous of all the commodities which are
brought into a market—as sensitive, and as subject
to variations, as is the fitful weather; and not
only has it a greater range of fluctuation, but vi-
brates in its price with far greater facility and frequency than the other commodities of trade. A
deficiency of one tenth in the crop, will raise the
price greatly more than one tenth. A deficiency
of one third will produce the alarm, and even
much of the actual suffering, of a famine.

Now, labour might be considered in the light
of a marketable commodity—the supply of which
is measured by the number of labourers—and the
price of which is regulated, as in other instances,
by the proportion between this supply, and the
demand. This price partakes, with that of the
necessaries of life, in being liable to great fluctuation; and on the same principle, too, but in a
sort of reverse direction. It is the urgent need
of subsistence which so raises articles of the first
necessity, even upon a very slight short-coming
from their usual quantity in the market. And it
is the same urgent need of subsistence which so
lowers the price of labour; and that, upon a very
slight overplus in the number of labourers. What,
in fact, looking to one side of the negotiation,
may be called the demand of the capitalists
for labour,—when looking to the other side of
it, may be called the demand of the labourers

for employment; and, in this latter demand, there may be all the importunity and vehemence of a demand for the necessaries of life. Employment, in fact, is the vehicle on which these necessaries are brought to their door; and should there be more hands than are wanted, rather than be thrown out of the competition altogether, there will be a general cheapening of their labour, and so that the fall in its price shall go greatly beyond the excess in the number of labourers. Men must have subsistence; and if employment be the essential stepping-stone to this, men must have employment;—and thus it is that capitalists have the same control over workmen, when there is an excess in their number, which the holders of the necessaries of life have over their customers, when there is a deficieney in the crop. And so, the price of labour too is a most tremulously variable element, and has as wide a range of fluctuation as the price of corn. A very small excess in the number of labourers will create a much greater proportional reduction in their wages. Should twenty thousand weavers of muslin be adequate, on a fair recompense for their work, to meet the natural demand that there is in that branch of manufacture, an additional thousand of these unemployed, and going about with their solicitations and offers among the master-manufacturers, would bring a fearful distress and deficiency on the circumstances of the whole body. The wages would fall by much more than a twentieth part of what they were originally; and thus, by a very trifling excess in the number of workmen, might a very sore and widely felt depression be brought upon the comfort and sufficiency of the lower orders.*

---

* The author had occasion to advert to this principle some years ago, at a time of great commercial distress in Glasgow, and when measures were under deliberation, for the relief of those numerous workmen who were then suffering under an unexampled depression of their wages. The following extract is from a small written exposition, which, to serve a temporary purpose, he made of this topic, and for which, it may be proper to add, that he obtained admission in the 66th Number of the Edinburgh Review.

" It ought to be kept in mind, that there are particular lines of employment, where a given excess of workmen is sure to create a much greater proportional reduction in the rate of their wages. Should twenty thousand labourers, in a given branch of industry, so meet the demand for their services, as to afford to each of them a fair remuneration, then an additional thousand coming into competition with those who are already at work, may very possibly lower, by much more than a twentieth part, the price of their labour. In other words, the consequent deficiency of wages might go greatly beyond the fractional addition that had thus been made to the number of labourers.

" It is thus that, in certain kinds of work, a very small excess of hands may bring a very heavy distress and depression upon a whole body of operatives. The urgency of a few more than are wanted, soliciting for employment, and satisfied with any terms, rather than be kept out of it, may bring down the terms, to the whole profession, in a ratio so large, that the entire maintenance of these additional applicants for work, would not nearly cost so much as is lost, upon the whole, by the body of their fellow-workmen in the shape of reduced wages. For example, should two shillings a day be a fair remuneration for labour, and should it be the actual remuneration earned by twenty thousand workmen at some particular kind of it, an additional thousand might be maintained at this rate daily for a hundred pounds. But we should not be surprised to find that the effect of their appearance, and of their competition, was to bring down the daily wages to eighteen pence. Now, this would degrade beneath the average of comfort, twenty-one thousand workmen, by sixpence a day to each, or

Now, however melancholy this contemplation
might be in the first instance, yet, by dwelling

---

by five hundred and twenty-five pounds a day to them all, taken collectively. In other words, a certain redundancy of men might entail a calamity upon their profession, which, when measured arithmetically, will be
found to exceed, by upwards of five times the whole expense, either of
maintaining them in idleness, or of giving them full and adequate wages
at another employment.

" The above statement, we are persuaded, will recommend itself to the
experience of all practical men;—nor do we think it difficult to apprehend
the rationale of it. Men must have a subsistence for themselves and their
families ; and if this is only to be had through the medium of employment,
men must have employment. If they cannot earn thereby a plentiful subsistence, they will rather put up with a scanty subsistence than have none
at all. And thus it is that a surplus thousand of labourers may cheapen
work, by a fraction greatly larger than the excess of their own number, over
the former number of labourers;—and thus, from the necessity of a few,
may there emanate an adverse influence which will spread itself over the
many—and, with a very slight importation of more hands into a branch of
industry already sufficiently occupied, may there be imported an evil so
weighty, as to overbear for a time the whole profession, and to call forth
from all the members of it, a general outcry of apprehension and distress.

" This view of the subject, if it contain in it matter of regret, that a cause
so trivial should operate a mischief so extensive, contains in it also matter
of consolation. As we have already travelled from the cause to the effect,
we have only to travel back again from the effect to the cause ; and if the
cause be trivial, it may be remedied by a trivial exertion. The actual magnitude of any present or existing distress amongst a body of workmen, will
not alarm us into a fear of its perpetuity, if we are right in tracing it to a
cause so remediable, as to a small fractional excess in the number of these
workmen. Should the addition of a thousand men on a branch of industry,
which affords sufficient maintenance to twenty thousand, have the effect of
reducing their maintenance by one-fourth, then, when a case of such grievous reduction actually occurs, it is fair to infer, that the transference or removal of a single twentieth part of these labourers, would operate as a
restorative to the comfort and circumstances of them all. And, when one
thinks of the many natural securities which there are for bringing about an
adjustment of those partial and temporary differences that obtain between
the demand for labour and the number of labourers, he may both admit the
severity of an existing pressure, and be foremost in every sound and prac-

upon it a little further, we shall be led to discover certain outlets and reparations, that might cause us to look more hopefully than ever on the future destinies of our species. One thing is clear, that if so small a fractional excess in the supply of labour, over its demand, is enough to account for a very great deficiency in its remuneration, then, after all, it may lie within the compass of a small fractional relief to bring back the remuneration to its proper level, and so restore the desirable equilibrium between the wages of a workman and the wants of his family. It is comfortable to know, that the misery of an overwrought trade is capable of being retrieved on such easy terms—and that could either the present small excess of labourers be otherwise disposed of, or their future annual supply be somewhat and slightly restored, then might well-paid, and well-conditioned industry, that most cheerful of all spectacles, again be realized. Could any expedient be devised by which the number of labourers might be more equalized to the need that there is for them, then, instead of the manufacturers having so oppressive a control over the workmen, workmen might in some degree have a control over manufacturers. We should certainly regard it as a far more healthful state of the community, if our workmen, instead of

ticable measure for its alleviation, without reading in it the symptoms of any great national catastrophe, or losing his confidence in the stability of his country's wealth and greatness."

having to seek employment, were to be sought after; and that masters had to go in quest of service,
rather than that labourers had to go a-begging for
it. It is most piteous to see a population lying
prostrate and overwhelmed under the weight of
their own numbers; nor are we aware of a finer
object, both for the wisdom and benevolence of
patriotism, than to devise a method by which
the lower orders might be rescued from this state
of apparent helplessness. This would be done, if
they were only relieved from the pressure of that
competition by which they now elbow out, or beat
down each other; but nothing more certain, than
that not till the number of workmen bears a less
proportion to the need which there is for them,
will they be able to treat more independently with
their employers, or make a stand against all such
terms of remuneration, as would degrade their families beneath the par of human comfort.

That a very small excess of workmen over the
need which there is for them, will create much
more than a proportional depression in their wages,
is just as true, as that a very small deficiency in
the supply of the corn-market will create much
more than a proportional rise in the price of that
commodity. Both are true, and on the same principle too. It is, in either case, a very sore mischief, traceable to a very slight cause; and which,
therefore, perhaps, may admit of being cured by
the application of a very slight corrective. It appears, by M'Pherson's Annals of Commerce, that

the average importation of corn, during a great
many years, exclusive of the two remarkable seasons of scarcity in 1800 and 1801, did not amount
to more than eleven days consumption annually;
and that even the greatest importation ever known,
did not amount to one-tenth of the consumption
of the island. These might appear but fractional
remedies, which could be easily dispensed with;
and so, the good of importation might come to be
under-rated. But minute as these annual supplies
may appear in themselves, they are momentous in
their consequences; and lower the price of corn in
the market, far more than they add to the stock of
it. And, it is even so, of the relation which subsists between the number of people in a country,
and the degree of comfort which they enjoy. A
very small excess in the number, will operate a very
great reduction upon the comfort. But just as
a slight importation will restore the price of necessaries to their fair and natural level,' so may either
a slight exportation of our people, such as to dispose of their small excess, or a slight change of
habits, such as to prevent their small excess, have
the effect of raising the lower orders to that condition, in which every generous friend of humanity
would rejoice to behold them.

It does not follow then, because there is a very
great depression in the circumstances of a people,
that, great as it is, it may not be removed either by
a very slight exportation, or by a very slight prevention, so as somewhat to diminish the number of

them. These two expedients of relief are so distinct, that the one, it is imagined by many, might entirely supersede the other. That emigration, by which the excess of our population might be disposed of, should, in their apprehension, do away the practical importance of those checks by which the excess might have been prevented. There is, at all events, a certain relation between these two expedients, which, as well as each of the expedients themselves, is worthy of consideration.

We cannot enter upon this argument without adverting, in the first instance, to the celebrated theory of Mr. Malthus, on the subject of population. And one thing at least is manifest, that the very comprehension of his views, has retarded the practical application of them to any question of political or domestic economy. He writes in reference to the species, and the world; and the mind of his reader, by being constantly directed to the population of the whole globe, and to the relative capacities for their subsistence, that are diffused over the surface of it, can make escape from his conclusions by roaming in imagination over the vast regions that are yet unpeopled, and the wilds that, however rich in nature's luxuriance, have been yet untrodden by human footsteps. The speculation is admitted by many to be true, who, nevertheless, would lie upon their oars till the last acre on the face of the earth was brought to its highest possible cultivation. The reply to an alleged excess of population in Britain, is, that

New Holland offers a space equal to twenty Britains, which has been yet unentered upon; and that till this space be fully occupied, there is only one expedient which we have to do with, even that of emigration—that, meanwhile, the other expedient, or a preventive check upon the increase of population, is wholly uncalled for, that it may lie in reserve for that futurity which is still at an indefinite distance from us—and that when agriculture shall have done its uttermost upon all lands, it will be fully soon enough to think of keeping the human species within that maximum of human subsistence which shall then have been arrived at.

But after all, it does not necessarily follow, that the pressure of the world's population upon the world's food, will remain unfelt, till the latter has attained its maximum. It is quite enough for this effect, that the tendency to an increase of population is greater than the tendency to an increase of food. When a moving body comes into contact with one that is stationary, it exerts upon it the force of a certain pressure—which may represent that of an increasing population upon means of subsistence now stationary, because now augmented to the uttermost. But when the moving body, instead of coming into contact with one that is stationary, overtakes one that is moving in the same direction with itself, but with less velocity—still there is a pressure, no doubt less than the former one, yet proportional to the difference be-

tween the velocities, and which may represent the
actual pressure, wherewith every population will
bear upon their means of subsistence, should they
but tend to increase faster than their means. It
all depends on the proportion which there is between the tendencies to an increase of population
and an increase of food; and hence, it is a possible thing, even now, for the population of the
world to press too hard upon its means of subsistence—and therefore, a desirable thing at this
moment, as well as centuries afterwards, that every
moral and salutary check were laid on the multiplication of our species. It is quite an imaginary
comfort to the suffering families of England, that
there are tracts in New Holland, capable of maintaining a tenfold population to that of the British
empire. They cannot transport themselves there
in an instant. They cannot raise at once the
means, either for their own emigration, or for the
cultivation of this unbroken territory—and if not
at once, then it must take a time ere this consummation is gained; and it is simply enough, for the
upholding of a continuous pressure, that during
that time, there is a greater force of progress in
the world's population than in the world's food.
Could we, by the lifting up of a magical wand,
cause a ripened harvest to arise and cover the whole
of earth's improvable surface, then every preventive check on the number of mankind, may, for the
present at least, be suspended. But if, in point
of fact, our species have to toil their way to this

accomplishment for many successive generations, then, by reason of the intervening obstacles, a pressure may be felt, and without the operation of a preventive check, the great human family may all along be in the misery of a straitened condition. The existence of such a country as New Holland may lighten this misery, but no more do it away than a similar tract of land in the moon or any of the planets, to which emigration is impossible. There may not be such a barrier, as shall intercept all emigration, and utterly close every outlet for our redundant people, but at least such a barrier as would impede the full tide of emigration requisite for our complete and total deliverance. Thousands of years may elapse ere all the facilities shall be opened, and the requisite capital shall so overflow, as to occupy the whole of that domain which has been yet unentered on. It is a gradual process, carried forward by the emigrations of each successive year; and, during the whole period, it may hold true, that many shall be in circumstances of distress, while few shall be in circumstances to emigrate. This is the real condition of every country that is sending forth its families, from time to time, to colonize distant territories. There are light and adventurous spirits that will move on every impulse ; but nothing, save actual and felt distress, will exile from their homes any considerable number of whole families. Those who do move, have the means to emigrate ; and others who have not, remain in straitness and suffering where they are. Even the aid of government cannot go beyond a certain limit; and, after it has done its uttermost, still there may be a distressed, because a redundant population. These successive ejections of the people, are like the successive escapes of steam by a safety-valve, which relieve the pressure that is within, but still it remains a pressure that is in equilibrium with the weight which is incumbent over it. Now, it is not desirable that there should be so strong an elastic pressure from within, as that the people shall be straitened and in durance, up to the point of being tempted to emigrate. A country is in a state of violence when at all comparable to a vessel, that is always on the eve of bursting, unless relieved by a constant efflux, or by successive discharges. To mitigate this violence is at all times desirable ; and it were surely a better and a blander community at home, if, instead of the people being urged on to the very margin of the country's capabilities to maintain them, they had rather ease, and amplitude, and sufficiency in their own native land, and were kept a good way within the point of emigration.

It says much for the soundness of the principles of Mr. Malthus, that they always become more evident the narrower the field is on which they are exemplified ; and, consequently, the nearer the inspection is to which they are submitted. When he affirms, in reference to the whole species, that there is an evil in premature marriages, for that the population of the world are thereby caused to press inconveniently on the food of the world, one finds a refuge from his conclusions, in the imagination of many fertile but yet unculti-vated tracts, that might yield the greatest possible scope to the outlet of families for centuries to come. Or, when he affirms the same thing, in reference to a kingdom, even apart from emigra-tion, there is still a refuge from his conclusions, in the yet unreclaimed wastes, and yet imperfect agriculture, of the land in which we dwell. But one needs not his philosophy to feel the whole force of his principle within the limits of a family, where the premature marriage of a son, who had rashly, and previously to any right establishment of himself in the world, entered upon this engage-ment, would be deplored by all the members of it as a most calamitous visitation; and that, too, both on account of the present expense, and also the eventual expense of a rising progeny. It would be no consolation, in these circumstances, to be told of the millions of acres, both at home and abroad, that could yet be turned to the suste-nance of millions of human beings. This will pass for a reply to the speculations of Mr. Malthus, when the question relates to the population of the globe, or to the population of our empire : but it will not be sustained as a dissuasive of any weight against the alarm that is felt, lest the improvident marriage of a son, who had no tenement of his own, should bring on the inconvenience of an over-peopled household. The danger and the imprudence are here distinctly apprehended; and no objection that can be alleged against his Theory of Population, when proposed in its abstract and universal form, can surely overbear those lessons of practical and experimental wisdom, that have been familiarly recognized as such by men of plain, yet substantial understanding, long before his theory was ever heard of. *

In like manner would we plead for an exemption from the obloquy that attaches to this Theory, when, instead of speculating and providing for the whole world, we concentrate our views on a single parish, and recal our scattered imagination from other continents and other climes, to that

---

* Mr. Malthus, in his chapter on the checks to population in the islands of the South Sea, says well of Otaheite, that " The difficulty here is reduced to so narrow a compass, is so clear, precise, and forcible, that we cannot escape from it. It cannot be answered in the usual vague and inconsiderate manner, by talking of emigration and further cultivation. In the present instance, we cannot but acknowledge that the one is impossible, and the other glaringly inadequate. The fullest conviction must stare us in the face, that the people on this groupe of islands could not continue to double their numbers every twenty-five years; and before we proceed to inquire into the state of society on them, we must be perfectly certain, that unless a perpetual miracle render the women barren, we shall be able to trace some very powerful checks to population in the habits of the people."

It is the narrowness of the compass which causes the operation of Mr. Malthus' principle to be so distinctly seen within the limits of a household, and also within the limits of a parish, if any barrier to emigration has been thrown around it. Now the poor laws have thrown an artificial barrier of this sort around an English parish; so that the miseries of a redundant population may there be most distinctly exemplified, and without escape from them, either in emigration, or in the further cultivation of distant parts of the world.

which lies directly and familiarly before us, among
the population of our own little vicinity. And
the truth is, that the poor laws of England tend
to isolate each of its parishes from the rest of the
world; and so, to bring it more clearly and definitely before us, as a separate object of contemplation. More particularly, do they throw a barrier around each, which, though not altogether
insuperable, has yet been of great efficacy in hem-
ming each population within its own boundaries,
and closing up the outlets to emigration. It is in
this way that the most encouraging offers of a settlement in distant lands, are often resisted by the
English peasantry. They are aware of a certain
right by the law of pauperism, upon their own
native soil; and this they are not willing to forego. They feel that they have a property at home,
which they would relinquish by the measure; and
that reasoning, therefore, which blinds the eye of
the reader against the truth of the general speculation, is not applicable in present circumstances
to the case that is before us. And the poor laws
not only check the egress of the redundant population to our distant colonies; they go a certain
way to impede and to lessen the free interchange
of people from one parish to another, both by begetting in each a jealousy of new settlers, and
augmenting the natural preference for home by
the superadded tie, that there they have their proper and their rightful inheritance; the benefit of
which can be got far more directly and conve-

niently when on the spot, than when they remove themselves to a distant part of the country. But even when so removed, they still hold on their own parish; and, like non-resident proprietors, can have their rent 'transmitted to them; and may, in fact, be as burdensome as if they still resided within its limits. It is thus that the vestry, whence the dispensations of pauperism proceed, may be regarded as a kind of adhesive nucleus, around which the people of each parish accumulate and settle, and so present us with as distinct an exemplification of the theory of Mr. Malthus, as if each were in itself a little world; the affairs and difficulties of which, may, at the same time, be considered without his theory being in our heads at all. It is not in the least necessary to blend with the argument any wide or general speculation. We happen to regard Mr. Malthus' Theory of Population as quite incontrovertible. Yet we do not link with it our reprobation of English pauperism, any more than we would link with it our reprobation of a precipitate marriage in a destitute and unprepared family. Let his theory be execrated as it may, let it even be out-argued by its adversaries, this will not overthrow any of those maxims of domestic prudence, that might be learned at the mouth of every ordinary housewife; and, neither, will it overthrow any demonstration of those evils in pauperism, which, with or without a philosophical treatise, are quite obvious to the home-bred sagacity of country squires and parish overseers.

CHAP. XVIII.

ON THE EFFECT OF A POOR RATE, WHEN APPLIED IN AID OF DEFECTIVE WAGES.

LET us therefore withdraw our regards from the extended speculations of Mr. Malthus, and confine them to the state and regimen of one parish—addressing ourselves to the current experience of plain and practical men, who both painfully feel, and clearly understand the mischiefs of their present economy; yet, whose understandings would only be mystified by the demonstrations of a political arithmetic, which took in a wider scope than that of their own humble community. In every such parish, there is a certain quantity of work to be done, and a certain number of labourers would suffice for the doing of it. Some of them may be imported from abroad; and, on the other hand, some of the native workmen may have gone beyond their own parochial limits in quest of employment. Still, with or without these movements, there is a certain number in the parish of able or available labourers, who, if barely adequate to the labour that is required, will be hired upon a fair remuneration; but who, if they exceed, will be glad to accept of an inferior remuneration, rather than want employment altogether. It is this competition which brings down the wages of labour;

and, on the principle that is already unfolded, a very small excess in the number of labourers may give rise to a very large reduction in the price of labour. It is in vain to say that this excess will naturally discharge itself upon other places. So it would, in a natural state of things. So it always does in those parishes of Scotland where a compulsory provision is unknown. But in England, where the practice is now established, of ministering from the poor rate, not merely to the indigence of age, and sickness, and impotency, but to the indigence of able-bodied, though ill-paid industry, this excess is not so easily disposed of. There is a principle of adherence in the system, which detains and fastens it upon every parish where once this excess has been formed; and we hold it very instructive, to look at the various expedients by which it has been met, and at the uniform failure which has attended them.

The distress of inferior wages, is, in the first instance, felt by the fathers of large families; and, accordingly, they are the first who have been benefitted by the extension of the legal charity of England beyond those cases, for which it has been alleged, by the defenders of the system as established by the act of Elizabeth, that it was strictly and originally intended. Certain it is, that if there really was any such limitation designed in the primary construction of the statute, it is now very generally disregarded, and there is nought more common, particularly in the southern counties, than a composition of wages and poor rate, both of which are made to enter into the maintenance of an able-bodied labourer. There are two questions generally asked of the applicant for parish relief, and which may be regarded as furnishing the data that fix the parish allowance: " What do you earn?" and " What is the number of the family that you have to maintain?" and, if the wages be held inadequate to the family, the deficiency, in most instances, is held to be as firm a ground of application, as the utter helplessness of impotency or disease. The defect in wages is eked out by a weekly allowance from the poor rate; and he, who in other circumstances would have been left as an independent workman upon his own resources, becomes, under this system, a dependent upon legal charity.*

---

* I have had the honour of receiving communications upon this subject, from the justly celebrated Thomas Clarkson. The following is his information of two methods, according to which they proceed in certain villages of the county of Suffolk, with regard to the allowance for parents of large families.

" In some villages they allow handsome and proper wages per week, say nine shillings to every man employed. Now, nine shillings will do very well, as far as a man, wife, and two children go; but will not be enough where the children are from three to six, or more. All, therefore, which the large families may want beyond the nine shillings, they pay out of the poor's rates. This is not unjust, because they give to every man a fair and equitable wage, according to the times; that is, as much as he can earn. The family man wants undoubtedly more than the single man, but still he cannot earn more; and, very often, not so much. All, then, have fair wages; and if there are wants beyond what the weekly wages will provide, they belong to the parish in common. The tailor, the shoemaker, &c. is equally bound with the farmer to contribute to the wants of the parish; and what reason have they to complain, when the farmer, after paying his men

This then is the first application of poor-rate to wages which claims our regard. Before that single and able-bodied men can have the benefit of this poor-rate, the parents of families must have been visited by its allowances; and that, just in proportion to the number of their offspring. It is a premium on population, and must serve to perpetuate the cause of that mischief which it is designed to alleviate. There is a general feeling, all over England, of something wrong in this composition of wages with the parish allowance; and, along with it, a sort of anxiety, in some places, to vindicate their management from the imputation of a practice that is felt to be discreditable; so that when the question is put, whether it be the habit

---

fair wages for their work, pays also his share towards their extraordinary wants?

"In Playford, again, we do differently. We do not pay all our men alike. We pay nine shillings per week, as far as a man, wife, and two children; but we pay all the family, or rather large family-men, by the piece, so as to make them earn ten, eleven, and twelve shillings per week. We differ again in another respect, for we pay all the surplus beyond nine shillings entirely out of our own pockets. We never go to the poor rates for this surplus, in order, if possible, to promote a spirit of independence among our labourers. Where the surplus is paid out of the poor rates, every labourer knows it; that is, he knows that he gets nine shillings from the farmer, and two or three from the parish: but in Playford, the labourer, when he takes his money home at the end of the week, has the pleasure of reflecting, that all the money is of his own earning, unmixed with any parish gift. This is so, except in a few cases; for, where a man has a wife, and seven or eight children, it would be hard upon a farmer to pay him twenty shillings per week, when the labourer could only earn ten or twelve. In such extraordinary cases as these, thére is a regular allowance for such pauper, beyond his wages, out of the parish funds, to do justice both to the man and to the master."

of the place to supplement defective wages out of the poor-rate, a very frequent reply is, that it is never done by them; and that nothing is ever given in consideration of a low wage, but only in consideration of a large family. This way of shifting it from one ground to another, though practically it makes no difference as to the effect of the regimen, yet is very instructive as to the rationale of its operation. Though Malthus had never written, there could not be a more complete exposition than is given by the answers of unlettered and unsophisticated men, of the bearing that English pauperism has upon population. We do not need to embarrass this contemplation with any argument respecting the soundness or unsoundness of his theory. Here we have parents paid out of a legal and compulsory fund, because of the largeness of their families; and we may safely appeal to the common sense and sagacity of the most unspeculative minds, whether this must not add to the number of marriages in a parish—whether it does not slacken all those prudential restraints, that else would have operated as a check upon their frequency—whether the hesitation and delay, that, in a natural state of things, are associated with this step, are not in a great measure overborne by the prospect thus held out, of a defence and a guarantee against the worst consequences of many a rash and misguided adventure. Must not marriages become earlier, and, therefore, more productive under such a system, than they otherwise would be? Or, in other words, is not this remedy for the low wages, induced by an excess of people, the likeliest instrument that could be devised, not only for keeping up the excess, but for causing it to press still more on the already urged and overburdened resources of this small parochial community? This mode of curing the disease is the most effectual for upholding it; and that, in constantly increasing vigour and virulency from one generation to another. And when one adverts to the principle that has already often been appealed to, that a very small excess of labourers is enough to account for a very great deficiency in the price of labour, it just ascertains and aggravates the conclusion the more, seeing, by how very slight an addition to the frequency of marriages, the mischief in question might be effectuated.*

---

* From the abstract of the returns sent to the Committee on Labourers' Wages, and ordered by the House of Commons to be printed on the 10th of May, 1825, it would appear that the practice of making an allowance to able-bodied labourers, according to the number of their families, obtains very extensively in the southern and midland counties. To the question, " Do any labourers in your district employed by the farmers, receive either the whole or any part of the wages of their labour out of the poor rates?" there seems to be a great majority of affirmative answers from many of the counties. The same holds true of the answers to the second question: " Is it usual, in your district, for married labourers having children, to receive assistance from the parish rate?" And to the third question: " If so, does such allowance begin when they have one child or more?" the answers are exceedingly various. In many cases they give to able-bodied labourers without children. Some parishes commence the allowance from the poor rate with one child; others when the family has attained the number of two, three, or four children. There is frequently a rule upon which they proceed, of calculating so much a head for each individual of the family, and if the earning do not amount to the computed sum, making up the dif-

One needs only to be versant in the familiar details of parish management in England, in order to
be convinced of the real practical effect that their
pauperism has on the frequency of marriages. In
some cases, the allowance is not given till the family have reached the extent of two or three children. But, in other cases, when the proper wages
have been still further depressed, and the habit obtains of compounding with them a still larger ingredient of poor-rate, the distinction between pensioned and unpensioned labourers takes place at
an earlier stage in the progress. Sometimes the
formal parish allowance begins immediately with
the event of matrimony. Insomuch, that single
men, on being refused the parochial aid for eking
out their miserable wages, have threatened to
marry—have put their threat into execution, and
been instantly preferred, in consequence, to a
place in the vestry roll, among those who have
qualified in like manner. When marriage is thus
made the qualification for an allowance from the
poor-rate, one does not see how the poor-rate can
escape the charge of being a bounty upon marriage.
And, accordingly, this evil is so much felt and deprecated, that, in certain places, they have resolved to abolish the distinction between the allowances to single and married men; and actually
pay all alike, though at a great additional expense

---

ference out of the poor rate. Hence this allowance is familiarly known, in
many parts of England, by the name of " head-money."

in the meantime—and this, to arrest and lighten, if possible, that coming tide of population wherewith they fear to be overwhelmed.*

---

* The following are the questions and replies of a correspondence with Mr. Smoothy, a farmer in the parish of Halsted in Essex:—

" Has not the shame of pauperism very much abated of late? Yes.

" Do not young men sometimes marry with the direct object of getting parish relief? It has been threatened, and I believe acted upon.

" Have they not threatened to marry that they may get an additional allowance? Yes.

" To employ idle hands, are you not often obliged to give useless work? And is not this parish-work very apt to introduce them into idleness and dissipation? We have expended large sums in useless labour, and the men became idle and dissipated.

" Does not a married man get six shillings a-week for working on the road? Yes.

" And is not this often made up to eight, nine, or ten shillings, when there are children? Yes.

" Have you not had occasion to send twenty, thirty, or forty men, round with a paper for employment? Yes.

" When you fail, do you not give four shillings a-week to a single man whom you keep idle? We do not now give so much; two shillings, or two shillings and sixpence.

" Have you not expended a great deal of money uselessly in finding labour? Yes; large sums.

" And do not all expedients often fail, and then you have to maintain them idle? Yes.

" Are not many of them idling about, and standing in the streets all the day long? Yes.

" Would not many of them be glad to get work at any wages? Yes, in some cases.

" Is there not a strong feeling of the helplessness and difficulty of your state of pauperism? Yes.

" Do not the farmers often refuse to have the work of these men, even though they might have it for nothing? Yes, in some instances.

" Do not the people often marry in very early life? Yes, quite boys.

" And do they not count on the additional allowance for a wife and children? I believe they do.

" Is it not difficult to arrive at the truth in the examination of the cir-

But we are not to suppose, that by this compromise between the payers of charity and the
payers of labour, all the able-bodied of a parish
are admitted to employment. There is a limit
to the work of a parish; but while this economy
lasts, there can be no limit to the number of
its workmen, who, of course, after various expedients and ingenuities have been practised, for
the purpose of intercepting them with something
to do, at length overflow into a state of total idleness. One of these expedients is to send round
the men who have not fallen into employment in
the regular and customary way, to send them
round among the farmers, with the lure of getting their work on very cheap terms, as the parish
will pay the difference between their low wages,
and the sum that might be deemed necessary for
their entire maintenance. It is no doubt an advantage to the farmer to have his work done cheaply
—but where is the advantage, if he have no work

---

cumstances of the applicants? Yes, very difficult. Pauperism is now no
shame, and every artifice is practised to get on the parish."

This correspondence took place in the latter end of 1822. A few months
afterwards he added, " We have, some months past, billetted the surplus
hands to different farmers and tradesmen, according to their occupations,
and pay them from the rate, yet in some instances they are refused.

" We billet about sixty in the week, and the numbers are increasing.

" We have about eight labourers to an hundred acres, (it seems five labourers are reckoned a sufficient complement for an hundred acres,) so that
I may safely say, we have a surplus of more than one-third, could the farmer
find the means of paying his five men to an hundred acres of land."

for them to do? Every one department may be already filled and supersaturated with labour. For the accommodation of idle hands, threshing machines may be put down, and a ruder and clumsier agriculture may have been perpetuated, and all ingenious devices by which the human mind could contrive to abridge labour, may have been prescribed, and just that human muscles may be kept in as full requisition as possible. Yet all is ineffectual; and many a weary circuit often have these roundsmen to make, knocking at every door for admittance, yet everywhere refused—till at length, after all their attempts are exhausted, they devolve the whole burden of their existence on the parish, and gather into a band of supernumeraries.*

---

* The following impressive statements on this subject are from the pen of Mr. Clarkson:—" I verily believe that every farmer with us takes as many as he can find money to pay, and that he gives his men competent wages, I mean his regular men, and not the supernumeraries; for these are labourers to the parish at a very inferior rate. The regular men were seldom better off of late years than they are now. I think that our farmers, if they had money, might employ between them three or four more regular labourers than they do; but I think they could not, even if they had money, find work for all; and, if this be the case now, what will it be in fifty years, if the poor laws remain unaltered, if the poor continue to increase as they have hitherto done, and if there be no vent for the surplus population, or if the population will take no pains to seek support for itself. I am sure the Suffolk farmers take as many as they can pay, and almost as many as they could employ, and yet leave a long list of supernumeraries: but, in some parts of the county, they do not pay their labourers so liberally as we do in ours, not by eighteenpence per week a man.

" We had seven supernumeraries in October 1822, but we have had more since: we had, in December and January, 1823, thirteen at one time. We

And, exceedingly various have been the devices for their employment. Sometimes they have been congregated into work-houses, where they are provided with any employment that can be got for them by the parish overseers. At other times they have been farmed out to a speculator, who has turned the work-house into a factory, and possesses himself of their services at a rate exceedingly beneath the market price of labour. At other times, they may be seen in a kind of disorderly band, labouring either upon parish roads, or in sand and gravel pits. The value of what they render in this way for their subsistence, is in general very insignificant. The truth is, that an increasing population can'no more be supplied indefinitely with profitable work, than they can be supplied indefinitely with money or with food. It is more for a moral effect, than for the worth of

---

have, however, not one at this moment (July, 1823); for the dry, windy weather, which we have had almost incessantly for the last seven weeks, has been the finest season for hoeing wheat, and other crops, almost ever known; and hoeing is a process indispensable in Suffolk. But I understand that five or six are likely to become supernumerary in a few days; and this number will increase, and be out of regular employ, more or less, till Harvest; and that even then, some of them will not have work; but that, after October or November, we shall have from eight to thirteen out of employ till Spring again. This will bring a great burthen on the Parish, and be a great calamity to the poor supernumerary; because, not having half the wages of the regular man, he will not have enough to support himself with any comfort; and this will probably lead to idleness and crime."

It is to be observed, that Playford, of which Mr. Clarkson writes, is a very small Parish, of only 264 inhabitants, by the census of 1821.

their labour, that these various modes of industry are laid upon them. Better give them something to do, than that they should be wholly idle. Though even this object is not always accomplished, and in many of the agricultural parishes, they may be seen lounging out a kind of lazzaroni life, upon a weekly pittance from the vestry, in the fields or on the highways.

There is one very sore evil in this system. It has distempered altogether the relationship between a master and his servants. The latter feel less obligation to the former for being taken into his employment, seeing that they have a refuge in poor-rates, from the destitution which in other countries attaches to a state of idleness. They are not so careful in seeking work for themselves, as the law has rendered them in some measure independent of it. It becomes more, in fact, the interest of the house and land occupiers in the parish that they shall have employment, than their own interest; and they, exempted in this way from the care of themselves, and from all those sobrieties and virtues which are thereby called into exercise, become reckless, and like to a difficult or unmanageable charge in the hand of guardians. The consequences are most mischievous, and more particularly in the bitterness and discomfort which have been introduced into all the departments of service. In like manner, as the anxiety of the lower orders to get employment is lessened under this system, so their anxiety to keep the employment is lessened also; and, in this way, the master loses a most important hold on their fidelity and good conduct. They care little though they should be dismissed; and this has often the effect of making them idle and insolent. They know, that even though it should come to the worst, they must be maintained; and one may well conceive all the harassments and heart-burnings of such a loose and ill-sorted alliance, between a master that has no authority, and servants that are under no dependence—the one in a state of constant irritation, or fearfulness—the other in a state of hardy defiance, and, in fact, inverting the relationship altogether, by the virtual subjection in which their employer is held by them.

For under this perverse and most unlucky arrangement of things, the master has little or no choice of servants, and no benefit from any competition of theirs for employment. It has the effect, in a certain manner, of limiting the market for labour, within the narrow boundaries of each distinct and isolated parish. In the present state of the agricultural districts, over-peopled as they are even to compression, a master cannot go for labourers into another parish, without as many being thrown totally idle at home, as he has imported from abroad, and whose total maintenance, therefore, must be devolved on that poor-rate to which he himself is a contributor. This is felt by himself in common with all the other payers, so that often there is a sort of tacit obligation on the part of farmers, to employ none but the hinds, or labourers, whose settlement and right of relief lie in the parish. This is well understood by the other party. They know that their masters have no other resource than to keep them in their service; and the utter carelessness of habit, which this must engender amongst them, may be easily imagined. Nature has established a mutual interest between man and man; and when left to herself, she maketh the checks, and the mutual influences that are dependent thereupon, most beautifully subservient to the well-being of all. But this injudicious policy of man has broken it up, and has now brought the society of England into a state of most fearful disorganization.

After all, the employment which is given for the purpose of mitigating the rate, is little better than idleness in disguise. In the case of roundsmen, the whole remuneration is made up, partly of wages from the master, and partly of an allowance from the parish; and there is nothing more common, than when they have wrought to a certain amount, or for so many hours in the day, to take the rest of the day very much to themselves—and though still under the semblance of doing something at an allotted task, literally to do nothing. It is a familiar saying amongst them, that " Our master has now got all that time in the day from us which he has paid for—what the parish pays for is our own!" and this proportion, even though fairly and accurately struck, leaves a sad vacancy in their hands,

which is often filled up with positive mischief. At
all events, it wholly corrupts and relaxes them as
labourers. They lose the tone and habit of good
workmen. Under this artificial economy, the interest and the industry of the labourer stand dis-
sociated the one from the other; and that wholesome discipline of penalties and rewards, which
nature hath instituted, is put an end to. They become ill-conditioned, both morally and economically; and the fabric of our ancient commonwealth
becomes unsound at its basis, as the olden character disappears, of a hearty, hard-working, well-
paid, and withal well-habited peasantry.

There is one very melancholy process connected
with this system, and that must transmit and accumulate this deterioration from one age to
another. As the young generation of numerous
and premature families rises up in a parish, and the
boys are veering towards manhood, they of course
swell and aggravate still more the already overdone
competition for employment. Now, it is regarded
as a higher place in labour to be admitted among
the regular servants of a farmer, than among the
roundsmen. The former are on the whole better
paid; and the latter look to any vacancy there, as
a sort of preferment, to which those of full-grown
manhood, and who have perhaps served months
and years in the capacity of roundsmen, have a
better claim than mere striplings who have come
out for the first time in quest of employment.
So that very generally, in many of the parishes,

the vacancies among the regular farm servants are filled by roundsmen, and the consequent vacancies among the roundsmen filled by the raw and unpractised youths from the general population. In other words, their first outset as labourers, is with those who have got into the idle and profligate habits to which their situation peculiarly exposes them—a circumstance most ruinous to their own future habit and character as workmen, and most directly fitted to perpetuate and augment the tide of corruption, as it bears downward from the present generation to the next. It is further a most grievous necessity in their state, that they should be forced to commence their life as paupers, that they should be familiarized, from a tender age, to the allowances of the parish vestry, that all generous and aspiring independence should be smothered when in embryo within them, and a new race should arise so fostered and prepared as to outstrip their predecessors in the rapacity, and the meanness, and all the sordid or degrading habits of pauperism.*

It comes to the same result, whether they are sent about as roundsmen, or are wholly paid and employed by the parish as supernumeraries. In the latter case, they may give their labour either

---

* In the Parliamentary Abstract, above referred to, the fourth question is, " Is it usual for the Overseers of the poor, to send to the farmers labourers who cannot find work—to be paid partly by the employer, and partly out of the poor-rates?" And, from the affirmative answers which are returned by the parishes of the midland and southern counties, it would appear, that this practice is a very general one.

in a work-house or out of doors. But both from
the difficulty of supplying work, and from the lax
superintendence into which the whole system is
so apt to degenerate, it may be regarded as a vast
nursery both of idleness and vice all over England. We do not hesitate to charge on the pauperism of England the vast majority of its crimes
—detaining by its promises, within the borders of
every parish, a greater number of families than it
can well and comfortably provide for—luring, as it
were, more into existence than it can meet with
the right and requisite supplies—and, after having
conducted them onward to manhood, leaving them
in a state of unsated appetency, and withal in leisure for the exercise of their ingenuities, by which
to devise its gratification. We cannot conceive a
state of the commonwealth more fermentative of
crime, from the thousand unnoticed and unnotice-
able pilferments, that, we fear, are in daily and
very extended operation among the labouring
classes, to the higher feats of villany, the midnight
enterprise, the rapine, sealed, if necessary, with
blood, the house assault, the highway depredation.*

---

* It is obviously a thing of some delicacy, to publish the representa-
tions which may be given of the state of morality in a neighbourhood—and
more especially, when furnished by one who is residing within its limits.
But we fear, that the following account, given by Mr. Clarkson, of the
decay of all right independence among the lower classes, will serve for a
great many of the neighbourhoods in England.

"The spirit of independence is not entirely, but nearly gone. It is not,
I believe, to be found in nine out of ten among the poor. Here and there
an old-fashioned labourer remains, who would suffer much, rather than ask

Simply, if labour were better paid, it would not be so. Were there room and occupancy for all the

---

for relief. I have two of this description, out of fourteen labourers; but I doubt if there are other three of the same sort, in the three other farms of the parish. Among the persons born of late years, from the age of ten to thirty, all hang upon the parish for support. No one of these blushes to ask for relief, but, on the other hand, they demand it unblushingly as a right. Poor-rates, as you know, were first established for the aged, sick, lame, blind, and impotent. No fault could reasonably be found with this part of the law; but afterwards, in the same reign, the Parishes were made to find work for the unemployed, however robust, active, and healthy. Here the great evil began; for poor people, after this, would not take the trouble of going to other places to look for work. Why should they travel about for a precarious subsistence, when there was an obligation to maintain them at home? Since this time, the poor have been making, slowly and by degrees, new demands and encroachments; and the Magistrates, having been generally men of humanity, and not having foreseen the consequences which have taken place, have generously yielded to them, till their concessions from time to time have grown into customs, and been falsely interpreted into laws. When a poor woman, for example, has been delivered of a child, the husband generally goes to the Overseer, and applies for relief for his wife. Some Overseers, timid or compassionate, acquiesce: others refuse. But it has now passed into a custom, that every lying-in woman should be relieved with her third or fourth child. Let us see what happens next. A young family rises up. The father of this family sometimes hears of a place for his son or his daughter, with some farmer of a neighbouring, or other parish. He then applies to the Overseer to fit out his child with clothes. Such applications have passed also into a custom; and it has become a custom to accede to them, on the principle, that they who look out for service for their children, ought to be encouraged, and that, if the child keeps his service for one year, he belongs to another parish. I have been frequently at Vestry Meetings, when such applications have been made for clothing. I have told the father,—
'The children are yours, and it is your duty to provide for them, or you ought not to have married.' The answer has always been, ' The children belong to you (the Parish); I cannot get for them what they want; you therefore must.' No one can beat it into their heads, that the children belong to them, not to the parish. I have been quite disgusted with their conversation at such meetings. I have often been inclined to think, that they have no natural affection for their children, and I have told them

demand after employment, and did that employment meet with a comfortable subsistence in return

---

so. Certain it is, that they do not consider themselves to be under any
obligation to bring up their children, at their own expense, beyond a certain age. They will tell you at once, ' I have brought up the boy so far.
I wish to get rid of him. (What an expression this!) He belongs to
you.' If the boy arrives at this age, and his father cannot find a service
for him, the father makes no hesitation to demand either a weekly allowance for him, or that work may be found for him, or that he may be
apprenticed out at the expense of the parish. Thus the parish is to do
every thing, and the father nothing. Thus generation follows generation,
and the notion is every where diffused, that the poor man is under no necessity to rely upon his own efforts. In fact, almost all our labourers hang
upon the parish for every thing. This hanging upon the parish, is discer-
nible in various ways that may be mentioned. If a man, for example, is
turned away by his master, for idleness, negligence, abusive language, supposed theft, &c. &c. he goes directly to the Overseer, and, though in some
degree a culprit, he has the assurance to ask for money or work. The
Overseer then sends him round (this is the usual practice,) to all the other
farmers in the parish (except the man who discharged him,) to see if any
of these will employ him. Perhaps he is two days in making the inquiry.
At length he returns. His report is, that no one has a vacancy for him.
He demands, therefore, again, either work or money; and, what will appear to you to be most extraordinary, he demands, without blushing, to be
paid for the two days he lost in looking out for new work, though he lost
his former seat of work by his own misconduct. The Overseer resists this
new demand. The consequence is, that the pauper generally pours forth
against him a torrent of abuse. The Overseer, however, remains firm in
this point, and then proceeds to speak to him thus: ' If you cannot, as
you say, get work in your own parish, you must go to the next town or
village to seek it.' What, think you, is the man's reply? He talks
about his rights. He refuses to go. ' No,' says he to the Overseer, ' It
is your business to find me with work. I will not budge a step out of the
parish. You must go yourself, and seek it.' This, I assure you, insolent as it is, is the general answer. The Overseer, after this, is obliged
to give him either a weekly allowance, or to make him a supernumerary;
that is, to set him upon some parish job. Here a new scene takes place
between the two. The pauper is usually dissatisfied with his allowance,
and therefore abuses the Overseer. He threatens to bring him before a
Magistrate, and proceeds to imprecations. This is not always, but almost

for it, we should forthwith see a more orderly, and tranquil, and safe population. It bears the expression of a kindness to the people, that, when all the regular departments of service are filled, and there is still left an overplus of hands, there should lie a legal obligation on each parish to harbour, either as roundsmen or as supernumeraries,

---

always the case. Some Overseers have been so timid, as to have made the best terms they could with the pauper. Others have taken him before a Magistrate, but this seldom happens; and he has been confined a few days in prison for his abuse. Other overseers, being strong men, and also men of great courage, have turned him by main force, or kicked him, out of their premises. These violent scenes have occurred every now and then, during the six years I have been in Playford. The supernumeraries are still insolent to the Overseer, as he happens to come in contact with them, either when he superintends their work, or pays them at the end of the week; but they are not in general so grossly or vehemently abusive, as they used to be four or five years ago, because the Magistrates, having begun to see the evil of the Poor-laws, have of late leaned more to the side of the farmers than of the paupers, but particularly in confirming lower allowances to the latter. In fact, the Poor-laws have taught the paupers to discard all dependence upon themselves, and to look to the parish for every thing they want. During the last three or four years, they have been making a new effort at encroachment. Several of them have applied to the Overseer to pay their rents for them, that is, the rents of their cottages; and such applications have increased. What will they want next? The more you give them, the more helpless you make them, or the more you lessen their dependence on their own exertions for their support. Let me now mention, that, besides all these demands, it is usual, when a man or woman dies, to apply for coffins for them; and it has passed into a custom for the parishes to allow these. The labourer never thinks of making any savings or provision for burying the dead; at least, for any coffin to hold the body.—Thus a pauper in England, though he has the finest chance in the world of providing for himself, in consequence of the free scope which the constitution of his Government gives him, can neither, as we have seen, come into the world, nor live in it, nor go out of it, without burdening his Parish."

the men who have not been so fortunate as to find the better occupation. It is not known how woful the amount of depression is, which a very few of these might bring upon the wages of agricultural labour. If there be any truth in the principle that we have already attempted to expound, a small fractional excess of workmen thus detained, and under the guise of humanity too, are enough to bring a sad discomfort and deficiency on the circumstances of the whole body. In the higgling for wages between the farmer and his servants, what a mighty advantage is given to the former, by the simple circumstance of their being a few outcasts from regular work, that would be glad of the very place which any of his present workmen may be threatening to leave, or refusing to accept of on his terms. On the other hand, had there been no supernumeraries and no roundsmen, or still more, a very few less in the parish than its farmers and capitalists have use for, what a mighty turning of the scale would this produce in favour of the other party. A very small difference, indeed, in the number of the people, would suffice to create this most important difference of relationship between them and their masters—whether they should seek for masters, or masters should seek for them. There is a tremulous balance here, that will be decided by a very slight difference either in the one or the other of these ways; and surely there is no enlightened or liberal friend of his species, who would not rejoice to see it decided in favour of the population. In this view of the matter, we may see at once the cruelty of a poor-rate : how, in the first instance, by the encouragement which it gives to precipitate marriage, it multiplies the people beyond the rate at which they would otherwise have multiplied—how, in the second instance, by holding out to all of them a right and a property in their native parish, it detains the people, and closes up, as it were, those outlets of emigration by which relief might have been obtained from the competition of a most hurtful excess—how, in the third instance, it provides for this surplus of labourers, but on terms which lie at the arbitration of the upper classes in society —how, in the fourth instance, it gives to the masters a mighty advantage over their regular labourers, and enables them to bring the general wages of husbandry indefinitely near to the parish allowance for roundsmen and supernumeraries*—thus,

---

* The following are notes of a communication from Mr. Maitland, an intelligent Scotch farmer in the neighbourhood of Sherborne, Dorsetshire, and on the estate of Earl Digby:—

" As to the difference between England and Scotland, in respect that the labourers of the former solicited employment from him in dozens, whereas in Scotland he had to hunt after them? The fact is well known by every Scotsman resident here, and strongly marks the great demand for labour in that part of the kingdom. It also has, in my opinion, a powerful tendency to destroy still farther that spirit of independence, the want of which is already so visible among English labourers."

" As to the inferior scale of work that is rendered by paupers, so as to make it more profitable that there should be a full wage to regularly paid labourers? It is particularly remarked by every Scotsman resident here, how difficult it is to make the labourers do their duty, when regularly em-

in fact, under the guise of kindness to the stragglers
of the community, operating a most injurious re-

---

ployed, not only by the day, but even when piece-work is given them; arising from their total want of honour and gratitude. It need not then sur-
prise, that work performed by paupers, should cost a great deal more. I
believe it may fairly be set down at one-half."

"As to the effects of poor-rates in augmenting the population? An
English labourer having no property, nor prospect of acquiring any—and
being accustomed from infancy in believing the parish is bound to provide
for his family—marries early in life; of course has a prospect of a numerous
offspring. It also makes marriages more numerous, and entered into without
prudence or forethought."

"The comparative comfort of English and Scots labourers? The comparison here is altogether in favour of Scotland. The English labourer,
trusting to the parish, lays nothing up for a bad day—his week's wages are
always spent at the week's end. This produces improvidence in all his
affairs; and having no cow, nor even a garden, he accounts beer his *sum-
mum bonum*. This he takes at the public house by himself, to the great
misery of his family; and knows nothing of those social enjoyments, so
esteemed by the Scottish peasant. The effects of this must be obvious
upon the morals too—it blunts every parental and filial affection. Children
see their parents go to the parish with the utmost indifference, and without
even an effort to prevent it; and fathers, with equal indifference, send their
wives and families the same road."

Mr. Clarkson has stated some additional samples of the inconvenience to
which an over-peopled parish is exposed.

"We used to employ our supernumeraries in raising gravel for the roads,
and in repairing the roads also. Since that time we erected a machine for
dressing flax, and we bought, and we even grew flax; and we dressed it, and
sold it when dressed. But the price for the article was so low during our
trial of it, that the concern was in all respects a losing one. We were
obliged therefore to give it up. Since that time we have raised gravel
again; but as nearly all the gravel in our parish has been dug up and sifted,
we fear that we shall have no other resource left us, in a short time, than
to allow our supernumeraries what we call "walking passes;" that is, to
pay each of them a small weekly pittance, according as he is a boy or a man,
or as he has a large or a small family—say, from half a crown to six shillings
each per week, and let him walk or go where he will, and earn what he can
besides, and take his earnings to himself.

duction on the state and comfort of the whole
body—grinding down the lower orders to the very
point of starvation, and with a malignity not the
less provoking, that it works by a system, on the
face of which there are constantly playing the
smiles of mercy, and in the support of which, the
sweetest poesy hath been heard to pour forth her
dulcet strains into the ear of weeping sentimental-
ism.

We do not need any thing half so ponderous as
a theory of population for the whole species, to be
assured, that at this moment there are more people
than can be maintained with comfort in our agricultural parishes. The thing is plainly felt all
over England ; and this is a feeling which cannot
be overborne by any argument, either for or against
a theory. The doubt which attaches to a speculation, ought not to overshadow a distinct experience that forces itself rather on the observation
of our senses than the conviction of our understanding. And, along with the palpable exhibition of
an over-peopled parish, there is the equally pal-

" The poor laws most undoubtedly prevent the benefit of a competition
for labourers. I could get more skilful, and better men, and better labourers,
than I have at present, but I cannot take them: because, if I were to take
them, I must pay them, and I should be obliged, besides, to help to maintain those whom I discarded, while they were doing nothing for me. We
must maintain those who belong to us, whether we want them or not—whether they are good or bad, industrious or idle, sober or drunken. We have
therefore no competition, except at too great an expense, beyond our own
parish."

pable habit both of most abandoned licentiousness, and most improvident marriages. The number of illegitimate children alone, superinduces such an excess upon the other population, as is quite adequate to a great and general reduction in the price of labour. And surely there is nought, either in the reasoning for, or in the ridicule against, the philosophy of Mr. Malthus, that can affect a matter of such plain and popular understanding, as the undoubted connection which there is between too early marriages and too large families; a thing that is true of a single household, and true of such a number of households as makes out a parish—beyond which any argument of ours does not require us to extend our contemplation. There may be ways of evading to be a Malthusian in reference to the world, but not in reference to a parish, where the people adhere, by the law of settlement, with a force and a tenacity as great as if drawn together and detained by the law of gravitation. The poor-rate, in fact, has isolated, in a great measure, each of the parishes in England, and turned it into a little world of its own, where we might see in model such an exemplification of the truth, as recommends itself even to the unlettered eye. And the question before us is not a right economy for the globe. It is not even at present a right economy for the whole empire; for this will at length be arrived at by committing to each parish the management of its own affairs, and that management is all which we are now called upon to attend to. *

---

* The latest parliamentary document which has been published on the subject of pauperism, is the Report from the Select Committee on Poor Rate Returns, ordered by the House of Commons to be printed on the 20th of May, 1825. It appears from this Report, that "the expenditure upon the poor in 1823–4, fell short of the amount in 1822–3, by £38,742 only," or by less than an hundred and fiftieth part of the whole annual expense.

It is unnecessary here to repeat our observations in the 260th, and some following pages of the second volume of this work. We there affirm the possibility of a very great reduction in the expenditure, by certain expedients, which have the interest of novelty, and of a yet untried experiment to recommend them, even though the expedients should be altogether superficial, and in no way reach to the principle of this great moral and political disease. Such an expedient is that of the select vestry act; and it is striking to remark, that though but recently adopted by many parishes, and still in the course of successive adoption by more, so slender an abridgment of the evil should have taken place. We predict, that the strenuousness of management in these parishes, where the abridgment has taken place, which is so natural at the outset of every new undertaking, and to which the temporary diminution of expense upon the whole is owing, will shortly relax, when the disease will again manifest its native virulence, and demonstrate, that nothing short of a blow at the root can permanently extenuate it, and far less ever effect its extermination.

To this Report are subjoined a few interesting notices, from parishes in the various counties of England; and from which it will appear that the mischief is making sure progress, although our present bright season of public and political prosperity has, for a time, diverted the attention of men from the subject. It only waits the next of these periodical reverses, to which every trading nation is exposed, when it will again assume its wonted prominency, as an evil of the first magnitude. The people of England are not, perhaps, to be argued out of their system by any power of reasoning; but they will at length be driven out of it, by the pressure of strong and felt necessity.

The composition of wages with poor rate, and its demoralizing effects, are well stated in the following extracts:—

" *Dalby Parva, in the County of Leicester.*—The custom which has pre-

It were a very crude legislation for giving effect
to the speculation of Mr. Malthus, to define the

---

vailed lately, of allowing labourers their wages according to their families,
whether they work or not, tends to encourage idleness and insubordination,
and is very hurtful and expensive to parishes."

"*Dalby Magna, in the same County.*—The method of paying for work
from the poor's rate, is very oppressive to the small occupiers of land; it
is a bad custom, and much practised here. For instance, a good labourer,
perhaps with four or five children, is allowed from eight pence to one shilling per diem, for his work, and goes to the overseer for an additional remuneration according to his family; the small occupiers get none of the
work, but must pay towards the support of his family; indeed, it is now very
customary for labourers to idle away their time, and earn no more than the
eight pence or one shilling. This is spoiling many a good husbandman, and
requires amendment."

"*Laughton, in Lincolnshire.*—Poor rates in this county are generally low,
except in considerable parishes, where the parishioners disagree, and consequent mismanagement arises. Those parishes that employ, or rather place
their poor on the roads to do nothing, and allow them to waste their time
in idleness or pilfering, and suffer them to begin their work and give over
when they please, have plenty of destitute poor, as they frequently prefer
going to the roads at nine shillings per week, to regular labour with the
farmers, at twelve shillings per week. It is the exorbitant power given
to Magistrates, and their folly and erroneous conduct, that have in a great
degree created an evil which it is now difficult to mitigate."

"*Barton Bendish, in Norfolk.*—The poor's rates gradually increase, from
the effects of bastardy, and other causes of increased population. The
county rates rapidly increase, as the proprietors of the soil have the sole
control of the monies expended in the county, and are but comparatively
small contributors. The system of the scale of allowance so tena-
ciously adhered to by the Magistrates, is a notorious cause of pauperism,
idleness, and theft, and causes a manifest disunion of the interests which
ought always to exist between the employer and the employed."

"*Harting, in Sussex.*—There is at this time scarcely a labourer in the
parish, who does not receive parochial assistance. All the children
above two in a family, are on the parish books, by an order of the Magistrates."

We think that we can perceive something like a glimmering of light in
the following observations—a call for a permissive process—the adoption
of which, even in the partial way that is here specified, might lead, in

earliest age at which people should marry. There is no doubt that, by postponing the average period of marriage, there behoved to be a relief from the increase of population; and it is not known

---

some future period, to that more complete and conclusive operation, which, in our fifteenth Chapter of this work, we have ventured to recommend.

" *Washingley, in Huntingdon.*—The less Magistrates interfere with parishes, the better the poor will be provided for. Let select vestries be appointed, and a fine imposed on those who are too indolent to attend them. The heads of a parish will always be the best judges of who are deserving of relief, from the character they bear. Head-money, as it is called, is only an encouragement of the early marriages of the most profligate;—the more children, the more head-money. We know the fact, that men, when they have been asked, how they could think of marrying, when they could not maintain themselves, their answer has been, the laws of the country would provide them a house, maintain their family, and pay the rent."

" *Leybourne, in Kent.*—We earnestly recommend the adoption of some such measure as that contained in the Report of the Committee of the House of Commons; viz. ' That the parishioners shall, if they think fit, draw up rules and regulations for the maintenance and employment of the poor; and when such rules are adjusted to the satisfaction of the Justices and parishioners, to be parochial law for one year.' "

" *Barton Bendish, in Norfolk.*—It would be much better for cultivators of land, if the sole management of the poor were taken from the Magistrates, and invested in the Minister, Churchwardens, and other respectable occupants in the parish. It would be a means of saving considerable expense, inasmuch as it would deprive the Magistrate's clerk of infamous fees and charges, which only tend to further disputes and contentions on the part of labourers and paupers; the husbandman would be much more contented and happy, by being compelled to have recourse to his industry for maintenance, in lieu of seeking an indolent and fraudulent subsistence from the parish fund."

Our last extract shall be from " *Holcombe, in Somerset.*—The poor's rate in this parish, is still on the advance; and although there is full employment (from the very flourishing state of the country) for every one, yet the poor say they will not work, unless the Overseers find it them at their own doors."

by how few months, or by how very few years of a later average, the whole amount of necessary relief would be gained. But, for the purpose of securing an average, it is not indispensable that each individual case should be rigidly fixed down to it. There might be a sure average, and, at the same time, the utmost freedom and variety of individual cases.

To enact any age for marriages, would be just attempting to neutralize one blunder in legislation by another. It were striving to bring about a right result by a compensation of errors; when it were surely better if both were expunged, and there remained no error to be compensated. The law of pauperism has given undue encouragement to matrimony: and it has been proposed, by a law of matrimony, to repress the encouragement. It is the excess of legislation which has done the mischief; and the best method of doing it away, is simply to lop off the excess, and not to counteract one foolish law by another. The tree that would have grown in an upright direction might rise obliquely, because of an artificial pressure on one side of it, though it is possible to correct this by an equal pressure on the other side: still it would have been preferable that it had grown free and unencumbered, without any pressure on either side, and that nature had been simply left to its own way. It is just so in the matter before us. We have only to commit back again to the wisdom of nature, that which ought never to have been meddled with by the wisdom of man. She balances the matter aright between the proneness to marriage, and the prudence that delays it; and the desirable result is brought about, not by the enactment of a new law, but by the cancelment of an old one. The abolition of the law of pauperism would translate the people into other circumstances, and in these circumstances they should be left to act freely.

There can be no doubt, that the abolition of the law of pauperism would bring on a somewhat later average of matrimony among the people. Should this abolition ever take place, and the consequent period of marriage become the subject of political arithmetic, there can be no doubt that its tables will exhibit a more advanced age, on the whole, at which females marry under the new system, than under the present one. This might safely be predicated on the general experience of human nature, although it is further satisfactory, to have had the connection so distinctly exhibited in the parishes of England, between the encouragements of pauperism, and the utter rashness and improvidence of marriages among the peasantry. Should these encouragements be done away, there would be rash and imprudent marriages as before, but not so many. There would, even without the law of pauperism, be a premature entry upon this alliance, but not so premature upon the whole. The evident tendency of a legal provision, is both to speed and to multiply marriages; and were this provision done away, they would be neither so early nor so frequent as they are now. Many still would be the outbreakings of irregularity and folly; but, if at all diminished, there would necessarily be a certain shift for the better in the average of matrimony; and it were in the face of all arithmetic, it were losing sight of the principles and the property of numbers altogether, to deny that this must tell on the births of a parish and its population. We do not say, that profligacy would be exterminated with the law of pauperism; but it would be checked, and, we venture to affirm, that were the supplies of pauperism withdrawn from all future illegitimates, there would be an instantaneous diminution of their number. In all these ways, the market for labour would be less crowded than it is now; and labourers would stand on a higher vantage-ground in the negotiation between them and their employers. There would be some fewer workmen than before, and this is enough to cause much higher wages. This is a most important compensation that awaits the lower classes of England, after that the dispensations of pauperism have been withdrawn from them.

In one part of his work, on the Nature and Causes of the Wealth of Nations, Dr. Adam Smith speaks lightly of political arithmetic. But he can only mean to reflect on the inaccuracy wherewith its data are often guessed at, and presumed upon, and not on the substantial importance of the data themselves. The average date of marriage, in

the various countries of the world, may not have
been precisely ascertained, in any one instance.
But still there is such a date, certain, though not
ascertained; and, furthermore, having a certain influence upon the population, in regard to the increase or diminution of their number. Whatever
postpones the date, must retard the increase; and,
let the obscurity be what it may, which rests upon
the numerical statements that have been exhibited
upon this subject, the connection is indisputable
between the prudence that would delay marriage,
and the relief that would thereby be given to an
overpeopled land. This were true, in the particular of each household, and just as true in the general of that aggregate of households which make up
a population. And we ought not to lose sight of
those elements which are known to have force and
substantive being in our land, though numerically
they are unknown to us. We cannot specify the
accurate proportion which obtains between the
money expended by the lower orders on dissipation, and that expended in pauperism. But there
is no doubt that the former bears a very great proportion to the latter, and, perhaps, overpasses it.
So that, even in the absence of all detail, it is a
most legitimate conclusion, that though pauperism
were abolished, there might still remain throughout the mass a capability for the subsistence of all
their families; and, that if an adequate impulse
were given first to the sobrieties, and then to the
sympathies of our population, there might still

exist such a sufficiency among all, as would, of it-self, prove an effectual guarantee against the starvation of any. It is obviously the direct tendency of such an abolition, to stimulate both their sobrieties and their sympathies; and it is further a comfort to know, from the general fact of the sums expended by the working classes on intemperance alone, that, after all, and apart from public charity, the *materiel* of an entire subsistence passes into their hands, and that nought but the *morale* is wanting, which, by the kindness and the economy that pauperism now supersedes, might impress a right distribution upon it.

But we are quite aware of the incredulity where-with all argument and affirmation are met, when proposed in terms so very general; and it is this which makes us the more solicitous for a tentative process in so many individual parishes. We have elsewhere sufficiently explained by what steps such a process might be obtained for the remedy of pauperism at large; and it would be found equally applicable to that more special abuse of it, which we have now attempted to expose. A few trial parishes, rightly conducted, would soon set the discussion at rest. Every thing would be gained by the success of the experiment; and no widely spread mischief could ensue from the failure of it. All who were actually roundsmen, and supernumeraries in a parish at the commencement of the retracing process, might, like all who were then actually paupers, continue to be treated as old cases—so that the only innovation would be in the treatment of the new applicants. And it should never be out of view, that these applicants must come on very gradually; and that there are many small manageable parishes, where the whole inconvenience would not amount to more perhaps than three or four, each having to wait a few months ere some regular vacancy in labour should occur for their accommodation. And meanwhile, it were well, that they had no right to any other accommodation—that they felt it to be their own business, to look out for work to themselves—that they should be kept on the alert, and on the inquiry for any openings which might occur—and in a word, that the whole matter regarding the employment of the rising youth in a parish, should simply be devolved on their respective families. This would instantly bring into play all the busy interests and activities of self; and under their wholesome operation, there is not a doubt that families would weather all the apprehended evils of this transition, and be at length landed in a state of greater comfort and sufficiency than before. Were each man left to the consequences of his own imprudence, there is a moral necessity for it, that the imprudence would at least be abridged; and if only some few marriages were suspended, and some few criminalities refrained from, it is arithmetically sure, that in a very few years the market for labour would be less loaded with this commodity, and the market price of labour would

yield a greater sufficiency to the families of workmen than before. And this is a benefit that
would be extended more and more, in proportion
to the wisdom and the virtue of our peasantry,
who might thus become the agents of their own
amelioration; and, through the medium of their
own intelligence and worth, be raised to a place
of greater security and comfort than they now
occupy.

There are many ways in which the transition
to a natural state could be smoothed and facilitated
in country parishes. Instances might be named,
of a single gentleman taking up all the supernumeraries of a parish, and giving them employment for months; and if ever such an effort can
be looked for, it is at the outset of a retracing
process, in the success of which so many of the
landlords and other parishioners must feel an interest. Nay, if they so willed it, it is quite possible, at such a crisis as this, to abolish at once the
whole system of composition between wages and
poor-rate, in the case of able-bodied labourers,
by simply translating their whole existing allowance into wages, and relieving the farmer by a
diminution of his levy to as great an amount, as is
the addition which he has made under this arrangement to the pay of his servants. In this way,
every vestige even of the old pauperism, might be
swept away *instanter* from the class of able-bodied
labourers—a thing of incalculable advantage in
warding off that corrupt influence by which the

people of many parishes in England have become almost *en masse* reconciled and assimilated to a state of pauperism. And if the existing supernumeraries could, in many instances, be so easily absorbed and provided for ; one cannot doubt that new cases, coming on as they would very gradually, might, for a time, be as easily disposed of. Meanwhile the right is abolished. Employment might be asked, but it could no longer be demanded. It would not now, be in such certain and unfailing reserve for the superfluous members of a family, as to supersede the necessity of their own shifts and their own expedients. In such circumstances as these, the precipitate marriage of one of their boys, and still more the seduction of a daughter, would be far more felt than it is now as a family visitation ; and thus a higher tone of virtue would spring up among them, almost as soon as the necessity which compels it. It is not yet known how very soon the state of the population would accommodate itself to this new state of things, or how soon labourers would attain to independent and well-earned comfort, and that simply because there would be fewer labourers.

Emigration to our colonies is worthy of the utmost support from Government, if connected with a process for the abolition of pauperism. But should the system of pauperism continue, it will operate no sensible relief to England. It has been likened to a safety-valve—but it is a valve, the very lifting and opening of which implies the elasticity

within of a state of compression and violence;
and up to this state it will remain, notwithstanding the successive escapes of a redundant population. The creative process will always maintain a
balance with the relieving process; and a people
must be in distress, when the difficulties of home
are so nearly in equilibrium with its charms, as to
place them on the eve of desire and deliberation
to renounce it for ever. And besides, the poor
laws act in an opposite direction to the offers and
the encouragements of emigration; though, if connected with any plan for the abolition of them, we
cannot conceive a better way both of smoothing
the transition, and of keeping the country in a
clear and healthful state after the transition has
been effected. It would, at all events, afford a
ready answer to the complaints and difficulties of
able-bodied men, who alleged a wânt of employment; if a parish were enabled, by the facilities
that government held out, to aid, upon easy terms,
the emigration of them. It were a test by which
to ascertain the truth of their complaints; and we
believe that, when the proposal of emigration was
made, it would be declined in by far the greater
number of instances. The parish would at least
stand acquitted; and it would afterwards be seen,
that a very small fraction of the labourers of a
parish stood in need after all of the resource of
emigration. On this account, it would not be very
expensive to government, though it held out very
great advantages to emigration; and it would

shield every parish from the charge of inhumanity, were it enabled to suggest this expedient to its unemployed labourers.

But it is to the reaction at home, that we look for our best securities against any shock or disaster that might be apprehended to our families from the overthrow of pauperism. When charity is altogether detached from the remuneration of labour, this of itself will keep off a very wide and wasting contamination from the spirit of our peasantry, and they will again recover the honest pride of independence. Still more would this feeling grow in strength and sensibility, were they trained to the habit of small but constant accumulation. It is at this crisis, that a parish saving-bank might achieve a wondrous transformation on the state of the people, by begetting a sense of property among labourers. A very few philanthropists could set it on foot. By a very few easy devices, at the outset of the retracing process, there could, in many places, be afforded as much employment and as liberal wages to all, as might enable them to deposit. Once that the turning point has been made from being a pauper to being a possessor, a new ambition is felt, and a new object comes to be intensely prosecuted. This is a better expedient for postponing the date of marriage than any act of parliament. The days were in Scotland, when it was customary, during the virtuous attachment of years, for the parties to fill up the interval with those frugalities and labours

by which they made a provision for their future
household; and there is no doubt, that a saving-
bank is fitted to inspire with a similar purpose
those who repair to it. If it did so with a few only,
still the average period of matrimony is somewhat
shifted for the better; the tide of population is
somewhat arrested; the excess in a few years is
somewhat reduced from what it would otherwise
have been; and the market price of labour is elevated in greater proportion. These are the sure
steps which lead from a growing virtue among the
people, to a still more rapidly growing prosperity
in their economic condition ; and by which a process that guides to sufficiency and comfort each
individual family who embark upon it, carries in it
a further and a wider blessing to the general mass of
the population.

We have already said, that nothing was easier
than to suit the law of settlement to that state of
things, which would take place in a parish, when
the law of pauperism was done away. To acquire
a right of settlement in the parish itself were altogether useless, when by it there is nothing to acquire. After that any given subject of right or of
distribution has vanished, the laws which relate to
it, cease to be of any significancy. And thus it is,
that the mutual law of settlement between parishes
is virtually abrogated, by the very act which re-
leases either the one or the other from the *legal*
obligation of maintaining its own poor. After
that the poor at home have been devolved on the

free charities of nature, in any given parish, it is
never to be imagined that the poor from abroad,
and who may have chosen to reside in that parish,
should have any other resource provided for them
there. And it is thus, that while two trial parishes
may freely exchange their people with each other,
neither would feel any addition to its legal burden
in consequence of this, because neither would lie
under any legal obligation.

The case is different, where one of the parishes
only has emerged from the old system, and the
other still remains under it. There may still be a
free reciprocal transit of families between them;
but it were not fair, if, while the families of the
latter acquire no right by passing within the confines of the former, those of the former should acquire any right by passing within the confines of
the latter. The emancipated parish comes under
no burden by the influx of people from other parishes; and, conversely, it is right that these parishes should not be exposed to any burden by the
efflux of people from that parish, which shall have
now exchanged the compulsory for the gratuitous
system of charity. This does away every apprehension, lest the rest of England should suffer from those
portions of it which are delivered of the poor-rate:
And, we have elsewhere argued abundantly for
our persuasion, that the emigrants from a trial
parish, though without any right on the parish
which they have left, and without any possibility
of acquiring a right on the parish into which they

have entered, will be generally found of a higher and better condition than the population by whom they are surrounded.

But while it is indispensable, that the parishes still under bondage of pauperism shall sustain no injury from the reformed parishes, there is a way, in which, without a certain modification in the law of settlements, the workmen of a reformed parish might sustain injury from the others. The mixing of poor-rate with wages, has depressed the allowance that is given in the name of wages, throughout all those parishes of England where this practice is in force; and should the practice be abolished in any parish, this allowance would forthwith be raised. It is not impossible, that while in one parish a workman earns eight shillings a week in the shape of wages, and receives four in the shape of poor-rate, the workmen of a contiguous parish, where the poor-rate has been done away, might earn the whole twelve shillings in wages alone. The difficulty, in this case, would be to protect the labourers of a reformed parish from the competition of those exotic labourers who might come in to reside amongst them, although they belonged, by settlement, to other parishes—men who might endeavour to compound the high wage of the one with the vestry allowance of the other, and might succeed for a time in the pocketing of both. Meanwhile, there might be an under-bidding of the native, by the imported workmen; and although, if England were wholly emancipated from poor-rate, wages might sustain a high level all over the country, which would not be trodden down by the freest movements of its people from one part to another; yet so long as the emancipation is only partial, there will be, at least, a tendency to the sinking of wages down to the low rate of the assessed parishes.

Perhaps the most effectual security against this evil, would be a law, by which every man capable of working, should forfeit all right of relief from his own parish, so long as he resided in any of the trial parishes. This would give, at least, a theoretical consistency to the whole arrangement; besides being a defence against the apprehended mischief, in all those cases where the mischief would have followed. We do not think, however, that practically it could ever be felt to any great extent. In those parishes, where the retracing process had been entered upon in the spirit of a pure and patriotic reformation, there would be a strong preference for the employment of their own people. And what is more to the purpose, we do not find that the prevalence of this abuse in one part of England, has compelled the adoption of it in another part of England. The northern counties are comparatively exempted from the evils that lie in the composition of a poor-rate with wages; and though exposed to competition both from the labourers of the south, and what, perhaps, is still more formidable, to the competition of Scotch and Irish labourers, they still maintain that high rate of wages, which enables them to ward off, in a great measure, the stigma of pauperism, from the healthy and able-bodied of their population.

But, after all, we should hold it quite a safe measure, to abolish, *instanter*, the application of poor-rate to the relief of all able-bodied labourers. We have no doubt, that there would be an immediate compensation in the rise of wages ;* and, at all events, that the change of circumstances, however sudden, would be followed by no distress, either of great intensity, or of great duration. Our preference is for gradual changes; but still our confidence is, that when the change is from a wrong to a right system, even though accomplished at once by the fiat of authority, the country will always right itself surprisingly soon, and without any great suffering ensuing from the transition. On this same subject, we have the experience of a change, *per saltum*, in the condition of all the Irish paupers resident in England, the great majority of

---

* The following extract is from the report of Mr. Vivian's examination before the Select Committee on the Poor-Laws in 1817. His Parish was Bushey in Hertfordshire.

" Is it not, then, the practice in your parish, to advance regularly, weekly, a sum in addition to the wages earned by your labourers ? Never: and to that I ascribe, almost as much as any thing, a diminution of the rates.—If a man has six young children, no one of which can maintain himself, you do not give any permanent relief beyond his wages? Never: occasional presents, and that very seldom.—How did you prevail on the parish to put an end to that practice ? By strong persuasion, and by desiring them to try the experiment; and it answered. They immediately got into task-work, and got twenty-five shillings a week."

whom chose to remain, and without any sensible inconvenience, and certainly without one authentic case of starvation occurring in consequence.* The speed and the facility wherewith the population accommodate themselves to some new condition, into which they are suddenly transported by some great and unlooked-for change in the circumstances of a country, are never more strikingly exemplified, than in the changes which take place in the direction of national industry, on passing from a war to a peace, or from a peace to a war establishment. Still we are unfriendly to all violence, even on the career of undoubted amelioration. And we only give this instance to prove, that legislators may, without danger, proceed with bolder footsteps than they are generally inclined to do, in the path of economic improvement.

And certain it is, that however impotent the relief may be which emigration could afford to a country, the system of whose pauperism still continued to give full license and encouragement for the increase of population, yet, as connected with a scheme for the abolition of pauperism, it might be of most useful auxiliary influence, for smoothing the transition in parishes, from a compulsory to a gratuitous system of charity. Emigration could afford no adequate relief to the miseries of an over-peopled land, where a legal provision for the destitute still continued to uphold

---

* See Vol. II. of this Work, pp. 287, et seq.

the recklessness of families. But emigration were an admirable expedient, both for tranquillizing the fears of the public lest labourers should starve, and also for meeting the complaints and applications of these labourers, when they alleged a want of employment. Apart from a process which pointed to the extinction of pauperism, it is altogether a superficial remedy for the disorders of an excessive population. But when attached to such a process, it might speed and facilitate the whole operation; and it is only when so attached, that a scheme of emigration will repay, by its blessings to the country, the expense which it might bring upon Government.

CHAP. XIX.

ON SAVINGS BANKS.

WITHOUT the co-operation of their own virtuous endeavours, there seems no possible way of doing good to the labouring classes, or of helping them upwards from a lower to a more secure and elevated place in the commonwealth. But we can see a very patent way to it, in such habits and such resources as, generally speaking, are within their reach. It is for them, and for them only, to regulate the supply of labourers. In the command which belongs to them of this mighty element, the price of labour may be regarded as the product of their collective voice, which pitches either high or low, in proportion to the amount of worth and intelligence and sobriety that are diffused throughout the population. Could we only imagine a nation of regular and well-habited families, where the folly of premature marriages, and the vice of illicit associations, were alike unknown—there would then be no inconvenient excess of labourers; no fall of wages beneath the par of human comfort, or at least, no fall that would not almost be instantly repaired by the reaction it would have on the principle and prudence of an enlightened peasantry. Now, though such a nation is not to be born in a day, yet in a single day might we at least begin the work of approximating thereunto. Every additional school for popular education brings us nearer to it. Every new deposit in a savings bank helps us on to it. The removal of the whole system of pauperism, were the removal of a sore obstruction in its way; an obstruction which, if suffered to remain, will, we honestly believe, seal the peasantry of our land to irrecoverable degradation. So sure do we esteem the operation of these principles, that we should look for the visible result of them in a very few years, in any parish, where the retracing process had been entered upon. It is this which makes us so desirous of the experiment in England. The comparison between two parishes on the old and new system, would flash more conviction on the public understanding than a thousand arguments.

The frugality of a workman might at length, through means of a savings bank, land him in a small capital; and there is one effect of a capital in the hands of the labouring classes, which must be quite obvious. It were a barrier between them and that urgent immediate necessity, which gives such advantage to their employers in the question of wages. A man on the brink of starvation has no command in this negotiation. He will gladly accept of such terms as are offered, rather than perish of hunger; and it is thus, by their improvidence and their reckless expenditure in prosperous times, that on the evil day they lie so much at the mercy and dictation of their superiors. The possession of a capital, and that not a very great one, by each individual labourer, or rather by each of a considerable number of labourers, would reverse the character of the negotiation entirely. They could stand out against miserable wages. They could afford to be idle; and while so, the stock of that commodity which they work, and wherewith the market is for the present glutted, would soon melt away; and the price of their labour be speedily restored to its fair and comfortable level. It were most delightful to see the lower orders, by dint of foresight and economy in good times, thus enabled to weather the depression of bad times, nay inconceivably to shorten the period of it, by simply living on their accumulated means, and abstaining to work for a wretched remuneration. Or if they should continue to work, they would, at least, not need to overwork. It is this, which so lengthens out at present the season of ill-paid labour. The low wages stimulate to a greater amount of industry, that a subsistence, if possible, might be forced from it to their starving families. The use of a capital in savings banks would be to prevent this. Men would not, while they had a resource in the earnings of past years, put themselves to an unnatural violence, in order that the current earnings might meet their current necessities.* At all

---

* " There cannot be conceived a more cruel dilemma for the poor operative, than that, in eking out a subsistence for his family, he should thus

events, the overstocked market would sooner be cleared of its surplus, and, with a brisker demand, there would quickly come round a better remuneration. And such a state of things would not only serve to reduce the inequalities in the condition of labourers ; but, on the whole, it would somewhat elevate their condition, and that permanently. If in possession of means that raised them above the urgencies of immediate want, they could treat more independently with their employers. They would not as now, be so much the parties that sought; but more at least than now, they would be the parties that were sought after. The whole platform of humble life would take a higher level than at present; and we repeat that, to every man who felt aright, it were a satisfaction and a triumph, then to recognize a hale and well-conditioned peasantry.

We are aware of a jealousy here; and how much it is that capitalists have suffered by unlooked-for conspiracies on the part of the workmen. We are also aware of the sums that have been subscribed by the latter, for the express purpose of

---

overwork himself, and, by that miserable effort, should only strengthen the barrier that lies in the way of his final deliverance; that for the relief of the present urgencies of nature, he should be compelled to put forth more than the strength of nature, and yet find, as the direct result of his exertion, a lengthening out of the period of his distress ; that the necessity should thus be laid upon him of what may be called a self-destroying process,—accumulating as he does, with his own hand, the materials of his own wretchedness, and so annoying and overwhelming the earth with the multitude of his commodities, that she looks upon his offerings as an offence, rather than an obligation, and refuses to sustain him."—*Edinburgh Review*, vol. xxxiii. p. 388.

maintaining all the members of the conspiracy in idleness, and so of holding out, till masters should surrender to their terms. It is on these considerations that an apprehension has been felt, in certain quarters, lest savings banks should arm the mechanics and workmen of our land with a dangerous power, and place at the mercy of their caprice the interest of all the other orders in society. This, at least, is a concession of the efficacy of these institutions for all the purposes on account of which we would argue in their favour; and they who fear lest provident banks should make the lower orders too rich, must at all events allow, that, with care and conduct on their part, there is a capability amongst them for becoming rich enough to be wholly independent of the supplies of pauperism. While we have no doubt that the power of becoming rich enough is in their own hands, we cannot sympathize with the feelings of those who fear lest they should be too rich. We should like to see them invested with a certain power of dictation as to their own wages. We should like to see them taking full advantage of all that they have fairly earned, in the negotiation with their employers. We should like to see a great stable independent property in the hands of the labouring classes, and their interest elevated to one of the high co-ordinate interests of the state. It were well, we think, if, by dint of education and virtue, they at length secured a more generous remuneration for labour, so as that wages should bear a much higher proportion than they do now to the rent of land, and the profit of stock, which form the other two ingredients in the value of a commodity. In this competition between capitalists and workmen, we profess ourselves to be on the side of the latter, and would rejoice in every advantage which their own industry and their own sobriety had won for them. Rather than that, at the basis of society, we should have a heartless, profligate, and mis-thriven crew, on the brink of starvation, and crouching under all the humiliations of pauperism, we should vastly prefer an erect, and sturdy, and withal well-paid and well-principled peasantry, even though they should be occasionally able to strike their tools, and to incommode their superiors by bringing industry to a stand. We have no doubt, at the same time, that the fear is altogether an extravagant one—that the two classes would soon come to a right adjustment—and that, in particular, the employers of labour would find it a far more comfortable management, when they had to do with a set of prosperous and respectable workmen, than when they have to do with the fiery and unreasonable spirits that so abound among a dissipated, ill-taught, and ill-conditioned population. In the strength of the principle of population, nature has provided a sufficient security against the prudential restraint upon marriages being carried too far; and we may, therefore, always be sure of an adequate supply of labourers for all the essential or important business of the land. But, through the law of pauperism, the restraint is not carried far enough, and now we are oppressed, in consequence, by a redundancy of numbers. By abolishing this law, we simply leave the adjustment of the balance to nature. Legislators vacillate, and are uncertain about the alternative of the people being either too rich or too poor. But nature, if unmeddled with by their interference, will so manage between the animal instincts on the one hand, and the urgencies of self-preservation, or the higher principles of the mind, upon the other, as that they shall neither be richer nor poorer than they ought to be.

This prejudice, however, against savings banks, and this alarm for the independence of the lower orders, are very much confined to capitalists of narrow views and narrow circumstances. There is a delightful experience upon this subject, that is multiplying and becoming more manifest every day, and which goes to prove how much the interest of the employer and that of the workman is at one. It is, that the expense of a well-paid labourer is in general more than made up by the superior worth and quality of his service. The farmer, in those parishes where there is a composition of poor-rate with wages, does not find his account in this system. The labour is cheaper, but far less valuable in proportion—the work that is underpaid, being done in a way so much more slovenly, as to annihilate any advantage that might otherwise have accrued to the master. It is an advantage grasped at by men of limited means, and who find a saving in their immediate outlay to be of some consequence to them. But in the large and liberal scale, either of a great manufactory, or of any agricultural operation in which a sufficient capital is embarked, it is found that, with well-paid and well-principled workmen, the prosperity both of masters and servants is most effectually consulted. There is something triumphant and cheering in the perspective that is opened up by such a contemplation; and we cannot but admire that wisdom of nature's mechanism, in virtue of which, if law would only recal its blunders, and philanthropy go forth in the work of indefinitely enlightening and moralising the lower orders, we should behold, in their extended sufficiency and comfort, nought to impair, but rather every thing to improve, the condition of all the other classes in society.

It holds out a seeming advantage to the lower orders, that when the wages of their labour fall short of their necessary subsistence, they should have the difference made good to them from a fund that is chiefly provided by the higher orders of the community. It is the boast of equitable law, that it both ordains rights for the poor man, and protects him as effectually from all encroachments upon them, as it would the possessors of highest rank or opulence in the land. He has the right of freedom, and the right of personal security, and the right of property in his wages, and in all that he accumulates from these wages: and when, additionally to these, there is enacted for him the right of levying from the other classes, that sum by which his wages are deficient from the maintenance of himself and of his family, it hath the appearance of rendering him a more securely, and a more abundantly privileged individual than he was before. But the last privilege is wholly neutralized, should it be made palpable; and that, by a very obvious political economy, that the law which enacts it, creates the very deficiency which it professes to provide for; that the right of parish relief just makes so much the less valuable to him the right of property, even by abridging this property at least to the full extent of its own allowances; that though it should only operate to increase the number of workmen by a very little, this is enough of itself to reduce the wages very much; and that therefore it would have been better for him, if law had ceased one step sooner from that series of enactments which has been made in his favour. It is quite undeniable, from the state of every parish in England, that marriages are greatly more precipitate, and that licentiousness is greatly more unrestrained, by the way in which the law of pauperism hath palliated the consequences both of vice and of imprudence, and that practically and really, in agricultural districts, a very great oppression is felt from the redundancy of labourers. And the consequent deficiency in their wages is made up at the judgment of the upper classes in society, whose tendency of course will be to rate the allowance as low as possible. It is thus that their state is subjected to the arbitration of others, when, under a better economy of things, it might have virtually been at their own arbitration.

It marks most strikingly the evil that ensues, when the wisdom of man offers to mend or to meddle with the wisdom of nature, that not alone have the rich suffered in their patrimony, but the poor have become more helpless and dependent, because of the violence that has been done to the original feelings of property, by the aggressions thereupon of an artificial legislation. A people under the imagination that law must provide for them, will spread and multiply beyond the possibility of them being upheld in comfort at all. A people under a law that undertakes no more than simply to protect them in their earnings, have a patent way for raising a perpetual barrier against that indigence, which law hath vainly endeavoured, by its direct and formal provisions, to avert from our borders.

The man who leans on the fancied sufficiency of the poor laws, to meet his necessities when the day of necessity cometh, has no inducement to economise. He spends as fast as he gains; and on an adverse fluctuation in the price of labour, he has nothing for it but to submit to the terms of his employer. It is true, that when the remuneration is very glaringly beneath the par of human subsistence, there is a certain allowance eked out to him from the legal charity of his parish; but in those seasons of dreary vicissitude, when hundreds beside himself are thrown out of profitable work, we may be sure that this allowance will form but a meagre subsistence to himself and his family. The peculiar hardship of such a condition, is, that in order to enlarge the now straitened comforts of his household, there is the utmost temptation to overworking; and what is done by him, is done by thousands more in the country beside himself—or, in other words, the excessive supply of the market with the commodities of their particular manufacture, continues to be kept up and be extended, at the very time when it is most desirable that the overplus under which it labours should be wholly cleared away. In these circumstances, it is quite obvious, that the evil of an overstocked market, with the consequent depression of wages, must be sorely aggravated by the reckless improvidence of labourers; who, without economy, are always from hand to mouth, and must therefore put forth a busier hand, at the time when it is most desirable for them that the production were lessened, instead of being augmented. It is thus, that in as far as a poor-rate adds to the improvidence of workmen, and in as far as it adds to the number of them, (and it most directly and intelligibly ministers to both these effects,) in so far does it aggravate the helplessness of their condition, on those melancholy occasions, when the manufacturer, oppressed and overpowered with the solicitation of

labourers for employment, can, in fact, hold them
in subjection to his own terms, and possess himself,
for the lowest possible recompense, of the time,
and strength, and services of a prostrate population.

This process may be most beautifully reversed
under another system of things that would stimulate the economy of the lower orders ; or, in other
words, under a system where, instead of leaning on
the fancied sufficiency of a legal provision, each
knew that he had nought but himself to lean upon.
Just conceive his little savings to be accumulated
into a stock that could at length uphold him for
months, even though the daily income was to be
arrested for the whole of that period. Let this,
we shall not say, be the universal, but let it ap-
proximate, in some degree, to the general habit
and condition of labourers—and then we cannot
fail to perceive that they will stand on a secure
and lofty vantage ground, whence it is that they
will be able, not only to weather, but also to control the fluctuations of the market. More particularly, in any season of mercantile distress, when,
because of the heavy accumulation of goods,
prices had fallen, and manufacturers were sure to
lose by bringing for a time any more of them to
market, how precisely accommodated to such a state
of things, is the simple capacity of labourers to uphold themselves for a season, without that helpless
dependence on the daily wage, which is felt by
those who, in virtue of their own reckless impro-

vidence, are ever standing upon the very brink of their resources. A set of workmen who must either work or starve, is a sad incumbrance in a situation like this; and it must be at once obvious how, in their hands, the calamity that weighs them down must be woefully aggravated and prolonged. A set of workmen again, who in the sufficiency of their own accumulated means, can afford to work less at a time of scanty remuneration, or could even go to play for a season, and refuse to touch one farthing of so miserable a hire; or (which is the likeliest direction for them to take in these circumstances) who could keep themselves a-going with other, though less lucrative work, that perhaps might never have been performed, but for the cheapness at which they are willing to undertake it—let such workmen, in one or other of these ways, simply withdraw from their own particular manufacture the labour which they wont to bestow upon it; and, with the production so lessened, while the consumption proceeds at its ordinary, or perhaps at a much faster rate, because of the existing low price of the article, the now overladen market must be speedily relieved, and the price of the commodity will again rise to its wonted level. The simple ability of the workman to maintain himself for so many weeks without his accustomed wages, is that which brings up these wages in a far shorter period, than they otherwise would to their customary level. A fair recompense for labour, speedily accrues, as before, to the labourer, whose past economy in fact, is the instrument of his present relief, and whose future economy, in like manner, will effectually shield him from all those coming adversities to which a fitful and fluctuating commerce is exposed.

But the growth of capital among the lower orders, would not only secure for them this occasional relief. It would be the instrument of a general and permanent elevation. They would not only be saved by it from those periodical descents to which they are else so liable; they would not only throw a passage for themselves across those abysses, through which they would otherwise have had to flounder their hazardous and uncertain way; but they could raise the whole platform of their condition, and lift up its average, as well as smooth or equalise its fluctuations. At any time let manufacturers have to treat with workmen who are not just dependent upon them for the subsistence of to-morrow, but who for weeks or months to come, could live upon the fruits of their past industry and good conduct; and they will meet a far greater difficulty and resistance in bringing them to their own terms. The workmen will be able to treat independently with their employers. They are not obliged, in such a state of things, to acquiesce in the low wage that they would gladly submit to in other circumstances; and it will take a higher wage than before to satisfy them. This they can attain to without a poor-rate; but with a poor-rate they

never will. It is through the medium of ther own
virtuous economy that the only patent and effectual way lies, for elevating the lower orders, and
that permanently, in the scale. The law of pauperism has all along, with her lying promises, acted
as a cheat to lure them from the only road to their
own stable independence and comfort. It has now
placed them, all over England, on the brink of a
most fearful emergency. The wages of agricultural labour have lamentably fallen beneath the
par of human subsistence; and, throughout the
great mass of the peasantry, there is a very general recourse to such little scantlings or supple-
ments as are reluctantly doled out to them in the
shape of beggarly ministration from the parish
vestry; and all this to men, who but for this ac-
cursed law, might, in the pure capacity of honest
and hard-working labourers, have, instead of being
arbitrated upon, been themselves the arbitrators of
their own state.

There is no institution then, more adapted to
the condition of a parish, at that juncture when it
enters upon the retracing process, which I have
elsewhere explained, than a savings bank. It is
then that every endeavour should be made for rear-
ing the people into a habit, utterly the opposite of
that by which they are now depressed and degraded.
The influential men of any little vicinity, could do
much by their countenance and liberality on such
an occasion. They could, at least, afford to give
each new applicant for work as much more in the

shape of wages, as they would then withhold from him in the shape of poor-rate. The nominal price of labour would rise by this difference; and with such a prospect before them, as an ultimate deliverance from the burden of the poor-rate altogether, some might add a little more to the wage, with a special view to the training of the young in the practice of accumulation. And certainly the motive to deposit would not as now be neutralised by the existence of a right to relief, which the new economy of things supposes to be done away. And when once they exchanged the feeling of paupers for the feeling of proprietors, the breath of another spirit would animate the people; and that principle, to which Dr. Adam Smith so often refers, the instant effort of every man to better his own condition, would have its free and full operation among them. When the general aim is to make the most of that right which every man possesses to parochial relief, from this must ensue a slothful, and beggarly, and worthless population, who will be kept in as low a condition as masters and overseers can reduce them to. When the general aim is to make the most of that right which every man has to his own earnings, from this must ensue a population the reverse of the former in all their characteristics, and who, by every new accession made to the capital of the working classes, will attain to higher wages than before. The best service which can be rendered to the lower orders, is to take away the former right altogether, and to turn to its utmost possible account the latter right; which, in truth, is the only one that can at all avail them. On the moment that they could afford to live for a given period without labour, from that moment the value of their services would rise in the labour market.* They would never need to overwork for the sake of an immediate subsistence ; nor, of course, to overdo the supply of any article of consumption. The proportion between the supply

---

* We are quite aware, that it is not by the operation of but a few savings banks, and a consequent capital in the hands of fractionally a very small number of our people, that a higher rate of wages will become general in the country. To work this effect, there must be a corresponding generality in the cause. There will not be this general elevation in the status of labourers, till there be a general habit of accumulation amongst them ; and however much the individuals who do accumulate may benefit themselves, they must bear a certain proportion to the whole mass of the community, ere they can work a sensible advancement upon the whole in the circumstances of the lower orders. Suppose a district of the land, where the peasantry had, by economy and good management, attained a measure of independence ; yet, if surrounded by other over-peopled districts, teeming with reckless and improvident families, this were enough to keep down the remuneration of labour, even in that place where labourers had universally become little capitalists. It is thus that the neighbourhood of Ireland will retard the progress of the lower orders in Britain, towards a permanently higher state of comfort and sufficiency than they now enjoy. And the only way of neutralizing the competition from that quarter, is just by carrying to them too the beneficent influences of education, and training the people to that style and habit of enjoyment which will at length bring later marriages, and a less oppressive weight of population along with it. We are abundantly sensible that the enlargement, which we now contemplate as awaiting our operative classes, must be the slow result of a moral improvement among themselves, which we fear will come on very gradually. But certain it is, that, tardy as this way may be of a people's amelioration, it is the only way; and, at all events, there is nothing in the tumult and stir of those popular combinations, which have so recently arisen in all parts of the land, that in the least degree is fitted to hasten it.

and the demand, would be generally in favour of the workmen; and wages would be made permanently to stand in a higher relation, both to rent and profits, than they ever can maintain in the hands of a reckless and improvident peasantry.*

---

* The disciples of Ricardo, who have adopted all his formulæ on the subject of rent, profit, and wages, and of the relation which these three elements bear to each other, while directly led to perceive how it is that wages may increase at the expense of profit, may not acquiesce so readily in the position, that wages may increase without any diminution of profit, and solely at the expense of rent. Now it should be observed, in the reasonings of this economist, that when he speaks of profit, and of it alone, falling by an increase of wages, he keeps out of view, for the time at least, that process which he himself describes so well, and by which it is that inferior soils are, one after another along the scale of descent, brought into cultivation. Now the truth is, that, connected with this movement, there is not the mutual action of wages and profit, but the mutual action of wages and rent, and also that of profit and rent, upon each other; and as, on the one hand, in the direct process of an extending cultivation, the landlord gains both upon the capitalist and the labourer, so, on the other hand, there is a reverse process, in which both the capitalist and the labourer may not only keep their ground, but even make head against the encroachments of the landlord.

For, what is it that " obliges a country to have recourse to land of a worse quality, to enable it to raise its supply of food?" It is " the progress of population." (Ricardo's Political Economy, p. 52, second edition.) Now, the circumstance of the land being worse, implies, that it yields a less return to the same quantity of labour. Previous to its being entered upon for the purpose of cultivation, there was a better land which paid no rent, and whose larger return went all to the wages of that labour, and the profit of that capital, which were applied to it. The reason why land which yields a less return to the same labour has been entered upon is, that either labourers were willing to marry, and perpetuate their numbers, upon inferior wages, or, that capitalists were willing to trade upon inferior profits. Both causes may have operated. And certain it is, that if, after land of a given quality had been cultivated, there was still such a " progress of population" as to force an entrance upon land of a worse quality, that progress must have been owing to the standard of ease and

The whole philosophy of a subject may be exemplified within a narrow space. In its practical

---

enjoyment together, among the people, having been lower than was sufficient to keep them stationary in point of numbers. They were willing, for the sake of earlier marriages than they would otherwise have formed, to surrender part of this ease or enjoyment; and thus they married so early as to increase the population, and hence to make it necessary that " land of an inferior degree of fertility should be taken into cultivation." (Ricardo, p. 51.)

Now, if, previous to the overflow of people upon this inferior soil, there had been such an influence, from education, and other moral or exalting causes, upon the lower ranks, as kept them from descending to a lower style or standard of enjoyment, this of itself would have restrained the population to later, and therefore to less prolific, marriages. It would have made a higher soil the extreme barrier, for the time, of cultivation. And thus it is, that, by connecting the standard of enjoyment among the working classes, with the limit to which agriculture is carried downward among the soils of worse quality, you make the wages of labour have a direct bearing, not on the profits of the capitalists alone, but also on the rent of the landlord.

And further, it can be conceived of the popular taste, that it might not only be preserved from sinking, but that, by the humanizing influences of scholarship and Christianity, it might even be elevated. As far as this cause operates, it must narrow the extent of cultivation. It must force the abandonment of those worse soils which could not yield the now higher wages, consequent on a now less numerous and overstocked population. It would require, after such a change in the habits of enjoyment among our people, a better soil, to furnish the requisite profit, and the requisite wages, without leaving any surplus of rent to the proprietor. This would of course diminish the rent of his whole land, and so prove an encroachment by the labourer on the income of the proprietor.

And as the population can thus keep their ground, and even make head against the landed proprietor, so there is a way in which capitalists can do the same thing. There are certain points of analogy between the two elements of capital and population, which have not been adverted to ; and the statement of which, therefore, might appear paradoxical. We are sensible that it would require a separate work fully to vindicate the statement—and yet we cannot at present refrain from making it. We shall afterwards refer to the suddenness and the spontaneous facility wherewith capital is replaced, so as to recover, as if by the force of elasticity, all its former ex-

effects, pauperism is co-extensive with our empire.
In its principles, and in the whole rationale of its

---

tent, after any great curtailment which, from violence or other causes, it
may have undergone. In this it resembles population, the blanks of which,
created by wars or epidemics, are so speedily repaired. This, combined
with the general fact, that population, so far from having to be fostered by
encouragement, tends of itself to press inconveniently on the food of a
country, has changed the policy of the state regarding it—insomuch that,
instead of watching solicitously over it, as if it were at once the most precious, and at the same time the most precarious element of national
prosperity, it is now justly regarded as one of those interests which
may, with all safety, be left to itself, and which can never be permanently short of the subsistence that is afforded in any given state of the
world.

Now, we are far from expecting the full or immediate sympathy of all
our readers, when we affirm of mercantile capital also, that it tends so
to reproduce and to extend itself, as to press inconveniently on the business which is afforded in any given state of the world. For the upholding
of this interest, there is no call for that strenuous parsimony which Dr.
Smith insists upon so urgently, throughout the whole of his work. There
need be no greater apprehension of a sufficient capital at all times for the
profitable business, than there is of a sufficient population for the food of
the world. And if it be desirable that population should be restrained
within narrower limits, for the object of a more plenteous allowance to
every single family, then may it also be desirable that mercantile capital
should be restrained from its tendencies to overgrowth, to assure a more
liberal profit to every single capitalist.

It may be an excess of population that compels the entry upon inferior
soils, and causes the people to be satisfied with their scantier produce, as
the fund out of which their now inferior wages can be paid. Or it may
be an excess of capital that compels the same entry, by causing capitalists
to be satisfied with an inferior profit. The way to check both of these
excesses, is, by a higher style of enjoyment, which prevents, in the one
class, too rapid an accumulation of people, and prevents, in the other, too
rapid an accumulation of capital. We confess, that we should not object
to the moral preventive check of Malthus being extended from labourers to
capitalists; and a higher style of enjoyment is the instrument, in both
cases, of putting it into operation. Ricardo has the sagacity to foresee
the tendency of things—which is, that profits shall fall indefinitely low, so
as that " almost the whole produce of the country, after paying the la-

operation, it may be effectually studied even on the limited field of a small parochial community. It then lies before us in more manageable compass; and we even think, that one might in this way acquire a truer discernment of the process—just as a process of mechanism is better understood by our regard being directed to the model, than to the ponderous and unwieldy engine itself. It is on this account that we prize so much the following little narrative by the overseer of Long Burton, in Dorsetshire; a parish with a population of only three hundred and twenty-seven, and therefore peculiarly adapted for the distinct exhibition of any influence which its parochial economy might have on the state of its inhabitants.

The overseer had three able-bodied men out of

---

bourers, will be the property of the owners of land, and the receivers of tithes and taxes." The mercantile classes of society have it in their power to retard, if not to prevent, this fall in the circumstances of their order. They *collectively* can uphold a higher profit, by means of a more profuse expenditure, and a higher style of living in their families—by turning a larger share of their gains to the object of immediate enjoyment, and a less share of them to the growth and extension of a capital, which, just in proportion to its magnitude, will diminish the profits of future years. The individual merchant may take to himself so liberal a share now of this world's enjoyments, as to trench on his enjoyments afterwards; but certain it is, that if, by a change in the average habits of the whole mercantile body, there was to be a more liberal expenditure among them, this, instead of wasting, would perpetuate to them the means of liberal expenditure in all time coming. It would keep the capital lower than it now is, and the profit higher; and thus it is, that by the collective will of capitalists, as well as by that of the peasantry, a limitation might be raised to the rent of the landlord—and all the three classes might share more equally in the produce of the country.

employment, and whom it fell upon him to dispose of. The farmers all saturated with workmen, could not take them in; and rather than send them to work upon the roads, he applied to a master mason in the neighbourhood, who engaged to take their services at the low rate of six shillings in the week—the parish to make up the deficiency to the three men, so as that they should, on the whole, have fifteen-pence a-week for each member of their families. The mason had previously in his employment, from seven to ten men, at the weekly wage of eight or nine shillings each. But no sooner did he take in these three supernumeraries from the parish at six shillings, than he began to treat anew with his old workmen, and threatened to discharge them if they would not consent to a lower wage. This of course would have thrown them all upon the parish, for the difference between their reduced and their present wages; upon perceiving which, the overseer instantly drew back his three men from the mason, and at length contrived to dispose of them otherwise.* Upon

---

* The following is an extract of a letter received from the overseer, Mr. Poole:—

"The facts respecting the three men at Long Burton, were as follows: we had three able men out of employ, and rather than send them on the roads to work, we engaged with Mr. Perratt, the mason, for them, at six shillings per week each. Mr. Perràtt was at that time giving his men (from seven to ten men) eight or nine shillings each. Mr. Perratt then saw he could get men at a lower rate, and informed some of his old hands that he should discharge and lower the wages; therefore, in consequence those men (or many of them) would, at their discharge, become very burthensome

this the wages of the journeymen masons reverted to what they were before.

Now this exemplifies the state of many agricultural parishes in England. There is a reserve of supernumeraries constantly on the eve of pouring forth over all the departments of regular labour, and on the instant of their doing so, forcing one and all of the regular workmen within the margin of pauperism. It is instructive to observe how very few supernumeraries will suffice to produce this effect; and by how very small an excess in the number of labourers, a very great and grievous reduction takes place in the wages of labour. It is not even necessary for this purpose, that there should be an actual breaking forth of supernumeraries on the already crowded departments of regular industry. It is enough that they are at all times in readiness to break forth. The consciousness of a few idle hands in every neighbourhood, gives an advantage to the master, and an inferiority to the servants, in all their negotiations with each other. It has the effect of bringing wages as far down as possible ; so low as to the very confines of beggary, and in many instances so low as in fact to beggar the great mass of the popu-

---

to the parish of Long Burton. We immediately saw our error, of letting him have men at a low rate, (for recollect, it was one or two shillings lower than the farmers were giving at that time,) and took the men back on the roads at certain prices, so as to make their earnings fifteen pence per head, for their families; which, with Mr. Perratt's six shillings per week, we were obliged to make up from the parish to fifteen pence per head, per week."

lation. So wretched a remuneration as that of eight or nine shillings a week to masons, and that even previous to the irruption of supernumeraries upon them, was still the effect of the existence of supernumeraries. It is this in fact which has so reduced the wages of agricultural labour over a great part of England ; and virtually placed the question of a workman's recompense at the disposal, and under the arbitration of parish overseers.

It will be seen how beautifully this process would be reversed under a system where a parish bank came in place of the parish vestry, and when the people, instead of a claim upon the one, had, what is far better, a capital in the other. Had these masons been free of the presence of all supernumeraries, and, moreover, had they been in possession of a fund which could have subsisted them, even but a few weeks, they would have stood to their employers in a much firmer and more independent attitude ; and the miserable pittance of nine shillings a week would not have satisfied them. It is a mere evasion of the argument to say, that the master could have reduced them to his own terms, by hiring in labourers from a distance. This is just saying, that ere a capital in the hand of labourers work its full effect upon their condition, it must be generally, and not partially diffused among them. There can be no doubt, that the vicinity of a population with inferior habits, that the vicinity of Ireland, for example, must retard the march of our working classes, to a greater sufficiency, and a higher status in the commonwealth. But this does not impair, it rather enhances the conclusion, that the high road to their advancement is the accumulation of such a capital as might enable them to weather all the adverse fluctuations of trade, and as might enable them, throughout every season, to treat more independently with their employers, than labourers can do, who, without resources, are constantly, to use a familiar phrase, from hand to mouth, or on the very brink of starvation. The establishment of so much as one savings bank is at least the beginning of such a progress, although it will require the establishment and the successful operation of many, ere a sensible effect can be wrought by them on the general economic condition of our peasantry. This, however, is the unfailing way of it; and in proportion to the length that it is carried, will be its effect in raising the price of labour.

We hold the following narrative, which relates to the distresses experienced some years ago in the town of Leicester and its neighbourhood, to be very rich in the principles of this question. It was given and authenticated by one of the most respectable citizens in the place.

The great employment of the population in that quarter is the manufacture of stockings; which manufacture, in the year 1817, was in a state of very great depression. It was at this period that Mr. Cort was applied to by the township of Smeaton Westorby, in the parish of Kibworth, Beau-

champ, for work to some of their people. He
succeeded in finding admittance for them to the
service of a hosier in the town of Leicester, who
agreed to pay each of them five shillings a-week;
and the township to which they belonged, were
very thankful to make up the deficiency in their
wages, according to the state and number of their
families. Mr. Cort was, in a few days afterwards,
called upon by a man whom he knew to have been
a regular servant in the establishment of this hosier, and who complained that, immediately after
the importation of the mechanics from the country, he and others had been dismissed from their
employment. On remonstrating with their master, and asking him how they were to live, he
replied that it was not his affair; an answer which,
however harshly it may sound in those countries
where pauperism is unknown, may signify no
more, in many parts of England, than simply a
committal of discarded workmen to their legal
right on the charity of the parish. Certain it is,
that the excess of workmen beyond the work in
demand, created a very melancholy reduction in
the wages of the whole; insomuch that, according
to the estimate of our very intelligent informer, in
the parish alone of St. Margaret's in Leicester,
the wages of the stocking trade sustained a decline
at the rate of at least £20,000 in the year. At the
time of greatest depression, the sum earned by an
able-bodied mechanic was five shillings and sixpence
in the week; to which there was added an allow-

ance from the parish, according to the circumstances of his family. In the case of a man, wife, and two children, it was made up to nine shillings in the week. This *allowance system,** as it is

---

* There is an able and judicious pamphlet published sometime ago, by the Reverend Mr. Brereton, of Little Massingham, in Norfolk, entitled, " Observations on the Administration of the Poor Laws in Agricultural Districts." It contains a striking exposition of the evils of what is termed the " allowance system;" or that system under which defective wages are supplemented out of the poor-rate. The following is an extract from this interesting little work :—

" The system of allowances thrusts its ruthless hand into the hearts of the people, and violates the ties of nature. Natural affection between parent and child is the corner stone of social happiness. In Scotland, it is said, that the children and relations of persons who are in danger of falling upon the parish, generally use their utmost endeavours to prevent such a disgrace to the family. This was the case in England till the year 1795. Now it has become necessary to make laws to compel parents to maintain their children, and children to maintain their indigent parents. Such enactments are a lamentable proof that the natural affection of the poor has fallen to a low ebb. There were two cases in this small parish, in which the children, though in good business, had neglected their aged parents, merely because the parish had been accustomed to find them bread. The anxiety of a father to provide for his children would stimulate his industry, sweeten his toil, and endear those children to his heart. But if the law will decree that the father and the mother cannot, or need not provide for their offspring, then may you expect that natural affection will cool, and lust usurp the dominion of virtuous love over the hearts of the people. If children are taught that from the day of their birth they have been sustained by an allowance from the parish—that as soon as they are able to work they are called upon to do so, not to assist their parents, but to relieve the parish charge—if as soon, or even before they attain the age of discretion, they are released by a decree of the magistrates from parental authority, and it becomes the interest of parent and child to separate all mutual connexion and concern, of course one must not expect filial affection or honour to parents. Who can read without pain, and even indignation, articles like the following, blazoned through our villages and cottages, with the signatures of the ministers of justice and the ministers of religion, in a Christian country ?

termed in some parts of the country, was persevered in for a considerable time, but was soon found

---

" ' Every child, 1s. 9d.' ' Every boy, 3s.'

" ' All the earnings of any part to be considered as part of the allowance !'

" When boys of 13, 14, or 15 years of age, begin to earn more than their
allowance, the allowance of the parent is diminished by that excess; and to
avoid that diminution, parents turn their children adrift upon the world,
just at the time when they most need advice and protection, and when their
industry should avail to their parents' comfort. I have seen father, and
mother, and daughter, pensioners of the parish, preserving their separate
allowance, separate purse, and separate cupboard, and quarrelling with each
other who shall provide the fire. It would be tedious to multiply illustrations here; but when puerile and unnecessary regulations violate the ties of
blood, and the duties of religion, who can regard without detestation such
an unrestricted system of pauperism? The rebuke of Jesus to those scribes
and priests who, by their own by-laws, perverted the law of nature, and of
nature's God, is very pointed: 'Ye say, if a man shall say to his father or
mother, it is Corban, by whatsoever thou mightest be profited by me, he
shall be free, and ye suffer him to do no more for his father and his mother,
making the word of God of none effect through your traditions, and many
such like things do ye.' "

" Honour and chastity in every rank, and especially among the poor, are
intimately connected with natural affection. On this point, however, I will
not enter into details, which could be only painful. It is sufficiently notorious, that promiscuous intercourse is become common from early age—that
marriage is seldom contracted with honour, and that illegitimacy has greatly
increased since the introduction of this system, and the existing laws of
bastardy.

" I requested the governor of a neighbouring hundred house to furnish me
with the number of children born within a certain period, distinguishing the
legitimate from the illegitimate. The account was, 77 children born:—23
legitimate—54 illegitimate.

" There is a woman belonging to this parish who has had four illegitimate
children, and is now pregnant with a fifth. During the last year her children have been supported almost entirely by the parish, partly through the
running away of the fathers, and partly through the negligence of the former
and the present overseers, who have either lost the orders, or neglected to
enforce them. The woman has, I believe, received more than the allowance of a widow in similar circumstances, and thus not only is profligacy

to aggravate the mischief which it was designed to alleviate. It obviously detains a much greater number at the work of the depressed manufacture, than would otherwise have adhered to it; and thereby has the effect of perpetuating and even augmenting the glut of its commodities in the market. It was thus found, that just in proportion as the parish extended its allowances, the manufacturers reduced their wages; for which wages, however, it was still an object, in the midst of their scanty means, that all the hands of the family should be pressed into the employment, and be exerted to the uttermost. In this style of management matters grew unavoidably worse, till the glut became quite oppressive, and was felt to be alike burdensome to the manufacturer and the operative. They tried, therefore, a new expedient; and, instead of making good the defect of wages by means of parochial aid, they resolved on a subscription for the purpose of detaching a large proportion of men from the employ altogether, whether by maintaining them in a state of total idleness, or by employing them at some agricultural work, for a very inferior wage, or even for nothing at all. In a single month, this way of it operated like a charm. The glut was soon cleared away, when the production of the article was thus

---

shielded from punishment, but a bounty is afforded it. If the law of bastardy should continue in its present shape, a few simple regulations would correct many abuses attending it."

limited; and just in virtue of a certain number being kept off from their own professional business of working stockings, there was speedily restored to that neighbourhood the cheering spectacle of well-paid industry, and a well-fed population.

The whole sum by which this restoration was achieved, amounted to nine thousand pounds; and this did not exceed twelve shillings for each individual engaged in the stocking manufacture in the town and environs of Leicester. Had there been a deposit then to this extent from each in a savings bank, they had the means of accomplishing a deliverance for their whole body, by supporting in idleness, or at other work, a certain part of them. But this is not the way in which, after that a habit of accumulation has been established among labourers, the product of that accumulation will be applied. For the purpose of working a good effect, it is not necessary that there should be any such combined or corporate movement; or any resource whatever to the plans and expedients of committee-ship. The thing works far best when it works naturally. The same effect is arrived at just by each individual being upon his own accumulation; and when a glut comes round, he will spontaneously work less when a miserable renumeration is going, than if he were depending for his daily subsistence on his daily labour. An overstocked market is either prevented or more speedily relieved, simply by so many of the workmen ceasing to work, or by a great many working moderately. It is thus, that a savings bank is the happiest of all expedients for filling up the gaps, and equalising the deficiencies, and shortening those dreary intervals of ill-paid work, which now occur so frequently to the great degradation and distress of every manufacturing population.

The subscription of nine thousand pounds at Leicester, just did for the population there, what, by the system of savings banks, any population might do for themselves. It would not of course take two or three thousand people off from their work, and keep them idle or otherwise employed for a month or two. But it would exempt all from the pressure of that immediate necessity which now urges them to work to excess. The effect in clearing away the glut would just be the same; and the people would owe to themselves a benefit that, in this instance, was conferred upon them by others. They would soon recover the level of their old and natural prices; nay, permanently raise this level, so as to obtain a permanently higher status in the commonwealth.

We conclude this chapter by the following extract from that article in the Edinburgh Review, which we have already alluded to.

" There is another and a far more excellent way—not to be attained, certainly, but by a change of habit among the workmen themselves—yet such a change as may be greatly promoted by those whose condition or character gives them influence in society. We have always been of opinion, that

the main use of a savings bank was, not to elevate
labourers into the class of capitalists, but to equal-
ize and improve their condition as labourers. We
should like them to have each a small capital, not
wherewith to become manufacturers, but wherewith to control manufacturers. It is in this way
(and we can see no other) that they will be enabled to weather all the fluctuations to which trade
is liable. It is the cruel necessity of overworking
which feeds the mischief of superabundant stock,
and which renders so very large a transference of
hands necessary ere the market can be relieved of
the load under which it groans and languishes.
Now, this is a necessity that can only be felt by
men on the brink of starvation, who live from hand
to mouth, and have scarcely more than a day's
earnings for the subsistence of the day. Let these
men only be enabled, on the produce of former
accumulations, to live through a season of depression while they work moderately, or, if any of them
should so choose it, while they do not work at all,
—and they would not only lighten such a period
of its wretchedness, but they would inconceivably
shorten its duration. The overplus of manufactured goods, which is the cause of miserable wages,
would soon clear away under that restriction of
work which would naturally follow on the part of
men who did not choose, because they did not
need, to work for miserable wages. What is now
a protracted season of suffering and discontent to
the lower orders, would, in these circumstances,

become to them a short but brilliant career of holiday enjoyment. The report of a heavy downfal of wages, instead of sounding like a knell of despair in their ears, would be their signal for rising up to play. We have heard, that there does not exist in our empire a more intellectual and accomplished order of workmen than the weavers of Paisley. It was their habit, we understand, to abandon their looms throughout the half or nearly the whole of each Saturday, and to spend this time in gardening, or in the enjoyment of a country walk. It is true, that such time might sometimes be viciously spent; but still we should rejoice in such a degree of sufficiency among our operatives, as that they could afford a lawful day of every week for their amusement, and still more, that they could afford whole months of relaxed and diminished industry, when industry was underpaid. This is the dignified posture which they might attain; but only after the return of better times, and through the medium of their own sober and determined economy. Every shilling laid up in store, and kept in reserve for the evil day, would strengthen the barrier against such a visitation of distress and difficulty as that from which we are yet scarcely emerging. The very habits too, which helped them to accumulate in the season of well-paid work, would form our best guarantee against the vicious or immoral abuse of this accumulation, in the season either of entire or comparative inactivity. We would expect an increase of reading, and the growth of literary cultivation, and the steady advancement of virtuous and religious habits,—and, altogether, a greater weight of character and influence among the labouring classes, as the permanent results of such a system. Instead of being the victims of every adverse movement in trade, they would become its most effective regulators.

" This is the eminence that the labourers of our nation are fully capable both of reaching and of maintaining. But it is neither the Poor-rate of England, nor the law of Parochial Aid in Scotland, that will help them on to it. These have only deceived them away from the path which leads to independence ; and amid all the complaints which have been raised against the system of a compulsory provision for the poor, nothing is more certain than that our poor, because underpaid operatives, are the principal sufferers by it. Every other class in society has its compensation. It is paid back again to the manufacturer in the shape of a reduction in the wages of his workmen, and to the landholder by a reduction in the price of all manufactured articles. It is only the operative himself, who appears to be pensioned by it, that is really impoverished. It has deadened all those incitements to accumulation which would have raised him and his fellow-labourers to a footing of permanent security in the state—And, not till their eyes have been opened to the whole mischief and cruelty of this delusion—not till they see where it is that their most powerful and malignant enemy is lying in ambush—not till they have learned that, under the guise of charity, there has been an influence at work for many years, which has arrested the march of the lower orders to the elevation that naturally and rightfully belongs to them, and till they come to understand that it is by their own exertion and self-denial alone that they can win their way to it—not, in short, till the popular cry is for the abolition, rather than the extension of pauperism, will our labouring classes have attained their full share of comfort and importance in the commonwealth."

CHAP. XX.

ON THE COMBINATIONS OF WORKMEN FOR THE PURPOSE OF RAISING WAGES.

We fear that the cause of savings banks may have sustained a temporary discredit from the recent conduct of workmen all over the country. The apprehension is, that, by a large united capital amongst them, they might get the upper hand of their employers altogether; that, in possession of means which could enable them to be idle, they may exercise a power most capriciously and most inconveniently for the other classes of society; that they may lay manufacturers under bondage by their impregnable combinations; and, striking work at the most critical and unexpected junctures, they may subject the whole economy of human life to jolts and sudden derangements which might be enough for its overthrow. These fears, enhanced though they have been of late by the outrages of workmen in various parts of the country, would speedily be dissipated, we believe, under the light of growing experience. The repeal of the combination laws has not even yet been adequately tried. The effervescence which has followed on that repeal, is the natural, and, we believe, the temporary effect of the anterior state of things. There was nothing more likely than that the people, when put in possession of a power which they felt to be altogether new, would take a delight in the exercise of it, and break forth into misplaced and most extravagant manifestations. But if the conduct of the one party have been extravagant, the alarm of the other party we conceive to have been equally extravagant. We trust that the alarm may have in part been dissipated, ere Government shall be induced to legislate any further upon the subject; or to trench, by any of its acts, on the great principle of every man being entitled to make the most of his own labour, and also of acting in concert with his fellows for the production of a general benefit, as great as they can possibly make out to the whole body of labourers.

The repeal of the combination laws in England has been attended with consequences which strongly remind us of the consequences that ensued, after the Revolution, from the repeal of the game laws in France. The whole population, thrown agog by their new privilege, poured forth upon the country, and, variously accoutred, made war, in grotesque and unpractised style, upon the fowls of the air and the beasts of the field. In a few months, however, the extravagance subsided, and the people returned to their old quiescent habits and natural occupations. We feel assured that, in like manner, this delirium of a newly awakened faculty among our British workmen will speedily pass away. They will at length become wise and temperate in the use of it. Neither party, in fact, well understand how to proceed in the unwonted relation wherein they now stand to each other. There is indefinite demand upon the one side; upon the other there are distrust, and a most sensitive dread of encroachment. They have not yet completed their trial of strength; and just because, in ignorance of each others' powers, there are yet the effort, and the excitation, and the busy rivalship, of a still undetermined conflict. If Parliament would but suffer the great principle upon which its repeal has been founded to have full and unfettered swing in the country, we have no doubt, that, after a very few vibrations, the matter would at length settle down into a right and a comfortable adjustment for all parties. The experience of the, evil that results to themselves from an overdone ambition, would far more effectually chasten and repress the obstinacy or the daring of workmen, than all the terrors of the statute-book ; and a harmony would soon be established in a natural way between those parties whom the laws of the state had only set at variance.

The whole of this subject seems resolvable into three great divisions. First, for the question, " What were the right enactment in regard to combinations, on the pure and abstract principles of law ?" Second, the inquiry whether, under such an enactment, all the practical mischief that is apprehended from combinations, would not be sufficiently provided against without further law, and just by the action and reaction of certain natural influences, that operate throughout society, and among the parties themselves. Third, the consideration of the fears and the prejudices of men upon this subject, which are grounded upon Economic Theories.

I. The great principle of law upon this, and upon every other subject, is, that it should quadrate as much as it can possibly be made to do, with obvious morality. It is most desirable, that whatever the legislature shall ordain to be a crime, and liable to punishment, should be felt as a crime by man's natural conscience. In every case when there is a want of sympathy between the enactments of the statute-book, and the dictates of natural virtue, there is an expenditure and loss of strength incurred by the government of a country, when it either ordains such enactments, or carries them into effect. It is sure to lose ground thereby, in public or popular estimation;—and when the arbitrary regulations of a state are thus made to thwart and run counter to the independent feelings and judgments of men, this is certain to infuse an element of weakness into the body politic. The heart-burnings of him who suffers the penalty, meet with powerful reinforcement, in the sympathy of all his fellows. He feels himself to be a martyr or a hero, and not a criminal; and, if treated as a criminal, this only puts a generous indignancy into his heart, in

which he is supported by a kindred sentiment
among all the free and noble spirits of the land.
It is thus that the stability of government, and
with it the cause of public order and tranquillity,
is put to hazard by every law which squares not
with the jurisprudence of Nature—and that some
strong case of expediency would need to be made
out, ere that should be held a crime in the eye of
the law, which is not a crime in the eye of Nature
also.

On the other hand, let law be on the side of
clear and unquestionable morality—let that which
it reckons with as a delinquency, be regarded as a
delinquency by every unsophisticated conscience
—let the offence against which its penalties are
directed, be felt as an offence against the natural
dictates of humanity and rectitude—let its voice
of rebuke or of threatening, be at one with the
voice of the heart, insomuch that all the denun-
ciations of the statute-book are echoed to by the
universal sense of justice in society; and every
act of such a legislation will inconceivably
strengthen the authority from which it emanates.
Even though a very numerous class of the community should be thwarted by it in some favourite
but iniquitous design, any discontent of theirs
would be overborne by the general and concur-
rent feeling of the whole community besides.
Nothing could withstand the force of law, if thus
aided by the force of public opinion; and any
government whose deeds are responded to by this

natural sense of equity among men, may surely count on such support and sympathy through the land, as shall make its authority to be quite irresistible.

Now, we fear that there have been times when both these principles were traversed by Government, in its management of combinations. For, first, there seems nothing criminal in the act of a man ceasing to work at the expiry of his engagement, because not satisfied with his present wage, and desirous of a higher; or in the act of men confederated and doing jointly, or together, the same thing. On the contrary, it seems altogether fair, that each should make as much as he can of his own labour; and that just as dealers of the same description meet and hold consultations for the purpose of enhancing the price of their commodity, so it should be equally competent for workmen to deliberate, and fix on any common, if it be not a criminal agreement, and that to enhance, if they can, the price of their own services. There really is nothing morally wrong in all this; and however a man may be treated on account of it as a delinquent by the law, he certainly is not regarded as a delinquent in the eye of natural conscience. It was because of this discrepancy between nature and the law, that we held it a good thing, when, by the repeal act, it was expunged from the statute book—and we hope that no subsequent act will again restore it. It is true, that while the whole statute law against combinations has been abrogated, they, by the last act of parliament, have again been made liable as before to prosecution and punishment under the common law.* Yet we fondly trust, that even the application of common law to the practice in question, will fall into desuetude, as a thing not suited to the spirit of the age†—an expiring relict of the

---

* By the act of 5th George IV. cap. 95, all the enactments against combinations, of which a long enumeration is given, are repealed; and they who enter into combinations, are declared to be not " subject or liable to any indictment or prosecution for conspiracy, or to any other criminal information or punishment whatever, under the *common* or the statute law.

By the act of 6th George IV. cap. 129, this last act is repealed; but there is enacted over again its repeal of all the old statutory enactments against combination. So that the statute law continues to be abrogated, as it was by the repeal act which has been superseded. The repeal of the common law, however, has not been enacted over again; so that it has been restored to its old authority against the simple offence of combinations.

† This natural sentiment, that it is a fair and legitimate thing for workmen to stand out against such wages as do not satisfy them, often breaks forth into open and undisguised expression in the evidence taken by the Select Committee on Combination Laws, during the spring of 1825. It is felt and recognized by masters as well as others. The following is from the examination of Mr. Eli Chadwick, a manufacturer in Huddersfield:—

" Did they finish the work they had in the loom? They stopped out as long as the law would allow them, eight days, then they came and finished the work in their loom.

" Then they gave you notice they meant to retire? Yes.

" Having postponed the finishing that work as long as they could? Yes; eight days.

" You must be aware that, having completed their contract with you, they were under no further obligation? Certainly not.

" It was therefore a matter of option with them, whether they would engage with you for the wages they had heretofore? Yes.

" And they were perfectly at liberty to ask what they considered a fit remuneration for their own labour? Undoubtedly.

" They choosing to retire, there was no reason why they should not retire if they thought proper? None whatever.

barbarity of other times. And accordingly, in almost all the prosecutions which have taken place ever since the repeal act was modified, and in part done away, it is not the simple deed of combination which is proceeded against, but certain obvious and undoubted criminalities which are charged upon the promoters or the agents of combination.

But, secondly, while Government on the one hand, by its penalties against the simple act of combination, put forth a rigour far beyond the natural dimensions of this alleged enormity, they, on

---

" Do you mean to say, that it was your opinion that a rise should not take place, or was that the opinion of the men? It was my own opinion, at least in our own manufactory.

" In selling your goods, do you decide for yourselves what price you will sell them at? Of course.

" You would not think it right for any other person to interfere and say this price is unreasonable, and you must sell them at a lower rate? It is often done in trade; people are often ready to say we ought to sell them lower.

" Do you, in point of fact, admit the interference of any persons to regulate your prices? Certainly not.

" Do you consider that it would be fair to allow you to regulate the sale of your own wares, and to prohibit the men from selling their own labour as they may think proper? By no means, we do not wish any thing of the kind; nor would I allege the shadow of any thing that should seem to say so."

The question which succeeds the last quoted, with its answer, marks out most specifically the only grievance of which masters have a right to complain, and the only legitimate object which Government should aim to secure :—

" Then what is it you wish to suggest to the Committee for them to do in the present case? That if the men in my employ do not choose to work at the wages I can afford to give them, I may be at liberty to obtain other men from the neighbourhood about me."

the other hand, have not been declared and rigorous enough against those real enormities, which are often attendant on combinations. If, in the one way, they have greatly outrun the sympathies of the country—in the other way, they, for a time, perhaps, as greatly fell short of them. A mere combination among those who are unwilling to work, is not in the eye of morality a crime. But the members of a combination proceed to a very great and undeniable crime, when they put forth a hand, or even utter dark and terrifying threats of violence to those who are willing to work. This is the point against which the whole force of legislation ought to be directed; and though the public cannot go along with those severities of imprisonment and exile, which law has inflicted for the naked offence of combination, yet they will go most readily along with far greater severities than have ever yet been inflicted for the outrage done to those who refuse to enter them.*

---

* If, on the one hand, it evince how much the public feeling is with labourers in all their fair attempts to better their condition, when it is admitted, as in an instance already quoted, even by their masters; so, on the other hand, it evinces how much the public feeling is against labourers in the outrages of which they have been guilty, when workmen themselves betray a strong anxiety, either to disguise or to disclaim them. In this view, we hold the following extracts from the minutes of evidence to be valuable.

The first is from the examination of John Swift, a journeyman weaver at Newsome, near Huddersfield.

" They would have been dismissed from the union?—Yes; I do not know of any case where a person has been dismissed, but they have invariably left the union.

This then is the point at which the legislature should put forth all their rigour—even to protect

---

" And forfeited the money they had paid ?—Yes, forfeited the threepence they had put in.

" That may have gone on for a considerable time ?—Certainly.

" They have forfeited all the contribution they have made?—Yes; there have been two or three cases in 5,000 men.

" Have they continued to work in the same place ?—Yes, with the same men.

" You mean now to state, that no arrangements have been made to prevent their continuing to work at those lower wages, for the same men and at the same prices? Yes, I do.

" You never heard of any case of the kind? No.

" Are you sure no instance has occurred within your knowledge, where a man has been willing to work at a lower rate of wages than the union had fixed, and where he had been prevented? I am sure there has not one.

" Have you ever heard of any brickbats having been thrown through the windows of the workshops when the men had struck? I have.

" In what cases? In one case, in Mr. William Norton's strike. I went over myself when I heard it, and said, ' I will give ten guineas to any man who will bring me word who threw that brickbat through the window, whether it was a union man or not;' and nothing could be found but a drunken man of one of the master manufacturers; and they said, this man, in a drunken fit, had thrown it at a weaver who was weaving.

" Was any person taken up in consequence of that outrage? Not one.

" During that strike at Mr. Norton's, was any personal violence or mischief done to any person whom you know? Not one.

" Did you ever hear of any complaint made respecting it? Not one."

The next is from the examination of Amos Cowgill, a weaver:—

" During that strike do you recollect any brick-bats being thrown against his premises? I do not remember, nor do I believe there were ; I never heard a complaint of the kind, but it was said about that time, that there was a brick-bat thrown through a window about two miles from his place, and the members of the union offered a certain reward to any person who would tell who had done it; some said it was a manufacturer's son, some one, and some another, and we could never get to know who it was.

" Are you prepared to say, that no act of violence has taken place during any of the strikes since the union? I am prepared to say, there has not an act of violence taken place in any part of the West Fancy Union."

those who abide in their employment, or who have
newly entered, from the hostility and violence of

The next is from the examination of Thomas Worsley, a cotton-spinner
at Stockport:—

" Do you know of the circumstance of a new spinner at Hyde being ill-
treated?—There was a spinner at Hyde ill-treated; but by whom, it was
never in my power to find out. I made strict inquiries among the spinners,
if ever they had sanctioned such a thing; and instead of sanctioning it, they
declared they had offered a reward for the persons to be brought to justice
who had committed the offence.

" What were the circumstances of ill-treatment?—The circumstance
stated in the newspapers was, that five men met him in disguise and struck
him on the head, and persons were taken up for it.

" Who was the man who was struck?—I have entirely forgotten his name.

" Had he been in the general business of the trade, previous to his having been struck?—I cannot speak to it.

" Do you mean to say, you cannot tell the Committee whether the person who was ill-used and ill-treated by these men, had been engaged in the
trade or was a new spinner?—He was not a spinner; my belief is, he was
an old hand in the trade, a rover.

" Had he refused to comply with the regulations of the union, and worked
for less wages?—Not to my knowledge.

" Then, in making the inquiries, did you learn nothing on the subject?—
No further than to inquire whether the spinners had given encouragement
for the assault committed on the man.

" What was the result of your inquiry?—The result of my inquiry was,
that I found the spinners had not concurred in such an act; and to show
they had not, they offered a reward for the purpose of bringing to justice
those who had done it."

The next is from the examination of William M'Alister, an operative collier at Kilmarnock:—

" Do you conceive it right and proper that colliers should interfere with
any individual coming from a distance, working for your master for any
wages that he may think fit?—No, I do not think the colliers have any
right of interfering.

" You think that Mr. Guthrie, or any other coal-master, might be at perfect liberty to employ any man he pleases, for wages even less than those
you have in his colliery?—Yes, he has liberty, and nobody says anything
against it.

those who have abandoned it. In consistency
with their own great and glorious principle of

" Has he ever done that?—No, he pays them all alike; but supposing he
employs a man for three shillings a day, and gives us four shillings, we have
nothing to say against that."

The next is from the examination of Philip Hardy, a shipwright :—
" Have you known any instances where men have been threatened by
the union for working since the strike?—Never one.
" Are you sure of that?—I never heard of an instance of it.
" Are there any at work now in Mr. Young's yard?—Yes, there are several.
" Do they belong to the union?—Some do, some do not."

The next is from the examination of John Gast, a shipwright:—
" Then do you mean to state, that the withdrawing from the different
yards has been the act of the men themselves, independently of any communication with the union?—If the Committee will leave the word union
out of the question, because the union is a general term.
" Either with the members of the committee, or with the general meeting of the union?—I mean to say, that every man's act, at least the acts of
the shipwrights in the River Thames, as respects the union, has been spontaneous.
" Are there no cases in which the men, after having returned to their
work, or when working under any given circumstances in any yards, have
been called to an account for it by the committee?—I really know of none,
I am not in possession of any case at all where they have been at work,
and called to any account at all, further than their own application, direct
or indirect, as to the nature of the case, and that has been always left to
themselves. Whenever they come to the committee upon any business, the
committee have invariably said, ' Why do you trouble us? we have nothing
at all to do with it, settle the matter with yourselves; we want to know
nothing of your business; whatever there has been, you and your employers
are at full liberty to settle it.' "
It is interesting to remark how much the *avowed* sentiments of the strike-
work shipwrights on the Thames are at one with the sentiments of natural
equity on this point. They at least disclaim all right of interference with
the freedom of individual workmen. It is not essential to our argument,
that they are honest in this disavowal. They indicate, at all events, a consciousness of such interference being wrong; and our Government might
proceed, with all safety, to legislate more rigorously than they have ever yet
done, against such acts as no one class of society can hold up their face to.

freedom, they should guard to the uttermost the freedom of those who are willing, from the ty-

---

The following is part of a letter from a committee of these shipwrights to the master builders :—

"1st March, 1825.

" Sir,—In answer to the question proposed to us, whether we concur in *recinding* from the rules and regulations of the Shipwrights' Provident Union, all articles whatever claiming or asserting the right of interfering in the internal regulations of any dock-yard, or claiming control over the freedom of action by which every individual workman should be at liberty to act for himself, as to the terms and conditions on which he will accept employment,—We beg leave to state, that there is no such *article or regulation in existence amongst us,* and we disclaim, on our part, the idea of interfering with the internal regulations of your establishments. It *as* been impressed on the minds of the shipwrights, that they ought to demand a sufficient remuneration for their labour, but at the same time they have been left at full liberty to act for themselves; the only demand that has been made, is to be paid at the rate of 12s. 6d. per hundred for making stages for stripping or coppering, 2s. 6d. for docking, and 1s. 6d. for undocking.

" Our opinion is, when a man or number of men agree with his master or foreman to perform a certain piece of work, and the master should want more hands on it, that we should have the choice of our mates, instead of having men forced on us against our inclination. It always was the *perogative,* and no man doubts the propriety of it, that the master should employ who he pleases; but after he has let a job to any man or set of men, then in that case it is our right, by law and custom, to get those people who are most agreeable to ourselves. We can appeal to most of the respectable builders on this point. The practice has invariably been, with one or two exceptions, when men *as* been wanted, for the foreman to call one of the people and tell him he wants more hands on the work; the reply generally is, ' Have you any men you wish to send,' and if he has, there is no objection. In this manner have we gone on till now, when a single arbitrary foreman says he will have his way, in *contridiction* to the wishes of upwards of 1,300 men ; and we have reason to believe that he is now using his endeavours to set every shipbuilder in the port of London against the people in their employ. In this we hope he will be disappointed. We are not so lost to our interests as not to know that a good understanding ought to exist between master and journeymen, for without it no good can result to either party; and it is our determination to cherish such an understanding as will be of mutual benefit. We further beg to state, that our committee

ranny and violence of those who are not willing
to work. It was in the spirit of kindness to the
working classes, that the act for the repeal of
the combination laws was passed ; and it would
appear, as if in the exuberance of this spirit, that
an unwonted gentleness and forbearance had been
made to run through all the provisions of it. The
punishment, whether for forcing, by violence, their
fellow-workmen to combinations along with them
—or for forcing, by violence, their masters into a

---

have no power whatever over us; they were appointed to draw up a statement of prices, and submit them to the general body for inspection.''

This was met by a series of resolutions on the part of the shipbuilders,
who manifest an equally just discernment of the natural equities, as is manifest in the following extract :—

" That disclaiming therefore entirely all intention or wish to exercise any
oppressive power over the workman, or to prevent his obtaining, by equitable means, the fair and just remuneration to which his labour is entitled, but
anxious alone for the restoration of freedom of individual opinion, and of the
open competition of labour consequent thereon, the shipbuilders present at
this meeting pledge themselves, individually and collectively, to use their
best exertions for the suppression of the union referred to, if, after a decided
appeal to the people, they shall refuse to rescind from their regulations and
bye-laws all articles whatever claiming or asserting the right of interference
in the internal regulation of any dock-yard, or controlling the privilege of
freedom of individual action among the workmen.''

When workmen, on the one hand, disclaim all right of interference with
the individual freedom of any of their fellows, and masters, on the other,
profess their acquiescence in every equitable effort on the part of servants to
better their condition, the legislature may with all safety proceed to embody
these principles in such enactments as might both proclaim and guard the
observation of them ; and, while leaving those who will to combine in any
way that is not directly criminal, it might, in full confidence of the nation's
sympathy, strengthen as far as it may be found necessary, all those sanctions and expedients of law by which those who do not will, shall be secured from the outrages of the associated workmen.

compliance with their own prescriptions, is a great deal too small. By a *prosecution under this act*, no violence to person or property, no destruction of machinery, tools, goods, wares, or work, is liable to any greater penalty than that of two months imprisonment and hard labour. It is true, that by the subsequent clauses, the penalty is extended to three months imprisonment and hard labour. And it is also true, that all these offences are liable to prosecution and punishment under the severer laws that were previously in operation. But it may help to account in part for the recent popular ebullitions, that the repeal act held out a more mild and merciful aspect than the law ever held out before, to the very offences which itself was calculated to provoke. It was to this act that workmen naturally looked, and by which they measured the hardships and the criminalities of all the violence which they might use to enforce their combinations.* To them, in the first instance,

---

* The following is an example of workmen having been deluded into an offence, by the milder treatment which it obtained under the Repeal Act, than it ought to obtain even on the principles of natural equity.

" Are you aware of the provisions of the Act of last session?—I have understood from the magistrates there is nothing in the Act which would punish a man for leaving his work unfinished.

" Are you not aware that that was provided for by an Act of the year preceding?—The magistrates in Dublin do not appear to be aware of that.

" Are you aware whether any prosecution has taken place against men for leaving their work unfinished?—No, I am not.

" Do you conceive, from any conversation you have had with the magistrates, that they are not aware of the existence of any such law?—I conceive so; I may have misunderstood them.

then, it may be said to have offered a temptation
to such violence ; nor are we to wonder, if anterior
to their experience of those heavier penalties,
which this act did not bring into view, they heedlessly broke forth into outrages that were alike
hurtful to the interest of their employers, and to
the interest of their fellow-workmen.

It would help to clear and to facilitate the determination of this whole problem, were it extri-
cated from that confusion of sentiment, in virtue
of which, the right and the wrong of combinations
have been blended together into one object of con-

" Are you aware that by the Act of last session persons entering into combinations, by threats or otherwise inducing men to quit their work, come under the regulations, are punishable by two months imprisonment only?—
Yes, I am ; but the punishment is not one that the men attend to much,
because they can be supported during that time, from the friends of their
body, in prison; and in the next place, from the difficulty of proving any
thing like threat, especially by two witnesses.

" Have you observed the 6th section of the Act in which are these words :
' Provided always, that nothing herein contained shall alter or affect any law
now in force for the prosecution and punishment of the said several offences :'
which offences, in the 5th and 6th sections, are denominated to be threats
or intimidation to force another to leave work, or to prevent any man from
going to work, from damnifying and spoiling the property, or injuring the
person of any one whatever?—I was not aware of the effects of such
clause."

We are further convinced, that the Act in question was fitted to do what
it actually did in the present instance, to delude men into the imagination,
that by leaving their work unfinished, they were not liable to punishment.
There is even too lenient a penalty for those who tempt to the commission
of the crime, while the penalty to be laid on the criminal himself is not adverted to. And it was most natural for him to think lightly of that enormity, when so light a punishment was awarded to the instigators of it. In
the proportion that the actual deviates from the natural jurisprudence, in
that proportion is it fitted to do mischief in society."

templation. The public indignation has been very much fostered against the cause of natural liberty in workmen, by the shameful outrages of which associated workmen have been guilty in many parts of the land. It is thus that we are hurried into a desire for the abridgement of that liberty, by barring with legal penalties the very act of combination. Whereas, in fact, it is by the perfecting and extending of natural liberty, that all the mischiefs of combination are most effectually neutralised. But legislators themselves participate in this confusion, and forget, that after they have resolved to leave untouched the freedom of those who are not willing to work, there lies with them the remaining duty of shielding to the uttermost the freedom of those who are willing. In such a career of legislation, they do not need to relinquish for a moment that fine aspect of liberality which characterised the outset of it. They do not need to recal any part of that boon which they granted to the labouring classes; but only to add to the boon of protection from the alleged tyranny of their masters, the further boon of protection from the far more severe and substantial tyranny which, if not restrained, they would exercise on each other. In the prosecution of this walk, they will find, how much it is that sound morality and sound legislation harmonize. There is nought, either in the joint or separate resolutions of workmen, not to work for their masters under certain wages, that should be enacted against; for in such resolutions there is truly nothing wrong. But there is a most glaring moral evil in the threats, or the annoyances, or the assaults that have been committed by them against their fellows; and, to put these down, the whole strength and wisdom of Government should be called into operation.*

---

* These outrages vary in their atrociousness, from the annoyance or threat, to deeds of most fearful enormity. The following are but a few specimens out of the many.

From the examination of Mr. John Buddle :—

" In point of fact, have you from the fitters, or any other persons, any knowledge that threats or intimidations have been used by sailors or others to prevent the regular execution of the law?—Yes, when I was at Sunderland, on the first of the month, some of Lord Londonderry's fitters were complaining that they had been threatened, and some of their vessels had been stopped from sailing until they complied with the rules of the Union.

" What was the nature of the compulsion; in what manner were they prevented ?—By menaces and threats from the body of seamen to the persons navigating a particular vessel.

" Do you know of any particular expressions or any particular act of menace which took place ?—No, I only heard a general complaint.

" You do not know whether it was from the general trade arising from the known object of the Union, or whether it was from particular threats applied?—The case I allude to was, I believe, from particular threats.

" You do not know the names of the parties ?—No.

" Was it a threat of violence ?—Yes, to the seamen, if they went on board and navigated the vessel without complying with the rules of the Union.

From the examination of Mr. Robert Hutton, coachmaker in Dublin :—

" Were any precautions taken to protect those men?—Yes; we purchased a house in the neighbourhood, and had a passage made from another house into our own factory.

" Have those people communicated to you the threats which have been made to them ?—Yes.

" What was the nature of those threats ?—Personal violence.

" Did they name any individuals who had made those threats?—They never knew the individuals; they said they had always been threatened by persons whom they did not know, and I believe that the persons who make those threats are generally persons unknown to the persons threatened.

It is of vital importance that any future effort
of legislation should be well directed; not against

" Was any such threat carried into execution ?—Not in our trade.

" Was it in consequence of that threat, or your apprehension in consequence of it, that you took that house for the men ?—In consequence of both."

" During the preceding years you have carried on business, have you ever had any disturbances with your men, on the score of wages, or any other cause ?—We have never had any, on the score of wages, with our workmen ; but we have had disturbances with other workmen on other accounts.

" Were those disturbances of a more serious nature than those you have just stated ?—One of them was of a more serious nature, because it was accompanied with a loss of nearly the life of an individual.

" In what year, and on what occasion, was that ?—In 1813.

" How did that originate ?—From a man whom we brought over from' England, of the name of Couchman.

" What was his trade ?—A painter.

" What was the result ?—He was assaulted and beaten.

" Was any person punished in consequence ?—Two men were punished.

" What were their names ?—Kelly and Conolly.

" What was this man beaten for ?—The men understood he was introducing a new and improved system, making alterations in the mode of carrying on the business.

" Was he materially hurt ?—Yes, so as to unable him to work ever afterwards ; and he is now living in England at our cost.

" You have maintained him on a pension ever since ?—Yes.

" That happened while the combination laws were in full force ?—It did.

" During the time you have been in business, have not combinations and strikes, amongst the trades in Dublin, been very frequent ?—Yes ; never, however, so frequent as within the last year.

" What was the character given to those strikes previous to the repeal of the laws, was it attended with outrage or violence, or were they peaceable ? —In general attended with outrage and violence.

" Have many cases occurred since the repeal of the combination laws ?— A great number ; two men have been murdered, and a great number assaulted.

" In what trade ?—Chambers, a carpenter ; and Daly, a sawyer.

" What were the circumstances attending those murders ?—Chambers, the carpenter, was an advocate amongst the men for making a gradation of rates, and finding he could not succeed, he withdrew from the body, and

the principle of workmen being at full liberty to
act both individually and conjointly in opposition

---

worked on piece work, which is one of the things the body have a great objection to, and he was assaulted and murdered.

" Has any person been taken up and punished for that murder?—I understand never.

" At what period was that?—In October last.   Daly, a sawyer, who supported himself and his family at some distance from Dublin, by sawing coffin
boards, was attacked and murdered, because it was conceived that the supply
of this timber, sawed out of Dublin, interfered with the business of the
sawyers.

" How was it known by whom he was murdered?—From his having had
threatening letters, and there being no hostility to him but on that account,
and that having been before expressed.

" Was he a quiet peaceable man?—So I understood.

" Have the police been able to apprehend the persons murdering him?—I
do not know.

" Was this murder accompanied with robbery of the person?—No; since
those two murders there has been a great accession of numbers to the
body, and the knowledge that those murders had been committed has answered the purpose of personal injury.

" There has been no individual injured by attacks of that kind since October last?—Oh! yes, a great many; I only meant to say, that it had answered the purpose to a certain degree.

" It has saved them the necessity of taking away more lives?—Yes;
there have been a great many assaulted; one man of the name of Toole
was assaulted a short time ago, I believe not more than six weeks ago."

From the examination of Mr. Michael Farrell, chief constable of police in
Dublin :—

" Have they latterly increased?—The outrages have not been so numerous, but they increased very much lately, since in or about June last; there
was not an outrage from in or about March until some time in the middle
of June.

" Can you state to the Committee the number of outrages which have
been committed since that period, up to the period of your quitting Dublin?—Of beating people in the streets I suppose between sixty and seventy
from that time.

Describe the nature of these offences.—Any man who differs from what
is called the Body, they watch him in a retired street, and either six or seven

to their masters, in every such way as is not criminal for a rise of wages, but against the practice of

---

are selected for the purpose of beating him. I have brought one of the weapons with me with which they beat him,—[*the witness produced a piece of wood of the length of about two feet, and very thick at one end, presenting three edges,*]—it is only their anxiety that preserves him, that saves his life, but they commonly break his bones. That was got in a seat in a public-house, on which some carpenters were sitting; we had information that they were to beat a man, and sent to see to frustrate it; it is only by the providence of God that any man can escape after getting a blow of that, for they mostly make at the head; there were two died from the beatings they got.

" Have there been only two individuals since June last who have died in consequence of those attacks?—Only two have died.

" What have been their names?—One man, the name of Daly, a sawyer; and Chambers, a carpenter.

" If it had been stated to this Committee that twenty people have lost their lives by being attacked in the streets of Dublin since July last, would that be correct?—No.

" Do you know how many people have had their skulls fractured?—I dare say, roughly speaking, there must have been forty.

" Who have received very serious bodily injury?—Yes, very dreadfully, but only two have died; but there are a great many that get severely beaten whom we never hear of, they are afraid to say any thing about it, for fear of incurring the displeasure of the Body.

" Of those sixty or seventy cases you refer to, how many have been brought before the police?—A great many; I believe there were twelve summarily convicted before the magistrate.

" Under what Act?—Under the late Acts for threats and intimidation; I know there were nine in one office, and there were three in our own.

" Have any been tried for their lives in consequence of the death of those individuals?—There were three men apprehended for the murder of Daly, but the law officers recommended them not to be tried, as the evidence would not be sufficient to convict, and hereafter evidence might be found.

" What was the nature of the crime committed by those nine or twelve who were found guilty?—They were chiefly nailers, going to the workshops of men, and threatening them; in one instance, they threw some vitriol into a man's shop, and about the place, and beat his men; there was one man convicted for that.

" Was he convicted under the last Act?—Yes; and the proof of the attack workmen putting forth the slightest violence, or committing the smallest outrage in their opposition

---

was evidence in that; but the others were for threats, when they came to a man's window and threatened his workmen.

" In this case in which the man was actually beaten, how came it that the offenders were only punished under the late Act?—Against one of them there was direct proof of assault, he was sent for trial, and the others were for using threatening language.

" In the cases where beating has taken place, have you ever obtained evidence of the persons by whom it was committed?—Yes, and there have been three convictions; one man got eighteen months imprisonment, and another man got six; and what is very extraordinary, the very night after these men were sentenced they beat one man at the Military-gate in Watling-street, and the very next night they beat another man, in the same employment, at the corner of the Circular-road in Clanbrassil-street, and broke his limbs, and mangled him in such a way, that surgeon M'Namara said, that one would imagine they had studied surgery, for they had gone as far as they could without taking his life; that was a man of the name of Butler.

" Do you find any greater difficulty in prosecuting to conviction people guilty of acts of violence, arising out of combination, than you do for other crimes, such as robberies, or common assaults?—Oh yes, more so than any other crime.

" If any body has stated to this Committee, that twenty lives, in the immediate vicinity of Dublin, have fallen victims to the combinations of workmen, since the repeal of the combination laws, would you say that was a correct statement?—Certainly not.

" Are you not aware of a man having been found in the canal last week? —I was not in Dublin at the time; but I have heard of the circumstance of a man being found in the canal.

" How many actual deaths have you known, arising out of attacks of assaults and combinations of workmen, since July last?—Two.

" Have any precautions been adopted by the police, to take up individuals guilty of acts of violence, arising out of those combinations?—Continually. I could give a great many instances where we saved lives; we have people who, in this country, would be called spies, for the purpose of knowing what they are about; they give us information, that a man is to be beaten; the great fear we have is, that we shall not be able to prevent it; we throw men into the neighbourhood to watch them, not letting the man know; but they get information of the police being there, and the man, therefore, is not beaten.

to each other. The thing to be desired, is, that any new act shall not contravene the expres-

---

" How do you get information of that?—By persons we employ to go amongst them.

" Do you think those acts of violence are determined on by the committee of trades, or by individuals?—I think some persons among them give the hard word to strike, and then they select the man; they are levied; a proof of that took place six weeks ago. There was a man of the name of Carroll, a dyer, had reared some men to the silk-dying business, contrary to the wish of the trade, a body of men rushed into his place looking for him, very luckily they met his son, who was able to bear the beating better than himself; they beat the son in a dreadful way, mistaking him for the father; they then began to break the furniture, and then walked off, which shows the men were hired, they did not know the man Carroll, but mistook his son for him.

" Were not instances of that kind frequent before the repeal of the laws? —They were.

" You do not consider that these acts arise immediately out of that repeal? —It is a continuation of the same system.

" You do not think it has increased since?—No; but that the combination has increased. The death of those two men so terrified all the working men that they complied immediately with what was required by the Body.

" Has it come to your knowledge that the attack upon those two men had been arranged by the committee?—Nothing beyond suspicion, and the character of the cases; Daly and his brother lived with their father, an old man, at Maynooth, eleven miles from Dublin, they used to cut up timber, and send it into Dublin for making coffins and car wheels; the sawyers at Dublin thought this was injuring their trade, and they selected a place called Island Bridge, within a mile and a half of Dublin, and at two o'clock in the open day they attacked these two men so severely that one died the next week in Stevens' Hospital.

" How many men attacked those men?—Seven; they leaped over the Park wall and gave two huzzas when they did it.

" Were none of those men taken up?—There were two men taken up, but there was not evidence sufficient to send them to trial.

" Did those two men belong to the sawyers trade?—They did.

" What was the other case?—Chambers was a man of great talent, as a working man; he thought it a hardship that a master should give the same wages to a bad man as to a good one, and he caused a division in the Body,

sion of the repeal act, which was altogether
framed in the spirit of an honest friendship to the

---

setting a value on men's labour; they were displeased with him for this, and they watched an opportunity when he went to see a man of the name of Hendrick, who was beaten the night before; he went to give money and relief to him, and just as he came out of the door where Hendrick lived, he was knocked down himself; and from what I can hear, in about half a minute he was so mangled that he died in the hospital in three days afterwards.

" Do you recollect the case of the gas works?—Yes; there was a man of the name of Craven convicted for that.

" What sentence was passed upon him?—Eighteen months imprisonment.

" Do you recollect an attack on a person of the name of Kennan, of Wine Tavern-street, a tanner?—Yes, in his own tan-yard, in the morning, at between eight and nine o'clock.

" By whom was that made?—It is not known; they were supposed to be tanners, for he had differed with the body, and taken in strange hands.

" Did not an examination take place at the police office on that subject? —There did; and there was a man committed to Newgate, tried before the recorder, and sentenced to nine months imprisonment.

" Who was the man; was he a tanner?—He was an old man, who had been a tanner; and it appeared he waited an opportunity and entered into a conversation, and that those men who appeared to have been hired, watched an opportunity and struck the man he spoke to.

" Hired by whom?—It is supposed by the journeymen of the trade.

" Did not the tanners trade offer a reward, and come forward themselves to prosecute, denying any cognizance whatever of any part of their trade? —I heard the curriers say they would do so; I went to the curriers meeting the next night they met.

" Have not you seen an advertisement to that effect?—No, but the magistrates recommended to them to do so; and I heard them say they would do so. Kennan's supposition was, that they instigated it; for he carried on the tanning and currying business together; and the wish of the trade was, to separate the two, to have them distinct trades.

" Do you know that the magistrates, after an inquiry into that case, returned the curriers thanks for the activity they had shown in discovering the person who attacked Kennan?—They showed a good disposition, for it was on the information that one of the curriers gave, that we arrested the man that was convicted.

labouring classes of society. Its design was to protect them from what, in the fervour of their indig-

---

" To what trade did that man belong?—He had been a tanner; he was past his labour.

" Are you aware that there is a difference between the tanners and the curriers?—Yes, between the master tanners, and the journeymen curriers.

" Was it by a member of the masters or the journeymen, that this man was beaten?—He supposed that he was beaten at the instigation of the curriers.

" It was a tanner that set him?—It was an old tanner that set him.

" Have you known any instances of any trade in Dublin refusing to concur with the police to discover any person suspected to have committed acts of violence?—They invariably plead ignorance of knowing of any act; they always deny it."

" You have stated, that on several occasions you have had information of an intended beating, from some persons who were present, and knew of the circumstance?—Yes; they were not present when the resolution took place that a man was to be beaten, but they were told that a meeting was to take place: the cant word for it was, Such a man is to be slated such a night; that is understood that he is to be beaten.

" Do you believe that that slating takes place in consequence of a resolution of the committee, or how do you understand it to be determined on?— The conduct of the man has displeased the committee, and an observation of displeasure is made upon it, and then some one speaks to those people who are ready to do such a business.

" That is done without a resolution of the committee?—Without any resolution at all."

From the examination of Mr. Chippendale.

" If you were to employ a number of coopers from Ireland, would you apprehend personal violence?—They would not suffer them to work, I am satisfied.

" What reason have you to suppose there would be personal injury?—On this ground: whenever a man has come into the yard, and they can find he has worked under the price, he will be scouted out of the yard."

From the examination of Mr. Thomas Hebblethwaite, near Wakefield.

" When did the men form themselves into an association?—I did not know of it till last November: we had heard of it before, but the men would not confess they had joined it till the very last day.

nation, they have often denominated the tyranny of their employers. The truth is, that they re-

---

"Are you certain no combination existed among your men previously to the repeal of the combination laws?—I believe not.

"You had no reason to suspect it?—None at all.

"Do you suppose the repeal of the laws tempted the men to form themselves into an association?—I think it did.

"Did they so form themselves into an association shortly after the repeal of those laws was known?—I cannot say how long after; but they have got a very large fund: they paid three halfpence a-week; they have got a fund which keeps them now for six weeks.

"When did they begin to form that fund?—I cannot say.

"Do they keep those matters secret from you?—Yes.

"Are there other manufacturers of the same description near you?—Not very near; there is about a mile off.

"Have the workmen in those other manufactories also struck?— Some of them have, but none since they turned out with us, because, as we did not submit to them, they have gone on at other places: if we had submitted, they would have turned out in the other two manufactories.

"What reason have you to believe that?—That is what the people in the union say; we have got part of our own family turned in again, and they call them black ones.

"What has become of the men who have retired from the works?—They have been walking about.

"And living upon the funds of their society?—Yes.

"Do you know what they receive?—Some of them receive nine shillings a-week, and three shillings for each child.

"How long have they continued to receive it?—There were many of them continued thirteen weeks; then they would not go any where else to seek work; then the committee said, that they would not pay them any more money, and then they turned in at their old wages."

From the examination of Mr. William Willans.

"Are you able to say whether there was any proof what particular men had thrown these brick-bats?—I am not able to say there was any proof of that. There is also the case of Peter Singleton, who was drinking with some of the union men, at a public-house in Rastrick. They were endeavouring to persuade him to enter into the union. He said, he was satisfied with the wages he was receiving. In consequence of which,

quire a still further protection; and that is, full
protection from a still more odious and oppressive

---

they abused him very much : he was knocked down, and so kicked, that
he was carried into a room, in a state of insensibility. He had the persons taken before a magistrate, where they were ordered to pay all the expenses, and to allow him 2s. per day till the surgeon reported him fit for
work."

From the examination of Mr. Chadwick.

" Have you any facts to state upon which that opinion of him or yourself
is founded?—I could account for the reasons by which he was actuated;
he stood between the men and myself, and, of course, wished to command
the approbation and confidence of both parties as much as possible; and,
therefore, he was well aware that in giving to me the names of parties, or
in standing by me in prosecuting the parties for threats, he was exposing
himself. I should have little hesitation in saying he was exposing his life
to risk.

" Is it not usual that, where prosecution has taken place in case of combination, the persons prosecuting have been set against?—Yes, they are
marked objects. In fact, he assured me, if he took the steps I wished him
to do, he must quit the neighbourhood.

" Do you know any instance of that nature of your own knowledge?—I
cannot speak to other manufacturers cases on this point.

" Has any circumstance taken place of a person appearing as a witness,
or prosecutor, having afterwards suffered for such conduct?—I am not aware
that there have been more than one or two; I believe there have been one
or two taken before the magistrates within the last three or four weeks, but
I cannot speak to the circumstances which have occurred as to the result.
My foreman, rather than stand by me in the brunt of the opposition, offered,
if I would give the advance to the men for two or three months, to get the
old hands reconciled to work with the new ones, to pay the advance out of
his own pocket."

From the examination of Lieutenant William Jones.

" Did you hear. any thing of a person being carried about the town,
painted, his face blackened, and insulted?—No. A circumstance has happened at Berwick; the company were determined to resist the Berwick
union, and went to Dunleary to hire sailors, and one of the masters hired
five men, and brought one or two with him into Berwick for his own
vessel. The other men were to follow after as they were wanted. The

tyranny which is apt to spring up among themselves. We can confidently appeal to the expe-

---

Berwick union men hearing that, walked out on the road to meet them, and met the men coming in a cart; they said, "You have come from Dunleary?" "Yes." "You are going to join the smacks?" "Yes." "You had better go back, one man has been murdered, we would advise you as friends to go back, and here is money to pay your expenses." The men were frightened, and fortunately a ship's commander forseeing this, sent men out with a constable, who undeceived them and brought them in."

From the examination of Mr. Henry Taylor, Ship-owner at Bristol.

" He engaged some men from Plymouth, and paid their expenses to Bristol; during this week the Bristol carpenters had a committee sitting daily, and they got knowledge of these men coming up from Plymouth; they waited for them, and told them they would not be allowed to work in Bristol; that their lives would be in danger if they walked the streets, and they persuaded them to go back immediately. I got some hint of it, and went to the next coach about to start for Plymouth, and I found the strangers on the top of the coach, on their return, and the committee of the Bristol carpenters round the coach. I remonstrated with these strangers on the impropriety of their conduct, in coming up at Mr. Scott's expense; and I asked them why they were going back. They told me that the carpenters had told them that they should not work in the city, and had sent them back. The Bristol carpenters had supplied them with plenty of spirits during the few hours they were in Bristol, and handed up spirits to them on the coach, desiring them to drink success to the carpenters' union.

" Did any of those persons whom you had brought, state to you that they were induced to return from having been told that their lives would not be safe, if they remained in Bristol?—Yes; and that they were desired by the carpenters to stop the others, if they met them on the road, and support the union.

" They did return accordingly? Yes; they all returned. One gentleman in the coach, who went back with them, told me afterwards, that they told him they were sent back at the expense of the club at Bristol, and that they had sufficient money put into their pockets to send them home."

From the examination of Mr. Fletcher, Ship-builder, London.

" Have any of these punishments been carried into effect?—I do not know how far they have been carried into effect, for such is the system of

rience of many workmen, whether they ever felt
so grievously thwarted and overborne out of their

---

terror over the minds of the men that they dare not rebel. Many have engaged themselves to go and work on work left by these men, and not a
single ship-wright dare come; they would do it at the peril of their lives.

"Do you get without difficulty workmen who do not belong to the union?—We cannot get any. We have eight or nine at work, some of whom
have been obliged to apply to a magistrate. We for protection endeavoured
to prevail on these to continue, and have succeeded in keeping them from
joining the union; but they have been annoyed extremely and assaulted by
the people. I was obliged to take one of the men up, to ensure peace and
protection.

" What protection was afforded?—The magistrate told the men, if they
were impeded or insulted, or prevented from coming to work, that he would
certainly send the offender to the treadmill, and he, the person now charged,
was to make that known to the rest of his associates. We have had one
instance since, where the men have been abused; I called the man in and
told him, that as the second offence would send the offender to the treadmill, and he was sufficiently punished by obeying the law of the committee,
I would not punish him for breaking the law of the land, and therefore I
forbore."

From the examination of Mr. William Rose Robinson, Sheriff-depute of
Lanarkshire.

" Can you name the persons whom they wished to wound or assassinate?—The persons whom they wished to wound or assassinate, subsequently to the Act, were D. M'Fee, Robert Watson, and John Graham;
and I may also state, that of the concurring statement of two of the witnesses, who went to be examined on the trial for shooting J. Graham;
they were waylaid, and fired at, a few days previously to the time when
they were to be brought forward to give evidence against the man who shot
Graham.

" You know, as a fact, that these witnesses were fired at?—I have the
statement of the men themselves, that they were fired at; and next morning, two pieces of lead, seemingly flattened against a wall, or other hard
substance, and of the weight of a pistol-bullet, were found near the spot
where the said men were fired at. The case of Robert Watson, was as
follows. Watson was fired at with a bullet, which grazed his back,
underneath the shoulder. This was after having been threatened, and
intimidated in a variety of ways. There is reason to suppose, that he

own free choice, as by the terrors of their own
association, whose secret and mysterious power

---

was fired at twice, as there were two holes through the back of his
jacket.

" By whom ?—Although it was done in the midst of a considerable
number of people, such was the co-operation, or effect of the intimidation
existing, that we could not obtain evidence who the person or persons were
who did it. The case of Graham was tried, and John Kean was found
guilty of having shot Graham with ten pellets of the largest species of
shot: eight of these are at present in his body. He is paralyzed in his
lower extremities, and there is no chance of his recovering; that is the opinion of the medical gentlemen.

" Why did the prosecution take place before the man was out of danger?
—Because he was likely to survive for a considerable time; and such is
the state of intimidation and actual violence at present existing in Glasgow, that it was necessary to bring forward the trial, lest material evidence
should be lost. It was necessary to keep the principal witnesses on the
trial in safety; and a subscription is pressntly going on with a view to removal to some other place of a witness named Bell, who seized Kean, and
was the main instrument of his apprehension and conviction.

" Have you any reason to suppose the man had been employed by other
people to commit the act?—I have no reason to doubt that he was employed by others, viz. the secret committee, and that he was to receive
money for doing it; and I state this upon the man's own authority, being a
confession voluntarily given since his conviction of the crime. The import
of his confession is, that he, along with several others employed, were to
assassinate Graham and some others. Four or five of the masters were
particularly pointed out. The assassins were to receive, I think, the sum
of £100, and if successful were to get more.

" You are possessed of this confession in writing?—I am possessed of the
confession, and will produce it.

" Was all this since Mr. Hume's Act?—All the cases which I have latterly detailed have taken place within these few months.

" Are there other acts ?—There are a variety of other assaults and acts of
intimidation, of which I am prepared to give the particulars, if required.

" What has been the effect of these acts of intimidation?—I think the
effect of the acts of intimidation, taken generally, has been to bind together,
and to create and give effect to the existing co-operation among these combinations. I think that without intimidation they would individually and
collectively more speedily fall to pieces, because it is through the medium

wielded a far more despotic sway over their imaginations, than ever did the old law in the pleni-

---

of intimidation that they, in a great measure, collect or obtain the funds
which they distribute in furtherance of their purposes.

" Have there been acts of assembling round manufactories to prevent
workmen going to work?—There have been various instances of that. I
have been obliged to issue proclamations, to employ additional constables,
and even to call the military, in consequence of persons congregating round
the manufactories, and annoying with missiles and abusive language the new
workers. The annoyance was such that they have been obliged to be
guided to the work, and protected back again to their own rooms."

From the examination of Mr. Robert M'Kechnie, Procurator Fiscal of
Stirlingshire.

" Did they suffer much injury?—Two of the men were most severely cut,
one of the name of James Corbet, and another of the name of John Moffat.
John Moffat was knocked down by a stone, and fell into a ditch by the side
of the road, and while lying in the ditch, the individual who struck him with
the stone, and several other colliers, came up and struck him repeatedly
on the head with sticks and paling stakes, and caused various fractures;
and at this moment the man is confined in the house, and not able to do
any thing.

" Was he left for dead at the time?—He was. He has been attended
daily since the assault by two surgeons, and I believe it is only within these
two or three weeks that he has been certified to be out of danger.

" Subsequent to this were any others of those labourers threatened or
dealt with in any way by those colliers?—Yes, they were.

" When, and where?—What I have stated was, that on March the 14th
an attack was made on those labourers. On the following forenoon there
was an assembly of colliers, the Rumford and Park Hall colliers, the whole
of his Grace's strike-work colliers, the colliers at Quarrol and Kinnaird, and
from collieries from Borrowstoness, took place, to the amount of from six
to eight hundred, all armed with bludgeons and sticks. They met at Reading Moor, just by the coal-works, and some of those colliers got hold of one
of the Duke's labourers.

" One of those men that you spoke of before? Yes, one of the sixty or
seventy.

" What was his name?—William Bishop. They threatened to cut his
throat if he did not instantly go back from whence he came; they seized
him and threw him on the ground, and some of them took out an instru-

tude of all its enforcements. We venture to affirm, that the dread of ruin to their families, and of injury to their persons, has been far more frequently inspired by this new despotism, within these few months, than has been done by the statutes against combinations among all the working classes put together for a whole century.* An act for the fur-

---

ment from his pocket, and while he was lying on the ground, they said they would save his life, provided he instantly went back to Hamilton, and told the whole of his comrades to do the same; they desired him to tell his comrades, if they did not go back likewise that they would be done for; the consequence was, he did tell his comrades that very day or the next, and they all refused to work, being afraid of their lives. They would have commenced on the Tuesday had not the foresaid assault taken place; but in consequence of it, and what happened to Bishop, they all refused to work, and continued the whole of that week without working. Mr. M'Donald, the sheriff-depute of the county, got notice of all this, and came upon Thursday morning the 17th, to his Grace's coal-works, attended by his fiscal and some sheriff-officers. He was for some weeks after this almost daily at the works; he encouraged the men to go to work, said that he would protect them, and that they (the strike-work colliers) dared not meddle with them; and by his daring activity, and making apprehensions of various individuals concerned in the assault of those two labourers, the sheriff got them the beginning of the following week, the whole of the labourers, to go to work."

Who can doubt, after such instances of atrocity, that should Government find it necessary to enact heavier penalties against all interference with the natural liberty of workmen, they will carry the whole sense and virtuous feeling of the country along with them?

* From the examination of Mr. Robert Hutton.

" As you conceive the combination is increased, do you conceive the system of intimidation amongst the men has increased? Yes, increased to a very great degree.

" Do you mean threats of violence, or threats of any other consequences? —Threats of every kind; a man who came over from Manchester and set up himself as a repairer of machinery has been threatened, his men have left him; he went out on Easter Monday, and his wife and sister were with him, and they were told, you had better let that man, stating his name,

ther protection of workmen from this regimen of
terror, so far from even the most distant approach

leave the country; we have all settled that he, and other Englishmen who
come over to interfere with our trade, shall be roasted on a gridiron.; those
threats to women of course have a very powerful influence."

From the examination of Mr. J. Fletcher.

" Has Husband, or any other of the men formerly employed in your yard,
directly or indirectly intimated to you any feeling of a wish to return, if it
were not for a dread of this union?—They have said so over and over again,
that they should be very glad indeed. They have told me collectively and
individually, that if I would give them the smallest colour on earth, that
would be a justification to them,—if I would only do any thing that would
justify them to the committee, they would all return to work; they would
leave price and every thing else to myself, as they had done, if I would
only do any thing that would give them a colour of justification. I said
to them at one of the meetings, ' I will not; if I were capable of doing
any thing colourable, I should lose my character with you; if you must do
something with our regulations, strike your pen through the printer's name,
that is all I can grant; you must come as you went away; but if you are
under the control of the committee, if you dare not act as free agents, you
must abide the consequences, and ruin yourselves and families.' I am
convinced of it,—I have no more doubt of it than of my own existence,—
that the only thing that keeps the shipwrights in our employ away, is the
dread they are under of the consequences from the union, and the threats
the committee have made."

From the examination of Mr. G. F. Young, a Ship-builder at Lime-
house.

" Is there any other circumstance you have to state?—A control attempted to be exercised, in numerous instances, over persons who made no
complaint whatever, and who had expressed their satisfaction with their
wages and their treatment, but who are deterred from remaining in the employ by the apprehensions under which they lie of personal violence, but
more frequently by that sort of intimidation which men are naturally averse
to expose themselves to. No longer ago than Saturday last, I recollect an
excellent workman in our employment came to me himself; he stated, " Sir,
I have been many years in your employ; I am grateful for all you have
done for me; I always found you a kind and a good master; but I am an
inhabitant of one of the alms-houses belonging to the Shipwrights Heart of

to a re-enactment of the Combination Laws, would,
in fact, be tantamount to a grant of additional

Oak Institution, and it has been intimated to me that if I do not leave your employ I shall be expelled from that alms-house." I pressed him exceedingly to tell me by whom this intimation had been given, but I could not succeed. I have been told by many other men that they have joined the union because they were treated as so degraded a caste by their fellows, that their lives were rendered wretched and miserable; that they were literally so far compelled by that description of influence which men in that station of life can hardly be expected to be proof against.

" Three or four of the men who were so employed on the Ruth, told me that a meeting had been called, in consequence of its being conceived by the general body of the people that they ought to have demanded an increase of price upon this ship, they having taken it upon the usual price of the yard; I pointed out to them what an outrage it was upon their independence, that they should not be considered capable of making an agreement for themselves. I asked them how they could allow an interference of other persons unconnected with them; they told me they regretted it exceedingly, but that it was impossible for them to control the views of the general body; that they were members of the union, and they must act with the union; but they did return to their work."

From the examination of Mr. Thomas Carter.

" What has been the nature of these conversations?—I had occasion, within this week past, to speak with a man for leaving some work in an incomplete state, and I asked him why he had done it. He said that he had been before the committee to request permission to finish it, and they had told him that he had no right to finish it, though in his own opinion he said he had; in fact, he was under a verbal contract to do it. This same man, when first the union was formed, objected to enter into it, and met with a great deal of ill treatment from his mates in consequence.

" Have you this from himself?—Yes.

" What sort of ill treatment?—Every time he went to his meals he was attacked. The shipwrights, most of them, work far from home, and consequently they go to a public-house to get their meals; then a man is exposed to the attack of all his mates. This man resisted for some time all the advice of the people respecting his joining the union, and at last they told him, that without he would enter into the union, every man would leave the ship upon which he was employed. There were a great many men employed on the ship; she was an East Indiaman, and much wanted. I removed the

liberty; and, notwithstanding all the clamour and
jealousy of the obstinately disaffected among them,

---

man to another ship, as the owners were pressing to have her finished; I
thought it better to take no more notice of it; I removed him to another
dock, or else I felt assured the whole of them would strike.

" Did the man afterwards enter into the union?—He felt himself compelled; he told me that no man would have worked with him. I have
taken frequent and almost hourly opportunities of speaking with the men;
he is not the only one, by scores, who have declared to me that fear alone
has compelled them to enter into the union. I have men now working in
the yard who are intimidated to a degree of which you have no conception, and who, if they dared, would very gladly have nothing more to do
with the union. I have taken daily and hourly opportunities of speaking
with those whom I thought the most quiet and well-disposed amongst
them."

From the examination of Mr. Joseph Nash:—

" Do you conceive that that statement was an invention of his for the
purpose of saving himself in the opinion of the union?—I do decidedly so,
because he stated to me, ' Nash,' says he, ' we would give any thing to be at
work, if we could get any little measure, so as to justify ourselves in the
eyes of our committee.'

" Did Husband at any time express to you that he should be very glad
to return to Mr. Fletcher's work if it was not for the apprehensions he en-
tertained from the union?—He never stated that he was kept from going to
work by apprehensions; but he has more than once, twice, or thrice, stated
to me as a friend, ' I wish I was at work; for Mr. Fletcher has offered
every thing necessary for our comfort; but now we are in the union we
cannot, unless we could get him to do something to justify ourselves in the
eyes of the committee.'

" You stated that you had frequent communication with the shipwrights,
is it your opinion that many of them would return to work if they were allowed to do so?—I am certain of it; but if they came to work now, they
must forfeit the benefit they expect to result from the union.

" In your opinion, are they apprehensive of any insult, or any assault, if
they were to return to their work?—Several of them stated that they would
be glad to go to work, was it not that they should be scoffed at and jeered
at by the rest of the union.

" And you believe they would?—I am certain they would.

would be substantially felt as such by the body at large. It were to be regretted, if Government, after having done so well by the repeal of these laws, should forfeit any portion of the popularity and real strength which it has thereby acquired; and, therefore, it is especially desirable, that any subsequent measure which might be necessary, should wear the appearance, as well as possess the reality of being a measure for still further defending the liberties and the interest of workmen.

By the repeal of the Combination Laws, full liberty has been granted, that workmen shall either singly, or in a body, cease to work till they obtain such superior remuneration as they may choose to fancy or to fix upon. But the liberty is imperfect, if any one, or more of these workmen, be not in full security, when they please to work for any inferior remuneration. The man who is willing to accept of a lower wage than his fellows, is the man who can least of them all afford to be idle. It is he who is most goaded by his own necessities, and those of his family, to an exertion for their subsistence; and he, therefore, is the individual, to whom the restraints of an association enforced as they often are by the persecution and violence of its agents,

---

" Has any thing of that kind taken place with those men that are at work in your yard?—Yes.

" In what way?—They have been called as bad as assassins; they have been accused by the people that have left, ' You are as bad as assassins, to go to work to take the bread out of our mouths when we are remaining out of work for your good.' "

are in fact the most gallingly and oppressively cruel. The members of a combination of workmen hold out their cause to be that of the poor against the rich, whom they would represent as the tyrants and oppressors of society. They reflect not on the tyranny which they are exercising all the while on those who are still poorer, and in a state of more pitiable helplessness than themselves—on the individuals of their own body, who are most immersed in debt, or whose children are farthest sunk in destitution, and who most gladly would labour in their behalf for the current wages, were it not for the rigours and the menaces of this worse than revolutionary despotism. The greatest mischief which has ensued from the repeal in question, can be met by a legislation that might stand forth, not in the character of opposition, but in the character of friendship and benignity to the lower orders; a legislation that took the side not of masters against servants, but of the poorest and most helpless of these servants, against that crowd of petty oppressors who were of somewhat elevated condition above them. A legislation of this sort, whose equity recommends itself to every man's conscience never can awaken any popular disaffection that will be at all hazardous; and we therefore would repeat it as our fondest hope, that Parliament will devise a method for putting down those outrages, that we suspect at the very worst are temporary, without at all impairing that fine aspect of liberality, which is not less consonant with the soundest economic wisdom, than it is in grateful harmony with the spirit of our age.*

The associated workmen with the cry of liberty in their mouths, have most glaringly traversed all the principles of liberty. They have erected themselves into so many little corporations, and are chargeable with all the monopoly and intolerance of the corporation spirit. They have endeavoured to narrow the field of competition for employment, by shutting the avenues to their respective trades against the general population. The same paltry selfishness which wont to characterise in other days, the exclusive companies of merchants, has now descended among our labourers, and with them has acquired a still more hideous complexion, from the savage cruelties wherewith it has been aggravated, and which have armed against their cause all that is generous and good in the feelings of the country. Still it is hoped that even misconduct so outrageous as theirs will not precipitate the legislature back

---

* The Act 6th George IV. c. 126th, is altogether in this spirit, and will go far to check in Scotland, the only evils of combination which are really formidable, or against which Government should ever array themselves. It is entitled " An Act to make provision in Scotland, for the further prevention of maliciously shooting and attempting to discharge loaded fire-arms, stabbing, cutting, wounding, poisoning, maiming, disfiguring, and disabling his Majesty's subjects." There is particularly specified in this Act, the offence of unlawfully throwing, or otherwise applying to any of his Majesty's subjects, any Sulphuric Acid, or other corrosive substance. This and certain other outrages, (named in this Act) with the intent to murder, maim, or do some other grievous bodily harm, are held to be capital, and liable to sentence of death accordingly.

again to those antiquated prejudices from which they had emerged; but well may it warrant them to utter a voice of greater decision, and lift an arm of greater strength than they have ever yet done, against such enormities as can never be endured in any Christian or civilized land.

Because government may have conceded to our artizans and mechanics the fullest liberty not to work, that is no reason why a power should be permitted to arise in another quarter, which might trench upon their liberty to work. Government has nought to do, but to assert itself the equal patron and defender of both kinds of liberty. By means of the one liberty, it will neutralise all the mischief which is apprehended from the other. It is not by a regimen which does violence to any of the principles of natural freedom, but by the equal and impartial maintenance of all its principles, that a wise government is enabled to uphold the best and most wholesome state of society.

And so far from any call for any peculiar delicacy or tenderness of legislation in this matter, there is a very peculiar reason, why in every manufacturing country, the attempt to molest or impede workmen in the free exercise of their callings, should be visited with a treatment the very opposite of that lenity, wherewith this offence seems to be regarded at least in the Repeal Act. It is not because of the alleged importance of our manufactures to the public and political strength of our nation; an advantage which we have long held to be quite imaginary; but it is because of the very great number of those whose interest and safety are involved in the protection of every workman from the aggression of his fellows. We allude to the workmen themselves. There is altogether as great propriety in it, that the crime of forcing or interrupting a labourer should be signalized above an ordinary assault, by the severer penalties which are annexed to it, as that the crime of forgery should be so signalized. The latter severity, over rigorous as it surely is, has been defended on the ground of the extensive mischief done by forgery to the merchants of a trading nation. The former might well be vindicated on the ground of a mischief as extensive, done, by the forcing of workmen, to the mechanics and artizans of a manufacturing nation. To provide a barrier against the outrages of associated workmen, it is not necessary to conjure up again the legislation of barbarous times. It can be done by a better legislation, which shall bear upon its forehead the impress both of kindness to the labourer, and of enlightened patriotism.

II. But what theoretically may appear to be a good law in the statute book, might turn out, after all, to be practically a powerless or inapplicable law in society; like a machine, that however beautiful and perfect in the model, might not work well in the manufactory. Therefore it is, that ere such an inquiry as the present can be completed, we must pass from the abstract jurisprudence of the question, to the gross and living experience of the question; and, going forth on the outer field of actual and concrete humanity, we must observe, there, what the forces and the interests are which come into busy play, and in how far such a law as we have argued for, is of sufficient control over them, for all right and salutary purposes. It is not by the mere categories of ethical science that such a question ought to be determined. Such a law as would suit the republic of Plato, or some similar Utopia, might be the whole fruit of one's studious excogitations at home. But it is only by a survey abroad, and over the domain of business and familiar life, that he learns to modify, when needful, the generalizations of abstract thought, by the demands of a felt and urgent expediency.

Let us now look, then, to this outer field of contemplation—not to the principles of the question in any system of natural law, but to the exemplifications of the question in the midst of living society; and we greatly mistake it, if it be not found that there is a most entire harmony between them; and that the complex workings of what may be termed the economic mechanism, are altogether at one with the simplicities of theory. We hold that there are certain natural securities for a right adjustment between masters and servants, in the very relationship itself, which ought to supersede the interference of Government;—we mean, its interference for any other object than the enforcement of justice between the parties, and the protection of both from all sorts of personal violence.

Even from the very history of some recent misguided adventures, on the part of workmen, we
may learn what these securities are, and how powerful and efficient they must ultimately prove in
their operation. So that the interference of Government, with the just and natural freedom of any
of the parties, is really superseded by those better
influences that lie in the mechanism and the spontaneous workings of human society.

The great compensation, then, for the evils of a
strike, is the power which masters have of replac-
ing those who have struck work by other hands.
We will not deny the very great temporary inconvenience of such an event to masters; but we
deny that it is such as to warrant a legislation,
which traverses any of the principles of an obvious
or natural equity. And besides, we are not to
estimate the inconvenience in all time coming, by
any degree of it which might be felt or experienced at present; for now the conflict is at its
height in many places ; and though, by this time,
subsided into quiescence in some quarters, yet, in
others, still in a state of busy and unsettled fermentation. Still, however, we have to wait the various terminations of this controversy, which the
repeal of the Combination Laws has so very naturally awakened all over the land, ere we shall
obtain the complete verification of its result. We
are yet in the suspense, and among the uncertainties of the experiment; and though gradually
brightening towards it, we have not yet arrived at

the full and finished experience. This experience, however, if waited for patiently, and for a sufficient length of time, will, we have no doubt, be in the highest degree tranquillizing to the combatants, and satisfactory to the public at large. Meanwhile, even from the already bygone history of these combinations, in places where the warfare has been stoutest and most alarming, might we gather, I apprehend, enough of argument why the great principles of natural justice and liberty ought not to be violated.

In the first place, then, on the event of a general strike in an industrious establishment, there have been frequent instances of the old hands being replaced by new ones, who were rendered effective in the course of a few weeks. This has been done, and with ultimate success, at collieries and cotton-mills, and in many other manufactories. At the Redding colliery, for example, belonging to the Duke of Hamilton, and where the disturbances assumed a very riotous character, this expedient was resorted to. By a series of questions and answers now before me, it appears that the manager there, on the defection of the old colliers, employed in their place such labourers as were about the work, and who were before employed in above-ground jobs, together with a few strangers who accidentally came. The labourers were instructed in their new occupation by three oversmen of the work, and a few other colliers (three or four, chiefly old) who did not join the association. They were allowed two shillings and six-pence a-day at the first, but in a few weeks most of them earned more by the piece; and the good hands, in a very few weeks, made five shillings, and even more per day.

This narrative is chiefly valuable as affording the example of a good termination to the strike, achieved by the mere vigour and promptitude of the Sheriff-depute of the county. We feel persuaded, that without any recurrence to an antiquated law, the whole mischief of these combinations might be neutralized by means of a greater spirit and energy on the part of our executive officers. A stronger or more efficient police might be necessary for the purpose of putting down all that is really bad in them; and this were far better than to call in the aid of a legislation that traversed any great principle of liberality or justice.*

---

* It seems that the sixty or seventy labourers who have been taken in to replace the colliers who had struck, refused to work in consequence of a grievious assault made by the latter on some of their body, when Mr. M'Donald, with a daring and determination that do him great honour, interposed for their protection, and prevailed on the whole of them to go to work.

Further extract from the examination of Mr. Robert M'Kechnie on this subject.

" After Mr. M'Donald, the sheriff-depute, arrived, did the old men, the strike-work men, return to their work?—No.

" Are they still out?—I stated before, that during the month of April twenty or thirty of those strike-work colliers came to Mr. Johnston, his Grace's manager, and mentioned that they were willing to begin: they wished him to take them back, which he did, and up to the period that I left Scotland there were parties of them making application to be taken back into the works.

" Those that returned, did they return on any different terms than those that existed in the colliery when they left?—Yes; I know from the information of the manager, they are getting now the wages that his Grace of-

The next narrative, more especially as extended in the notes below, serves to demonstate how much,

---

fered them at the time of the strike, a rise of wages not, however, to the extent that they wanted. I believe they were allowed 2s. a ton previous to the strike, and at or immediately after the strike they were offered 2s. 7d. which they refused. They wished 3s. 6d., and I believe now they are getting 2s. 6d. or 2s. 7d.

" Since the 15th of March, when they threatened Bishop, has there been any disturbance, or act of violence committed by any of them, on any of the men now at work?—None at his Grace's works; but an act of violence was committed at Quarrol and Kinnaird's works, about three miles to the north of the Redding collieries.

" What is the other assault that you mention?—A family of the name of Hotchkis, who had been among his Grace's strike-work colliers in December, had renewed their engagements with his Grace, and on the 16th day of April last they went to Carron shore, on a visit to some relations there; while in their friend's house, a number of the Quarrol and Kinnaird colliers, understanding that they were there, came and surrounded the house, and called upon the family to send them out, &c. this was about ten o'clock at night, and they assaulted the house by throwing stones at the door, going round to the back of it, and breaking the windows, and throwing in at the party of the Hotchkises large pailing stakes as thick as my arm, and from two to three feet in length, and which struck some of the party sitting in the room.

" What followed?—In consequence of that assault, Mr. M'Donald the sheriff came to Falkirk on Monday, and went to the Redding collieries along with myself, when we heard of it the first time, we instantly went down to the collieries at Quarrol, on the Monday evening the 18th, and from the information we got, I drew out a petition and complaint, as the Procurator Fiscal, against the individuals who were alleged to have committed the assault; two of them were that night apprehended, examined, and sent to Stirling gaol, and since then, other four or five have been apprehended and sent to gaol till they should find bail to answer for the assault.

" How were they repelled from the house?—They appeared to have gone off of their own accord; the Hotchkises remained in the house, and kept the door barred as well as they could; they remained there till the Sunday morning; two or three of them slept all night there; one or two went out to another relation's, and when they went out all was quiet, the parties who made the assault having gone away.

without the aid either of law or of police, might be accomplished by a mere spirit of determination on the part of masters. It exhibits a fine miniature specimen of the progress and the natural expiry of combinations, by the action alone of those natural forces and interests which are involved in them. We think that it goes to establish the safety wherewith (after Government has fulfilled its duty of protection from all outrages) the whole matter might be left to its own issues: and we do think it hard that the legislature should be called upon, either to brave the odium, or to sustain the burden, of a management which devolves more properly on capitalists themselves.

The following is the extract of a letter from a gentleman connected with a colliery near Ayr :—
" Being firmly determined to withstand this system of dictation, we looked about us for the means of counteracting their measures; and nothing appearing to us so effectual as the taking or employing of

---

" The labourers?—In consequence of Mr. M'Donald's activity and exertions in making repeated apprehensions of the persons who had been guilty of the assault, and his coming almost daily upon the collieries, they all returned to their work, but I may mention that his Grace's manager was obliged to keep up what is called an armed force during the night-time to protect the machinery, he being afraid that a great body of colliers might have come and destroyed these, but the labourers have been going on from the week following the foresaid assault up to the time I left Scotland.

" Since that period when you and Mr. M'Donald were there, have any attacks in fact been made on the machinery, or on those labourers so employed?—Not to my knowledge.

" Is there an armed force now kept up?—-It was kept up partially to the very day that I left Scotland.

" Watchmen?—Yes, armed watchmen."

new hands, we instantly set about preparing tools, and engaging every labouring man we could obtain. In about three weeks, we had introduced seventy men into our pits; and the produce of our colliery daily increasing, it became evident that we were ultimately to prevail in the struggle. The men whom we employed were mostly Irishmen, but were picked up by us about the place. Had we not succeeded in getting them in that way, we had determined to send a person to Ireland to recruit there. Our old hands, at least such as we have chosen to employ, have returned to their work, and have, in a submissive manner, renounced the system of associations. Our new colliers continue with us, and are doing well."*

---

* The worth and importance of Mr. Taylor's evidence, have induced us to present it to the reader entire.

" Are you concerned in extensive collieries in the county of Ayr?—I am.

" Have you conducted those collieries for a considerable period?—Yes, for a considerable period; above twenty years.

" Have you occasion to know the number of colliers in the county of Ayr, occupied in your own and other collieries?—I believe about 1,400; I do not know precisely the number.

" Have you at any period been subjected, in conducting your collieries, to any inconvenience from associations among your workmen?—We have, at various periods.

" At what periods have you experienced such inconvenience?—We have frequently had small combinations, but not to a great extent: the first great combination we had, commenced the 15th of November, 1817.

" Can you state to the Committee any particulars respecting the combination in 1817?—It was in consequence of a general association of the colliers about Glasgow, and in Ayrshire; it was principally originated by a weaver of the name of Fallhouse Wilson; in consequence of that association, all the colliers in Ayrshire resolved to strike work upon a fixed day. When our colliers told us they should strike at a fortnight's notice, we told them we would dispense with the fortnight's notice; that, if they were to

These are only two examples, selected almost at random from the mass that lies before us, and

strike, they might strike immediately. Accordingly, they did strike immediately. That continued from the 15th of November, to the 1st of December, when they all returned to their employment. We did not, nor ever thought of applying for legal proceedings, or legal measures, to put down combinations ; we met it, by endeavouring to engage other workmen to execute the labour which those men had deserted; and it was in consequence of the numbers which were entering our work, and labourers becoming colliers, that we were enabled to put down that combination.

" What was their demand ?—I do not remember the demand in 1817; it was for a rise of wages.

" Did they obtain that rise ?—They did not.

" Was that attended with any acts of violence, or interference with you, to prevent your men working ?—No, it was not.

" It was amicably settled at the end of that period ?—It was.

" How many new men had you brought in ?—About forty at that period.

" How many had you working at that time ?—Above a hundred.

" Were those, whom you brought in to work, allowed to continue to work, after the old hands returned ?—They were; such as chose to remain.

" And no acts of violence were committed ?—No.

" Was there any other occasion, subsequent to 1817, in which the men demanded terms, which you were not disposed to give them ?—Not any great strike was the consequence. When the colliers wish to obtain an increase of wages, their general mode is, by continuing to work, and endeavouring, by every way possible, to thwart the masters. When they observe a master has a demand for coals, they limit their supply, and perhaps will only do half work, and for days decline to raise coal altogether; in this way thwarting him so much, that they generally obtain their ends. When they follow that system, they will pursue it for a very long period of time, with a view of obtaining ultimately what they seek for.

" Are the men engaged in this colliery by the day, or per year, or piece work ?—They are engaged for piece work.

" For what period are they engaged ?—We consider them free to go at the end of each fortnight, when they are paid.

" What is the nature of their engagement ; by the ton ?—Yes, by the ton.

which serve to demonstrate the facility wherewith
raw and unpractised labourers can be rendered ef-

" What do you reckon a ton?—Our ton weighs about twenty-eight hundred weight; indeed we seldom have occasion to weigh, because our engagement is only to deliver a certain measure.

" Has any thing occurred from 1817 up to a late period?—No strike at
all; occasionally thwarting in the manner I have mentioned, to obtain
their ends.

" Has any union or association taken place within the last year, different
from what before existed?—Yes.

" State the time at which, and the circumstances under which, that association took place.—An association of the colliers in Ayrshire was formed,
in which our workmen joined.

" At what period was that?—It might be in November last, I should
think. The object of that association was to obtain in general a rise of
wages, and to exclude other workmen from entering the pits.

" New men?—People that were not colliers before, but labourers.

" Were any demands made of you, on behalf of the men, your refusal
to comply with which was stated as a ground of complaint by the association?—No; some time about the end of November, we voluntarily gave
them a rise of wages, with which they were perfectly satisfied at the time.
We deemed it proper, in consequence of the change of circumstances
of the country, and the demand for labour, voluntarily to raise their
wages.

" What was the rate of wages before such rise was made?—It was eight
shillings per five waggons of coal; that was increased to nine shillings.

" What is the quantity in each waggon?—About twenty-eight hundred
weight, I believe.

" Do you keep to the same weight nearly?—We sell by measure; we
seldom have occasion to weigh them; the measure is regular.

" Can you state the rate of wages which your men were in general able
to earn, at the rate of payment which you have mentioned?—From
twelve to twenty shillings a-week, according as they chose to work.

" Before the rise?—Yes, I should think so.

" Did the average exceed half-a-guinea?—Yes; it greatly exceeded that.

" Did it exceed fifteen shillings?—No, I should think fifteen shillings
might be about the average before the increase; but at the same time, if
the workmen have any discontent hanging upon their minds, they will not
work freely, so that we cannot say what it would be if they were giving
their minds cheerfully to their work.

fective at least in this important branch of industry.
In many other branches masters have precisely

" On occasions where there is no discontent, and they are satisfied, and
work fairly, what might the fair average earnings of the men be?—I conceive, at present, good workmen can earn from four to five shillings a day.
Our wages are one ninth part greater than they were at that period.

" How long had that rate of eight shillings continued?—It had been for,
I should think, about two years.

" How many hours do you reckon that they must work to earn fifteen shillings a-week, under the old rate of eight shillings?—I should suppose about
eight or nine hours. Sometimes the workmen are longer in the pit. The
rule is, to relieve the collier of his coals in rotation : a collier who gets his
coals taken first from him to-day, is second on the day following, and so it
goes on till the last; and that last is detained in the pit a considerable period of time.

" What was the date of the voluntary advance?—It was about the end
of November.

" When did the men express any dissatisfaction after that period?—
About the 11th of December.

" In what manner did they express to you that dissatisfaction?—By a
letter written.

" What was the nature of that letter?

[*The witness delivered in the same, which was read as follows:*]

" Ayr Colliery, Dec. the 11th, 1824.

" Mr. Deir Sir, this is to inform you that we want our Miser mad accorden to the standrt, and if not we well not work no mor until you but
forten days after thies. Deir sir, we do not think that no man or set of
men will thank that our Demands is on Just, for thier is no man or set of
men that have goods to sell, eather by weight or misure, but would like
to see their own Goods gaven away, but that have not bein the Cass with
us, for we have bein Dennied that privilig thus two or three yeiars back;
but, sir we wish to gave you the 32 bushel to the wagon, or 26 hunder-
wight, as you have marked upon your wagons, but we wish for to see the
mesur oursalves accorden to the standert sir; and their is a nother theng
that we will not gave untoo, and that is, the being orf to the score when
you are not bingin sir. As you have the mens nems you can sand for
anney two men out of each pet that you pleias, to gave them an answar;
but thier is nine pance which belongs to the kanel pet, on account of them

the same resource; but instead of encumbering
the text with any new cases, we refer for all our

---

gaven 25 to scor, which we wish to obten; and their is 6 pance more which
belongs to the we pit, which they wish to obten.

" We Rimens, yours, &c.

(*Signed by* 84 *persons.*)

" What is the standard by which you regulate? You state it at twenty-
eight hundred weight?—No, I stated it to be by measure. The dimensions of the waggons I do not at present bear in mind, but they are all of
one size.

" Are not the waggons by law obliged to contain a certain quantity?
—No.

" Is there any mark on your waggons of the quantity they should contain?—There is.

" What is that?—It is that stated in that letter. The mark is not put
on by us, but by the Custom-house. At one period, the Custom-house
marked our waggons twenty-six hundred weight and a half; on a subsequent marking, they marked them twenty-six hundred weight; but I know
our coals were always more than twenty six hundred weight, from the
manner in which they discharged in Ireland; the Custom-house were not
accurate in that.

" What was the nature of the demand the men made for an alteration in
the manner in which their work should be measured?—By that letter,
they intended that the coals should be taken by weight, and that that
weight should be twenty-six hundred weight; that we should be obliged
to take the inaccurate weight affixed by the Custom-house officers upon
our coals.

" They thought that whatever weight was marked upon the waggon
should be the rule for you to go by, and that their wages should be regulated by that standard?—Yes; but our coals are sold by measure, and not
by weight.

" Was there any increase in the measure of your coals at the time they
brought forward their complaint, compared with what had been the practice at your colliery for many years past?—I believe there was a small
increase of measure. A period of great dulness followed on the repeal of
the distillery laws: we were obliged to store our coals; and the other collieries in the neighbourhood increased their measure, by which we were
obliged to do the same: and for two years previous to that time, I believe
a small increase of measure had taken place.

additional ones to the notes which are appended
below.

" Had not that increase extended to twenty-nine hundred weight, by
which the men were paid?—The men were paid by the same measure at
which we sold.

" Did you then sell the coals at twenty-nine hundrd weight, the same as
you paid the men for?—The same as we paid the men.

" If you had not stored the coals in the manner you have stated, would
it not have been matter of necessity that you should have discharged a considerable number of your men?—It would.

" Is it not a rule with you to store?—Only at some collieries. At
others, the men are prevented from working, unless they can sell. Some
coal-masters will not store coals, because there is a loss upon them, a
waste.

" What took place upon the receipt of the letter you have produced?—
We stated to the colliers the same as we had said in 1817; that, if they
were to strike, they might do it immediately.

" Did you refuse to comply with the demands herein stated?—We determined to listen to no demand made under that combination. That demand
was made in consequence of directions issued at a general meeting of colliers at Kilmarnock: the object was, to attack the collieries in Ayrshire
individually, and reduce them one by one to their measures.

" In what way do you know that orders were given by the association to
the effect you have stated?—I cannot well say how I know it: I know it
from the report of the colliers who had attended at that meeting, and from
many of our workmen; the greater part of our workmen were extremely
unwilling to strike, but it was forced upon them by the other colliers of the
county.

" Did you understand that your colliery had been selected by the general
meeting at Kilmarnock, as that at which the men had been desired first to
strike?—I did.

" Why did you prefer an immediate strike to taking time to consider
whether an arrangement could be made with the men?—Because we resolved on employing other men.

" You stated that part of your men unwillingly acceded to this; what
consequences did they apprehend from refusing to join in it?—They apprehended personal consequences to themselves.

" Have any acts taken place of personal violence?—No.

" Were there any direct threats of personal violence?—Very few.
There were some, and some few acts of violence; but not to any great
extent.

But, secondly, we are aware that, in the greater number of trades, a labourer from the general

---

" Were there acts sufficient to induce the men to think that, if they persevered, there would be violence committed?—There was, but no act of violence.

" Was there any other object the men had in view but a rise of wages? —Yes; the great object was the exclusion of other work-people. I sent for the men to meet me. After receiving that letter, they assembled to meet me; but I was delayed for a very few minutes, by a gentleman on business, and the hour passed at which I had appointed to meet with them: they were waiting not fifty yards from me; and, under the direction of their leaders, when they found the hour had expired, they resolved not to wait one minute longer, but to take me at a minute's warning, and they went away. I felt very much displeased with them for such conduct, and I gave out that not one of them need return to their work.

" How did you give that out, by a written letter?—No, verbally to a few of the men.

" That they should not be allowed to work?—Yes.

" Did you mean the whole of them?—No: I do not remember the express terms I made use of; I meant all those who adhered to the combination, or the association.

" Was your object, by the conduct then pursued, rather to induce them by your firmness to agree to continue to work than to force them to leave? —My intention was, to state to them that I would not agree to any terms made under that combination.

" You had no wish to meet them afterwards?—None.

" You did not send to ask them to meet you again?—No.

" What took place?—They struck work; there was no more work of course by those men, and we set about immediately employing other workmen.

" What occurred in consequence of this?—In about a fortnight or three weeks we were enabled to raise very nearly half the quantity of coals which we had been doing previously by new workmen, principally Irishmen, whom we induced to go down to become colliers.

" Had all your own men left you?—Yes; those were all new men.

" The old men were forbidden to work?—They were forbidden to work unless they renounced the association; and we continued in this way increasing the number of our men until the 2d of February, when a number of the association came in and renounced the association, declaring that they population is not so speedily convertible to use as in collieries; and that, therefore, with even

---

would have nothing hereafter to do with it, and that they had been misled and deceived.

" Did you take those men on?—We did.

" How many?—There were about twenty of them.

" From the time of that strike up to the 2d of February, had the men who had left you attempted by any acts of violence to prevent the men you had at work from working?—No; there were one or two acts of violence, but so trifling as not to be deserving of notice. On the 17th of February a still greater number came in; I may say all of them came in on the 17th of February, all whom we desired to take in, and they were all obliged to declare that they would hereafter join no association.

" Have they worked from that time to this quietly?—They have.

" You have had no disturbance and trouble with them?—No; and they harmonize very well with the new men; that was part of the obligation under which they were taken back.

" There was no violence to the new men?—No; they attempted to seduce the new men, and there is no doubt threats of violence were thrown out, but we showed that we were determined to protect the new men. I have great satisfaction in saying, that there is now great good temper among the men.

" What reason have you for saying that the men had been threatened?—It was reported to me by the men: one reported that he had been struck and abused, but that was to so trifling an extent as not to be deserving of notice, and only proceeding from the very worst of our men.

" This difference between you and your men has been amicably settled in consequence of the exertions you made to provide others?—Yes.

" Are there any other coal-masters in your neighbourhood?—There are.

" Is there any understanding between you and them in regard either to the rate or manner of working, or the rate you shall pay your men?—None.

" Has there never been?—Never.

" Has there been no agreement between you on the present occasion, that you would resist the demands of the men?—There was a meeting, which took place on the 18th of November.

" Where was that held?—At Ayr.

" Was it held by public notice, or by private letters sent about?—By private letters.

" Were the letters addressed to all the masters in Ayrshire?—I believe to the greater number.

full security for the new workmen, a time must
elapse, and loss must be incurred, and a most in-

" Who attended?—I do not bear a precise recollection now of the names
of all who attended; there were about thirteen or fourteen.

" Who took the chair?—I did.

" What took place at that meeting?—At that meeting it was resolved,
that for six months no coal-master should engage those belonging to a
neighbouring colliery, without he brought permission in writing.

" Unless he received a certificate of good conduct?—Yes, and of being
discharged.

" Have you any copy of those resolutions?—I have not; I have only
notes of them. It was further resolved, to oppose all interference on the
part of the workmen in the management or the conduct of the work; but
part of the resolution declared, that that was not to apply or prevent any
master from giving such advance of wages as might appear to him to be rea-
sonable in the altered circumstances of the country; it was only to prevent
an interference in the regulations of the work, not to prevent a rise of wages.

" But to prevent any man belonging to the colliers club or association
from being employed by you?—Those masters agreed not to employ each
other's men.

" Did you come to a resolution, that you would not employ any man belonging to the colliers club or association?—No, we did not come to any resolution of that kind.

" What induced you, as there was no such resolution at that meeting of
masters, to declare that you would employ no person belonging to the colliers association?—I said so, from a feeling of my own, that we never could
have any satisfaction with our workmen while they were under an association of that kind; I conceived there could be no harmony or good understanding between masters and men where the interference of others was
permitted; it was not against any combination of our own workmen that I
felt so strongly, but against the interference of strangers, and a committee,
sitting perhaps at Kilmarnock, directing the manner in which our workmen
should conduct themselves.

" Do you know whether the same regulation was adopted by any other
master collier than yourself?—I understand that the Duke of Hamilton has
followed the same plan which we did at Ayr, of engaging no men in associations.

" The question was confined to any of those who had been requested to
attend, or did actually attend, that meeting in November?—There was no
other strike took place; the rest of the colliers of the county waited to see
the result of the strike at our work.

convenient suspension of the manufacture must
take place, ere it can again be set a-going in the

" Then the Committee are to understand that the colliers, save and except that attempt upon you, have been regularly at work all the time?—I understand so.

" Was not that attempt upon you in consequence of a general resolution? —Yes.

" That was the fruit of a general conspiracy?—Yes.

" The conduct of the masters, through you, prevented their carrying their object into effect?—It did.

" Have you seen the resolutions of the association at Kilmarnock?—I have.

" Can you state that that is a copy of them?—[*A paper being shown to the witness.*]—This is a copy of the resolutions, [*producing another.*]

" When your men were not in work did they receive pecuniary allowance from the association at Kilmarnock?—They did for about six or seven weeks; they received in all about £360.

" Among what number of men was that money distributed?—I believe between 140 and 150.

" Do you conceive the arrangements you have now made are such that you have no apprehension of fresh difficulty from your men?—I have no apprehension of it.

" Do you conceive, if a similar proceeding took place to that which took place last autumn, you should overcome it in a similar manner?—I conceive so.

" Do you know the Act respecting the wages of colliers that existed in Scotland, the Collier Act as it has been called?—There has been no Collier Act in operation for many years; I am not aware of the substance of any Act.

" You are not aware that there was an Act called the Colliers Act, passed in 1799, for regulating wages and disputes between master colliers and their men?—No, I am not.

" It never came to your knowledge that that Act had been repealed last year?—It did not; it never was acted upon in Scotland to my knowledge.

" The repeal of that Act as regarding coal, not being known to you, could have no effect on the measure which took place?—None whatever.

" You knew there were Acts against combinations?—No; I believed till lately that the combination laws had not extended to Scotland, and such was the understanding in Scotland till within this very short period, when I believe the Court of Justiciary in Scotland, on a late case, declared combina-

same effective way as before. The old workmen
who have struck, cannot all at once be replaced by

---

tions to be a crime in Scotland; it was not before imagined to be so, and
Scotland has not laboured under the idea of being under the combination
laws until a very late period indeed.

" Do you speak of a decision in 1810, or the decision in 1817?—I believe
the decision might be in 1817; indeed I did not know of that decision till
very lately.

" In fact the combination laws have never been a matter before your
notice?—Never; they never influenced me at all.

" Do you think it has ever influenced others?—I do not think it has
ever weighed upon the minds of the masters, or any operative class in Scotland.

" What has been the price of your coals during the last year, was there
any great increase took place in the price last year?—The price increased
from 9s. a waggon to 10s.

" No greater increase?—No greater increase.

" Has that been the rate during the last two years?—No, it was 9s. until December, and since December it has been 10s.

" It continues at that price ?—It does.

" Did you make any alteration in the mode in which you paid the men
for their work, as to the measure or weight of the coals they worked, or did
that remain as it was before?—We remain as we did before. In winter
time we usually stock coals; and in winter time we take one to the score to
hold out the measure; after a certain time in spring we give over that,
when our demand commences; and we do not exact that from the colliers
in spring, summer or autumn, nor again till the winter time comes round.

" Has that mode of measuring been a subject of complaint on the part of
the men to you at any period before the present?—I believe the men at all
times complain of the measure, they wish the measure always to be smaller,
but they are at present in a state of high content; I have never known them
so contented or satisfied as they are at present.

" Have not the men been anxious that a fixed rate or measure should be
adopted, by which they should know that they are to be paid?—There is a
fixed measure by which they are paid.

" You stated that it varied?—It varied in consequence of that great depression on our trade; circumstances of that kind will always occasion vari-
ances; and we were obliged to follow the small increase which was given at
the neighbouring collieries, in order to keep those very people in employment, who could not otherwise have been employed.

the same number; and the new workmen who
succeed them, cannot all at once acquire the habit

" Do not you conceive that you have at various times made efforts to
keep your men employed, which you could not have been induced to make
from your own feelings of interest?—Certainly, we had to prevent the imposing on the men the hardship of being discharged.

" Have you never discharged your men in cases of failure of trade?—We
have sometimes, but not to any great extent; we have had a large stock of
coals for two years on our hills.

If it was stated that the average of the wages of the men in your employ
had been before the increase, from 10s. to 11s. a week, should you consider
that as correct?—I would not.

" Do not your coals deteriorate considerably from lying exposed to the
air?—I do not consider that our coals deteriorate much from being exposed
to the air.

" Do they waste much?—I do not think they do to any great degree.

" Then why do you exact one in twenty from your workmen, if they do
not diminish in quality or quantity?—Such has been the practice of our
work, and such has been the practice of the whole country; it is part of the
arrangement under which those men are engaged; a part of the understanding.

" Do you know any thing more of the history of the association at Kilmarnock; have they any oaths?—Not that I know of. Since our men returned to work we have increased the number of our men greatly.

The demand for coals has been sufficient to enable you to keep those additional men?—Yes. I would never think of applying to legal measures to
put down combinations if I could possibly do without.

" Are there any points of your evidence that you wish to explain?—
There was one point of additional evidence that I wished to give. Formerly, as the law was understood in Scotland, there was a summary process,
by which a workman could be called upon to fulfil any engagement which
he had entered upon: as the law is now explained, there is no means by
which an engagement can be put in force, except through an action for
damages, which renders all engagements in the country quite abortive, quite
inefficient; there is the expense of an action for damages against a man who
has not a shilling to lose. I know only one instance where an action of
damages has been brought, and the master incurred an expense of between
£40 and £50 in the prosecution of the suit.

" Are you not aware that there is an Act of Parliament, the 34 Geo. 3.
giving power to all masters, by summary process before magistrates, to compel the fulfilment of every contract?—No, I am not.

and skill of their predecessors.   It is certainly relieving to observe how soon an ordinary labourer

---

" And in point of fact it has not been acted upon in Scotland?—No, it
has not.   An application was made by some people in Kilmarnock to force
an engagement, and the matter was sent to the crown lawyers in Edinburgh
for their opinion, and their answer was, no proceedings could take place except through an action for damages.

" Had regular articles or engagements been entered into?—I know not
the species of engagement which had been entered into by these Kilmarnock
people, but an engagement of some kind had subsisted, and the answer was,
that no redress could be got but through an action of damages; the person
I applied to was the procurator fiscal.

" Is it your opinion, that if no law exist it would be convenient to have
summary process, compelling the fulfilment on the part of the men of their
engagements to their master?—I should think so; I think the ordinary redress by an action for damages is wholly useless to the master.

" Is there any other addition you wish to make to your evidence?—By
an Act of Parliament which was passed in the year 1799, a collier is not
liable for any debt he may contract to his master; I beg leave only to suggest that for the consideration of the Committee.

" Is that what is called the Collier Act?—I do not precisely recollect
what the Act is called, but I understand it to have been passed in the year
1799.

" Is that what is called the Collier Act in Scotland?—I answered you
just now, I do not know what the Act is called.   It has been very little
acted upon in Scotland, even before it was repealed; as a man was supplied with money, and the master got it in the best way he could.

" Is their any further explanation you wish to make?—A very aggravated
case of combination occurred two years ago in the neighbourhood of Edinburgh.

" State shortly what combination?—It was by the colliers, at a colliery
near Edinburgh; it subsisted for upwards of six months, and the colliers
were maintained by the colliers belonging to the neighbouring colliery;
that was a regular system of combination; the law was not resorted to, to
put it down; acts of extreme violence took place; several men's ears were
cut off.

" Was it a combination to resist the reduction of wages, or to demand an
increase?—To demand an increase.

" How was it put down?—The workmen, after six or eight months resistance, gave way.

can be transformed into a good collier, and even made serviceable in many of the branches of cotton-spinning. Yet there can be no doubt, that in all those crafts and occupations which require a long apprenticeship to be accomplished in their mysteries, there might be a cessation of work which, if persisted in beyond a certain length, might be inconvenient to master manufacturers, and still more inconvenient to their customers. To look fairly and openly at all the possibilities, one can conceive a great extent of inconvenience from a universal strike of shipwrights, or house-carpenters, and still more, perhaps, of clothiers and shoemakers, and all classes of workmen that cannot be so instantly replaced, as some others, out of the general population.

Now, in the nature of the case itself, there is a sufficient protection even against this evil, alarming as it may appear; and that without any express interference of parliament in the matter. We mean the certainty, that, sooner or latter, the workmen who have struck must surrender themselves to terms of agreement with their employers. They cannot hold out against this self-inflicted blockade beyond a certain period. There must

---

" During the last year no such acts of violence have taken place?—I was informed by the master of the colliery, the matter was regularly debated which of these colliers should put him to death.

" Has any thing of the kind come to your knowledge in the proceedings of the colliers during the last year?—Nothing of the kind; we never had acts of violence in the western parts of Scotland."

of course be a rapid expenditure of their means; and, if living without work, and therefore without wages, their resources must soon melt away. No associated fund can, for a great length of time, afford the indispensable allowances to the men, and their families, of a very numerous combination; and so, of necessity, the combination must sooner or later be broken up. They may submit to very great privations, and put their faculty of suffering to its uttermost endurance, ere they will again resign themselves to a treaty with their employers. But stern necessity must at length prevail over their resistance; and a visit, in the first instance, from one or two stragglers, or the offer of some new and modified terms, will be the sure precursor to a general surrender of the whole body. It is altogether misplaced and unnecessary for government to meddle, but for the prevention or punishment of crime, with the steps of a process that will so surely terminate in the very result which it can be the only object of government to effectuate.*

---

* So far back as a good many months ago, the run of several of these combinations was finished in this way, and many more have since given in; and, we have no doubt, left a lesson of efficacy behind them, which will do more to tranquillize the working classes, than law could possibly do with all the terror of its penalties. The Minutes of Evidence taken before the Select Committee record some of the earlier instances, beside being rich in such disclosures respecting the state of many of the existing combinations, as afford the surest presage of their inevitable and speedy termination.

From the examination of Mr. T. Hebblethwaite:—

" When did the men form themselves into an association?—I did not

And what we hold to be of prime importance
in this argument, is, that the result brought about

---

know of it till last November; we had heard of it before, but the men
would not confess they had joined it till the very last day.

" Are you certain no combination existed among your men previously to
the repeal of the combination laws?—I believe not.

" You had no reason to suspect it?—None at all.

" Do you suppose the repeal of the laws tempted the men to form themselves into an association?—I think it did.

" Did they so form themselves into an association shortly after the repeal
of those laws was known?—I cannot say how long after; but they have got
a very large fund, they paid three halfpence a week; they have got a fund
which keeps them now for six weeks.

" When did they begin to form that fund?—I cannot say.

" Do they keep those matters secret from you?—Yes.

" Are there other manufacturers of the same description near you?—Not
very near, there is about a mile off.

" Have the workmen in those other manufactories also struck?—Some
of them have, but none since they turned out with us, because as we did
not submit to them, they have gone on at other places; if we had submitted
they would have turned out in the other two manufactories.

" What reason have you to believe that?—That is what the people in the
union say; we have got part of our own family turned in again, and they
call them black ones.

" What has become of the men who have retired from the works?—They
have been walking about.

" And living upon the funds of their society?—Yes.

" Do you know what they receive?—Some of them receive nine shillings
a week, and three shillings for each child.

" How long have they continued to receive it?—There were many of
them continued thirteen weeks; then they would not go any where else to
seek work; then the committee said, that they would not pay them any
more money; and then they turned in at their old wages."

From the examination of Mr. Alexander Guthrie, at Mount, near Kilmarnock:—

" Had you many strikes with your men before the year 1824?—Yes, I
had one strike about ten years ago.

" What was the cause of that strike?—They wanted more wages, and I
would not give it.

in this natural way, has a far more permanent and pacifying effect upon the workmen, than

---

" What was the consequence of that?—They lay idle probably about eight or ten days.

" Was there any mischief done by them at that time?—No, I do not recollect any."

From the examination of Mr. William M'Allister:—

" Is it the intention of your association to continue and to enforce in future the regulations contained in that printed paper?—How long or how short it will continue, I cannot say; it seems in a wavering situation at the present moment; perhaps it is the last meeting that will ever be.

" Do you wish the Committee to understand that the association is at an end?—I cannot say that it is at an end, but it is declining fast in numbers."

" For what purpose do you consider it necessary to have this association, and pay money out of your very small wages towards a fund?—It was just for that purpose of getting our wages advanced.

" Is the book you have presented a correct account of the receipts?—That is a full account of the whole monies we have ever received.

" On the 20th of December there appears the sum of £51 : 15s. received, how was that collected?—One shilling was required to make up that amount of every associated member.

" To what purpose was that applied?—To Mr. Taylor's men, to pay a hundred and forty-eight of them eight shillings a week during the time of strike.

" After making that week's payment, that left in the treasurer's hands two shillings and ninepence?—Yes.

" Was that account examined and settled in the association?—Yes, they have been all signed and settled, every one of them: there are the dates of each settlement.

" Is this an account of the ten weeks that Mr. Taylor's men struck?—Yes.

" What is the sum collected in that time?—£495 : 7 : 6d.

" How was it disbursed?—All to Mr. Taylor's men.

" That is attested by the delegates present, who sign their names?—Yes.

" What is the cash in hand?—£6.

" What became of Mr. Taylor's men after that?—About sixty of them went to Glasgow.

" Have you had any contribution since that?—No.

when overborne out of their combination by the
force of legal restraints, and the terror of legal

" You are to have no funds until you require them again?—No.

" Do not you think it would be desirable for you to abstain altogether
from the association, and to let it drop?—I think it was very near dying a
natural death if they had let it alone; if the masters had not interfered, by
their agitating it, and bringing men up to London, summoning them to
London, and so on; that will agitate the men's minds against their masters."

From the examination of Adam Brown, one of Mr. Taylor's workmen:—
" Have you returned to the work?—Yes.

" Did you get what you wanted?—No, we did not.

" How came you to return?—I do not know precisely the reason.

" Did you think it best to give up?—Yes, I thought it was best to return,
and there were many who were of the same notion.

" Is not Mr. Taylor always a good master?—I never saw any thing else.

" Were you discharged?—The whole body was discharged.

" He would not agree to any alteration?—No.

" Did you report to the association?—Yes.

" Did they make you any allowance?—Yes, we received eight shillings a
week for a time.

" After that period what did you do?—There were a good many went
away to different places, and some returned, and I returned.

" Did you return to work in the same manner that you had done before,
or was there any alteration made in the measure?—There was a little alteration made, but it was on the same footing.

" Had any neutral men come into the pit during the time you were out
of it?—Yes, there were.

" What were they?—The greater part of them were Irishmen.

" When you returned, did those who belonged to the association interfere
with those neutral men, or did they allow them to go on working?—They
allowed them to go on working.

" Had any of them joined the association?—No, the works are distinct
from the association altogether."

" Do you think you have got any advantage by having belonged to the
association?—No, I cannot say that I have.

" Should you not think it would be better for you to refrain from joining
yourself again to such an association?—I will not think of that till I see
better about it.

penalties. It will be of far more quiescent and satisfying power, when it is the result of their

---

" Do not you think these associations will soon fall to pieces; that the men will not continue to pay money, unless they see masters likely to take advantage of them?—I think if it was let alone, it would die a natural death.

" Has any body meddled with it?—Calling us up here.

" Do you think the stir about the combination laws has tended to keep up these associations?—I do not know whether it has not; but I know nothing about the proceedings of the association, I was only a few weeks in it altogether.

" You are all satisfied now, and every thing is going on quietly and peaceably?—Yes."

From the examination of John Swift.

" What makes a member?—3d. paid.

" How often?—He pays 3d. in the commencement, and subscribes 3d. a week till he subscribes £1, and then his subscription ceases, except in case of any strike for advance of wages, and then he takes his part of it, but that is kept as a regular fund; £1 each member.

" How many days did the men stand out?—Perhaps three days.

" You paid the wages of those three days out of the fund?—We did.

" What wages did you pay out of the fund?—We allow a married man who has a wife and one child, 9s. a week."

From the examination of Mr. Henry Taylor.

" Do you know whether at any prior period strangers were admitted to come to Bristol and work there without any objection being made on the part of the club?—Yes, the last four or five years, but not previously to that; for the last four or five years they had no money.

" Then if there was a long strike, from what source do you apprehend they could get funds to enable them to go on?—I have heard they could get it from London. I know they have it not of themselves. They could not stand out long in Bristol."

From the examination of Mr. Joseph Fletcher.

" Was that combination broken up?—It wore itself out by their having no money left. They had accumulated together, some said, as much as 15 or £20,000, the loss to the shipwrights on the river at that time could not be computed at less than £90,000, in labour, out of the pockets of the working people."

own experiment. They will be greatly more
manageable, after having themselves made full

From the examination of Benjamin Lomax, Shipwright.

" You collect funds in your association?—Yes.

" How are they collected?—Men, when at work, pay a penny per day to
the funds; if not at work, nothing.

" Do you know the amount of the fund?—We have not much fund now,
because we have had such very heavy calls upon it.—I do not know exactly
what balance we have now, but not above £200, or £300.

" You were asked a question just now respecting the amount of funds ;
can you state what was the largest amount of funds at any one period?—I
do not think at any time we have had £500, in our possession."

From the examination of Charles Husband, Shipwright.

" Then, with the exception of those four days, and the fortnight you were
at Mr. Castles', you have been out of employment?—Yes.

" What did you receive during that time from the Union?—I received
one or two weeks at the rate of a guinea, and one I received at the rate
of 12s.

" What was the reason of the difference?—Because our funds would not
allow of it. I got about four or five days work for an owner of a ship; I
believe four days and a half."

Of course these combinations must vary in greater or less degrees of obstinacy; and perhaps the following extract from the minutes of evidence
before the Commons' Committee, furnishes us with one of the strongest
cases of determination on the part of workmen.

From the examination of Mr. W. Richmond, Ship-owner in North-
Shields.

" Do you think the ship-owners should be allowed to fix any rate of
wages they think proper for the men, and the men should not be allowed
to make what demands, or fix what rate they think proper?—The men
have an undoubted right to demand what they please, and we surely ought
to have a similar right to offer what we please; but if we will not give
what the men demand, the influence of the committee is so strong, they
will endure starvation and hunger, to my knowledge, rather than not carry
their point.

" You think it hard that they will rather starve than work on your terms?
—I am not capable of expressing myself upon that question."

" Have those resolutions been attended to?—No, we found it in vain, trial of their own impotency, than when festering under a sense of the injustice and hostility wherewith, under the old combination laws, they conceived that the hand of government was lifted up against the interests and natural rights of their order. It was quite to be expected, that there should be frequent, and even fierce out-breakings on their part, after the repeal of these laws; but, most assuredly, this general experience of the upshot will be of far more healing influence, than any thing so fitted to exasperate and tantalize, as the re-enactment of them. And it should fur-

---

because the men are consistent and united in their purpose, even to the extent of starvation to themselves; and I am afraid masters never can or will successfully combine against their workmen.

"Do you mean they would rather starve, than work against the regulations which they thought right for their own protection?—I do really think so."

We feel quite assured that nought but perseverance is requisite in such a case as this, for bringing the men to a surrender; if they indeed demand more than the fair market price of labour in a free state of things.

From the examination of Robert Raven, a Cooper.

"Do you think your funds amount to £500?—No.

"£300?—No, nor £200, I think.

"How could you pay 18s. a week to seven hundred of the trade, even for one week?—If it would not amount to that we should not pay them; we could not do more.

"If that fund was exhausted, have you any means to resort to to raise more?—No.

"Have you come to any resolution what amount the persons striking on Wednesday are to receive?—They are to receive according to the regular rule as long as the stock may last.

"What is the regular rule?—18s. I have stated."

What earthly call is there for legislating against people so helpless; or of superadding the penalties of law to those still more effectual penalties wherewith nature visits every unfair combination in the shape of sore and unavoidable privations?

ther be recollected, that, when freely left, first, to their own experiment, and then to their own experience of its failure, all the accompaniments of the process are such as serve to deter from the repetition of it. They will not be so readily tempted to place reliance again upon an association that has failed, and from very powerlessness, to make good any of those plans and promises which had so deceived them. And they will be still further alienated from such an enterprise, by their recollection of the miseries to which it already had exposed them—of the hardships which they had to suffer while it lasted—and, finally, of the humiliating prostration of themselves to their masters, in which it terminated. For they will not forget, that, should the perseverance of their employers outlast their own, it places them on high vantage-ground, and themselves in a state of most submissive helplessness. Should the master have but partially replaced them by new workmen during the strike, then he may not have room for all, after the strike is over; and he might signalize the ringleaders of the opposition by a determined exclusion of them; and he might re-admit the rest on less favourable terms than before.* Under all these recollections, the

---

* It should be observed, that the success even of one master, over his own special combination, must have a paralyzing effect on all other combinations, and more especially in the same trade. Should he have replaced so many of his strike-work men by new hands, and rejected as many after they have given in; these are thrown upon the country in a state of idleness, and will naturally go in quest of employment, to other establishments of a simi-

proposal for another combination may be repeated, in the course of years, but it will not just have the same charms for them. And better security far, we affirm, for the quiescence of our working classes, that they should be conducted to it, at length, by the lessons of their own experience, than that they should be constrained to it, at once, by the laws of authority.

And it is really not for the interest of the masters, that there should be a revival of these laws. Greatly better for them too, that there should have been a trial of strength, after which both parties are landed in that state of settlement and repose, which comes after a battle that has been decisively terminated. We are aware of the spirit which is now abroad among the workmen, and that it is going forth in succession through the manufacturing districts of the land. But,

---

lar kind to that from which they have been discarded; and so bring a force of competition to bear upon other combinations besides that which has just been broken up. And as a very few unemployed workmen agreeable to the principles that we have tried to expound, can effect a very grievous reduction on the wages of a whole body of tradesmen, it has the effect of aggravating the natural penalty of these combinations, by making the reaction all the more tremendous.

From the examination of Mr. Alexander Guthrie.

" Do you expect that this association will endeavour to carry into effect its regulations, with reference to the workmen employed in collieries in the county of Ayr?—I cannot say exactly; I think that the check they got by Mr. Taylor's success will have a considerable effect in keeping them quiet for some time.

" You do not apprehend any trouble from them at present?—No, not for some time."

truly, we contemplate the progress of these out-breakings with no other feelings, and no other anticipations, than we should regard the progress of an ambulatory school, whose office it is to spread the lessons of a practical wisdom over the face of the country; and the peace and meekness of wisdom will be the inevitable results of it. Accordingly, we do find that the earlier combinations have been dispersed, and given place to the re-establishment of a good understanding between the workmen and their employers; while other and more recent combinations are still in progress. This is just to say, that in some places they have acquired the lesson, while in others they are only learning it. The country is still at school upon this subject; and it were a pity that she was not permitted to finish her education.* For ourselves

---

* We feel assured that, at this moment, there is a more pacific habit, the fruit of their recent experience, among the workmen of Glasgow, than among those of many parts in England; and that among the capitalists of the former place, there is a more general conviction, the fruit, also, of recent experience, that combinations, if simply let alone, will soon work themselves out, and that no other legislative remedy is called for than a sufficient protection against the violence of the outstanding workmen.

Besides, it appears very evident that the lesson is making rapid progress, and will, in all probability, if it meet with no interruption, be perfected in a very few months. We found this affirmation upon such articles of daily intelligence as the following:—

" We are happy to state that the proprietors of coal-works in Renfrew-shire are discomfiting, in grand style, the colliers' confederation. Mr. Houston's works are fast filling with new men; and, from the quality of the coal, most of them will become expert colliers within a month. They are to be allowed at the rate of three shillings per day wages. They are to work from eight to ten hours, according to the work done, and which is to

we feel persuaded, that a lasting tranquillity will
be the effect of troubles which shall soon pass

---

be judged of by the oversmen. Each man to be furnished with what tools
may be considered necessary for carrying on the work; which tools are to
be sharped and upheld by Mr. Houston, and to be delivered back upon the
men leaving his employment, they paying for what may be deficient."

" The contest between the master manufacturers and their workmen at
Bradford, is happily at an end. The good advice given to the men has been
taken. On Saturday, in the afternoon, nearly a hundred of the union men
applied to Mr. Wood, one of the principal spinners in the town, for work at
the old wages; and this morning, the combers and weavers generally followed their example. On Saturday the weekly allowance was, for the most
part, paid to the turn-outs by the Union Committee, sitting at the Roebuck
Inn ; but the hopeless nature of the contest, as demonstrated in this paper
of the 29th ult., had diminished the supplies, while the approach of winter
was daily increasing the demands upon their funds, which could not be answered by a less sum than twelve or fourteen hundred pounds a-week. The
danger of losing their work entirely by the introduction of machinery, and
the arrival of workmen from other places, had its influence on their decision. The committee, bowing to circumstances, left the workmen to re-
sume their work; and the masters seem disposed to receive as many of
them as they can employ, which may be about one-half the number. The
town of Bradford is, in the mean time, in a state of considerable excitation.
The streets are filled with groupes of workmen, some of them deliberating
upon the course to be taken, and others reporting the success or failure of
their applications to their former employers. The inhabitants generally are
congratulating each other very cordially upon the termination of the contest, and anticipating the revival of that prosperity which, for the last twenty
years, has rendered Bradford one of the most flourishing and increasing
places of its size in the kingdom."

" The meeting at Fair Weather Green took place this afternoon, John
Yester in the chair. After some preliminary explanations relating to the
conflicting statements which had been published on the subject of the
amount of wages earned by the combers before the strike, the chairman announced, that, having found that the masters could not afford an advance of
wages, at the price at which manufactured stuff goods. were now selling, a
number of men had applied for work at the former prices, and some of them
had succeeded; others, it was hoped, would be equally fortunate, and those
who could not obtain work would still continue to be paid the usual allowance
from the union funds. In conclusion, they were congratulated on the re-

away.   But, for this purpose, it is indispensable
that they should work themselves out by their own

---

cognition of the union society by the masters, so far as not to require any of
their workmen to disown it.   With this explanation, and this consolation,
the meeting, which consisted of from 1200 to 1500 workmen, seemed satisfied; and a vote of thanks was carried unanimously, on the motion of Mr.
Yester, seconded by Mr. Walworth, to Mr. Wood and Messrs. Read, for
the readiness they had shown to meet the men on the present occasion, and
for their liberal conduct towards their workmen.   The meeting dispersed in
perfect good humour at nightfall, it having been previously announced from
the chair, that no further meetings would be held at this place."

"We commence the printing of a second edition at a late hour, to an-
nounce to the public the gratifying information, that the long existing differences between the master manufacturers of this town and their men are
now rapidly drawing to a close. This afternoon a deputation of Mr. Wood's
men waited upon him, and made a tender of their services at the old prices.
To this Mr. Wood has acceded; and many of his men have this evening
fetched their combs, to be ready to commence their work on Monday morning.   Mr. Wood is one of the largest worsted spinners in the town, and,
of course, the number of men in his employ is proportionably great; so that,
in fact, we may now consider the union at an end, and things in a fair way
to revert to their former channel.

"We are glad that Mr. Wood's men have at length seen their own interests in the proper light ; and the manly and handsome manner in which
they have come forward to effect this reconciliation, reflects the highest credit upon them.   We have no doubt that next week the example will be followed by the men who were employed by other manufacturers ; and we
trust they will be met in the same handsome manner as they were by Mr.
Wood.   The lateness of the hour prevents our saying more than that we
hope, in our next number, to have the pleasure of announcing that the differences between all the masters and their men are consigned to oblivion,
and the men engaged in their work as usual.

"Mr. Wood had previously, in the course of the week, engaged one hundred and twenty combers in the neighbourhood of Kildwick, (a village about
fifteen miles from Bradford,) and the eighty which have returned to their
employment to day· make the number he has set on this week two hundred."

"During last week, upwards of a thousand combers, and a number of the
Bradford weavers, have obtained work, leaving more than a thousand combers unemployed, and about half that number of weavers.   The committee

natural effervescence, instead of being forcibly repressed by the hand of authority. One conse-

---

of the union society, now considerably diminished, for the purpose of saving
expenses, still continue their sitting at the Roebuck Inn, and their principal
endeavours are directed to supplying the unemployed workmen with such
sums of money as the funds they have at their disposal enable them to ap-
portion out."

It is with the utmost pleasure that we present the following extract, as
recording an act of liberality on the part of the masters—the fruit, we have
no doubt, of that spontaneous kindness which so frequently comes into play
between parties after reconciliation :—

" We hail as a favourable omen the resolution taken by a number of the
principal worsted spinners in Bradford, to diminish the rate of labour in the
mills. Hitherto, forty minutes only have been allowed in the day for
meals ; but, in future, the work-people are to have an hour for dinner,
and twenty minutes for breakfast. The honour of originating this improvement is, we understand, due to Mr. John Wood, junior ; but the humane
suggestion has been cheerfully adopted by Messrs. J. Read and Sons,
Messrs. Penison and Whitehead, and Messrs. W. and J. Marshall."

Our concluding extract on this subject, we hold to be peculiarly instructive, as offering to our notice the weight of those penalties which Nature,
and the necessity of things, have annexed to combinations ; which penalties, we affirm, constitute a far more powerful and salutary check than any
which law can devise.

A Bradford paper, alluding to the late dissensions in that quarter between the masters and their workmen, makes the following remarks :—

" It is now ascertained, that the number of men, women, and children,
out of employment, amounts to no less than 3,280 ; and, as the Union
funds admit of but one shilling a-week to each man, and two shillings if
there be a large family, it is obvious, that the sufferings and privations of
these individuals must be great. Difficulties, no doubt, present themselves
in the adoption of any plan for their relief ; and yet we are very certain,
that there is no humane person, who will not feel disposed to extend relief, in some shape, to the wretched wives and children of these misguided
men. Whatever is resolved upon, it seems desirable that relief, if afforded
at all, should be by supplies of food, not of money."

The above article refers to the still outstanding workmen, who either
persisted in the strike, or who were refused admittance to their old employment, because now supplanted by other workmen. Surely this severe
natural chastisement supersedes the necessity of any legal one ; and the

quence is very obvious. It will serve to bring out
more singly, and therefore more impressively, to

---

remembrance of it will do more for the future peace of the community,
than could be done in a legal way by all the wisdom of Parliament.

We cannot refrain from the insertion of one notice more upon this subject, as being quite conclusive of the point, that the chastisements of Nature and Necessity on rash combinations are severe enough in themselves,
and require not the superadded chastisements of law.

" Disasters of the Bradford Turn-outs.

" We stated last week," says the Leeds Intelligencer, " that about 1,700
of those misguided men found it impossible, on any terms, to obtain employment, and that the resources of the Union were entirely drained. It
now appears, that, including the wives and children of the unfortunate beings, the total number at present in a state of the most abject destitution,
is nearly 3,000. All hope, too, we believe, of collecting from the working classes sums capable of affording this vast mass of sufferers as much as
one penny a-week each in future, are vanished. The appalling extremity
of distress and despair into which they have fallen, is described by an eye-
witness in terms that freeze the soul. They are said to be without fires,
without beds, nearly naked, and many of them entirely destitute of food.
Two instances are particularized. One, of a family at White Abbey, who
have not a bed to lie on; the other, of a family living near the White
Sheaf, which a neighbour went to see on Thursday, and found them without either fire or coals, without a morsel of any thing to eat or drink,
without money, and without employment. This family consisted of a
man, his wife, and five small children. Innumerable instances of a similar nature might be produced; but the heart sickens at such details of
misery."

The following extract illustrates how beautifully the natural mechanism
of trade brings round again, even to these wretched outcasts, the comfort
and sufficiency of their former days—making the correction, after all,
temporary, though severe—and so causing it to purify, and not to destroy. We have no doubt, that the now brisker demand for work and
workmen, is the result of a market now very much cleared of its commodities.

" The following letter we received last night from our correspondent.

" Bradford, Nov. 23d, 1825.

" The number of workmen out of employment is gradually diminishing.
A meeting has been called, to be held in the Court-House this afternoon,

the view of workmen, the natural control and ascendancy which masters have over them. It has an influence the very reverse of pacific, when servants are led to regard their master in the light of one who is invested, by arbitrary laws, with the power of a tyrant. But let Government and the laws be kept out of this controversy altogether. Let it be reduced to a single-handed contest between the power which should belong to the one party of giving or withholding employment, and the power which should equally belong to the other party, of giving or withholding their services. Let Parliament not meddle in this altercation at all; and it is impossible, but that at length, by the simple operation of its own rival and conflicting forces, a fair adjustment must come out of it. And a solid peace will be the fruit of this adjustment. After the artificial checks to combination have been withdrawn, workmen will be taught, and become intelligent as to the real power and operation of the natural checks; and they will not be so readily thrown agog by the plausibilities which now so

---

to devise some means of immediate relief to the suffering unemployed workmen and their families; and I have no doubt but what can be effected by the kind benevolence of the gentlemen and tradesmen of the town and neighbourhood, will be done in mitigation of the present extreme distress."

"We are happy to find that the demand for stuff goods in the Bradford market, on the last two market days, has been nearly equal to that of the five months preceding; and though there is not yet any material improvement in prices, the indications of an improving trade are already too clear to be at all mistaken."

mislead and agitate them. More especially, they will come to perceive, that apart from the authority of law altogether, there is a natural power which belongs to the holders of capital; and we are persuaded, that the demonstrations which have been recently given of it in the defeat of many associations, will do more to compose the turbulence of workmen, than all the threats and penalties of the statute-book. And better, greatly better for the masters, that their security should be founded upon this, than upon any odious and unpopular legislation, which has the effect of alienating from their persons, the respect and gratitude of their own servants. Let this hateful intermeddling of law be withdrawn from their negotiations; and, on both sides, there will at length be felt the sweets and the ties of a natural relationship. The mutual dependence, and the mutual obligation will be far better understood. And employers will never be on so secure and kindly a footing with their workmen, as when the latter have been taught, by sad experience, precisely to estimate how much they have to fear from any scheme of hostility against the interest of the former, and how much it is they owe for admission and continuance in their service.*

On every view then of this question, we feel as

---

* In Mr. Taylor's testimony it appears, that there was, after the entire defeat of the combination against him, "a great good temper among the men." We hold it quite in keeping with human nature, that when, instead of firm

if there was nothing so much to be abjured and
deprecated, as any regress, on the part of Government, towards the combination laws.   It were en-
dangering the peace of the country for the interest,
and that, too, the imaginary interest, of merchants
and master manufacturers.   It were bringing upon
Government the burden of a popular odium, which,
for the cement and security of the social fabric,
every friend of public order should rejoice in seeing it delivered from.   It were setting the authorities of the land in array against the population;
and that, for a purpose which is abundantly provided for by the workings and the influences, and
the actions and re-actions of the natural mechanism of society, if that mechanism were only left to
its own free operation.   We are reminded, while
on this argument, of the delusions which have been
so well exposed by Dr. Smith; and which were
practised by the traders of other days upon Government, when they attempted, and but too successfully, to enlist her on the side of their own peculiar interests.   Hence the wretched jealousies of

---

resistance, there was partially a giving way to the men, and some concessions made in their behalf, there should still be an unquelled spirit of turbulence and discontent.

The following is from the examination of Mr. Alexander Guthrie:—
" What answer did you give to the delegates?—I told them to work away
peaceably, and come to no strike; and that if we could see the means of
raising our prices we would raise theirs also.
" Since you made the advance, the men are working satisfactorily?—
Yes; they are grumbling sometimes, but they work pretty fairly.
" Do they belong to the association?—Yes."

that mercantile system, which is now verging to an overthrow; and by which the relation of Great Britain with all foreign nations, was placed on a footing the most vulnerable and precarious. In like manner, there are certain home jealousies, to which we trust that Government will not lend herself as the instrument of any subserviency whatever, else her own relation to the plebeian orders of the community, which it were so desirable should be a relation of kindness on the one side, and of grateful and confiding attachment on the other, might be turned into a relation of hostility and discontent. By the late enlightened reformations of her economical code, she has done much to propitiate the favour of people abroad; and of consequence she is now strong in the admiration and approving regards of all Europe. Let her proceed in the career upon which she has entered, of economical improvement at home, and higher achievement still, she will become equally strong in the affections of her own population.

The mercantile system, with its competitions and jealousies, has been the fertile source of many foreign wars, which we now trust will not be so easily or so frequently kindled as in past generations. And the same system turned inwardly upon ourselves, has been the prolific source of many intestine divisions, which we trust, by the wisdom of a more enlightened policy, will henceforth be effectually superseded. It is too much, that Government, to appease the premature and ex-

aggerated alarm of our capitalists, should be
called forth to interfere in such a way, as must
excite against her the heart-burnings of a whole
population. Her wisdom is forbearance; and
save for the punishment of crime, or the defence
of obvious and natural equity, she might safely
leave the whole question to the determination of
the parties themselves, to the adjustment, in which
it will of its own accord settle down by the way, in
which the claims of the one are met and limited
by the counteractions of the other.

Government might, with all confidence, leave the
price of labour to find its own level, in common
with all other marketable commodities. The recent outrages that have arisen from the repeal of
the combination laws, called most certainly for an
exercise of legislation, but an exercise altogether
distinct from that by which any great principle
of natural liberty is trenched upon or violated.
It will really be too much, if any premature or
imaginary alarm on the part of interested capitalists, shall precipitate our rulers into a departure
from that wise and liberal policy, by which they
have earned both the attachment of the people,
and the admiration of all those who are any way
versant in the philosophy of human affairs. The
best friends of peace and order in our land, will
ever regret that most useless waste of popularity
which they must incur, if they give way to the
sensitive fears, or the sordid wishes of traders and
manufacturers upon this subject—a class of men,

who, centuries ago, led our lawgivers into that Ishmaelitish policy, which laid us open to the hostility of all surrounding nations; and some of whom would now have us to brave the hazards of a still more fearful hostility at home, and despoil our truly paternal Government of her fair and natural inheritance in the affections of her own children.*

* There can be no doubt, however, that a very great number, and, perhaps, even the majority of our capitalists, desiderate no enactment whatever against combinations, and would be abundantly satisfied with security against the violence of the outstanding workmen.

The following is from the examination of Mr. Walter Glascock, proprietor of the Irish Times Newspaper:—

" Is it within your own knowledge, that in former years outrages arising out of combination took place in Dublin?—I have been so very short a time employing operatives, that I could not say from my own knowledge; but I understand, from other people, that while the combination laws existed there was always a great deal of that going on in Dublin; but I can assure the Committee that it is not the idea of any gentlemen that employ people in Dublin, that there should be any thing more done by the Legislature than that they should prevent this system of outrage; for they, every one, to a man, consider that the trade ought to be as open as possible; all they say is, if a man can earn but 5s. he shall have but 5s.; or if he can earn but 1s. he shall have but 1s.; and that he shall take what he knows he earns without afterwards resorting to any measures of outrage."

CHAP. XXI.

THE SAME SUBJECT CONTINUED.

It is competent for masters too, to frame such articles of agreement with their workmen, as shall protect them in a great measure from any sudden or unlooked-for cessations; and for the violation of which, these workmen shall bring down upon themselves, not the arbitrary, but the rightful penalties of law; and which penalties, should it be found necessary, might be still further aggravated, without any offence to the principles of an obvious or natural morality. They could engage their labourers for a service of months, instead of weeks or days, and then put forth a most legitimate strength to compel their fulfilment of the stipulated period. To make the security more effectual, they could hire their workmen in separate classes at all separate periods; so that, at worst, it could only be a partial, and never a universal strike at any one time. They could further ascertain beforehand, as in domestic service, whether any of them mean to leave their employment at the termination of their bargain; and thus masters, with time to look about for new workmen, could never be caught unprepared. We do not imagine that all these devices will be found necessary, but it is well that they lie in reserve, as so many natural expedients for preventing a mischief, the prevention of which, ought not to be the office of law, but the office of the parties concerned. All that law has to do, is to avenge violence and to redress injustice; and a master, secure of these, should make no further demand upon Government, but take upon himself the burden of his own arrangements, for the right and the prosperous conduct of his own affairs.*

---

* Perhaps there might be additional law requisite, to enforce, with more adequate penalties, the fulfilling of engagements on the part of workmen; and this were altogether in a right spirit of legislation.

From the examination of Mr. W. Richmond:—

" Have you any power by law to compel these men to fulfil their engagements?—Yes, I believe there is, on application to the magistrates; but it is an inefficient remedy in such a case.

" Was any application made to magistrates to compel the men in this case to fulfil their engagements and proceed on the voyage?—I should think not; I am pretty sure there was not.

" Are we to understand that the demand on the part of the men was yielded to by the owner rather than take the men before a magistrate to compel the execution of their contract?—The affidavit gives as a reason, that she was a large ship, and if she had lost that opportunity of sailing, she might have laid there a very long time at that season of the year.

" Was there time for the master of the ship to have made a regular complaint before the magistrate, so as to have got his ship to sea?—I do not know how far that might be the case, as it was near high water. The magistrate could not have compelled them to go to sea; he could only commit them; nor would any other men have come and taken their places. That is a principle amongst them, which nothing will induce them to deviate from."

From the examination of Mr. Henry Heath:—

" You are aware that there is a new Act enabling you to bring any seaman, who shall refuse to perform the articles he has signed, to immediate punishment?—Yes, I stated I was aware of it. I beg to state that I be-

And, more than this, such is the plenitude of his means for the counteraction of his associated workmen, that he can not only protect himself from them, by the system of prevention which we have now adverted to; but, failing this, there is a way in which he may find compensation for any losses which he may have sustained by the suspension of his works. Masters and manufacturers can lay an assessment on the wages of the re-admitted workmen, or, which is the same thing, can take them in again upon reduced wages, till they have recovered, by the difference, a complete indemnification for all that they have suffered by the interruption of the manufacture. This has often been held out as a threat, although we are not aware of any instance in which it has been put into execution. Still it is an available method, which, if adopted, would at once make up for the strike, and afford another security against the repetition of it. It were a competent, and, in many cases we believe, a fair chastisement inflicted by the employers upon their workmen, and so would serve to increase the weight of all the other chastisements, which, by the very nature and necessity of the case, are sure to follow in the train of such a combina-

---

lieve the Act only runs in this way, that if any seaman should refuse, after having signed the articles, to proceed to sea, he may be taken before a magistrate, and he hears him; and on his continuing to refuse, the magistrate may then commit him to the house of correction. So far the Act is certainly defective: it does not punish the act of refusal if the man afterwards thinks proper to go."

tion. There is no need that to these there should be superadded the terrors of the law, or that masters, with such a weight of natural ascendency as belongs to them, should call in the aid of Government for the settlement of their own private quarrels with their workmen. They have ample means for this in their own hands; nor is it fair to saddle our legislature with the odium and the responsibility of a most objectionable law; and that, for the purpose of bringing about a result which their own power and their own spirit should fully enable them to achieve.

At the very worst, and though masters should not be wholly able to protect themselves from inconvenience and loss by combination, this should just be regarded as one out of many other hazards to which their business is exposed. Manifold are the casualties to which they are subjected, whether from fire or shipwreck, or unlooked-for fluctuations in the state of the market. It is not more the part of Government to interfere for their defence against the uncertainties of the market for labour, than against the uncertainties of the market for those commodities in which they deal—against the fitful elements of discontent or cupidity in the minds of their workmen, than against the fitful agitations of the weather or of the ocean. It is for them to lay their account with the chances and the changes in the price of labour, as well as in the price, whether of their raw material or of their finished commodity, and just to charge or to cal-

culate accordingly. In a word, it is altogether
their own affair; and Government has acquitted
itself fully of all its duties to them, if, watching
over the preservation of the peace, it simply protects all, and provides for all, in the exercise of
that full natural liberty which belongs to them.*

But what completely exonerates Government
from the duty of protecting masters against the
losses that may arise from simple combination is,
that, in the mere workings and effects of such a
transaction, there does naturally, and at length,
cast up a most liberal compensation, we will not
say to each individual master, but certainly to the
general body; so that their interest, viewed as a
whole, does not suffer by it. The master, in truth,
is only the ostensible, or at worst the temporary
sufferer by this conspiracy of his workmen; and
if there be any sufferer at all in the long run, it is
not he but the customer. He loses profit for a
season; but it is all made up to him by the eventual rise of profit that ensues on the production of

---

* This is somewhat brought out in the examination of Mr. Eli Chadwick.

" If I might be allowed to make an observation, this case involves a more
serious inconvenience to us than seems to be apprehended; for our orders
were taken at a certain price, and we were obliged to give an advance that
interfered most seriously with our profits.

" You made no contract with your men?—No.

" Would you not suffer the same inconvenience if a rise in the raw material was to take place after you had made a contract?—We were labouring
under that at the time.

" Have you suffered that inconvenience also?—Yes."

his commodity being suspended. This is the well-known effect of a general strike among operatives. It relieves the overladen market of the glut under which it labours, and, by the time that workmen at length give in, the manufacturer enters upon what to him is the most enriching of all harvests, the harvest of a brisk demand upon empty warehouses. These cessations are the very calms which not only precede, but ensure the gales of prosperity that come in between them. This paltry attempt of the legislature, to regulate and restrain the monsoons of the trading world, works nothing beneficial to the one party, while it hurts and harasses the feelings of the other. Would they but withhold that perpetual interference by which they are ever cramping and constraining the liberty of things, they would find how much better the laws of nature, and the laws of political economy, provide for the great interests of human life, when unchecked by the laws of parliament.*

---

* Even during the currency of a partial strike, masters may find a harvest in combinations. This is exemplified in nothing more remarkably than in coals. The smaller quantity which is thrown out of the pits, in consequence of the colliers working less than their masters would have them, or in consequence of inefficiency on the part of the new men who have been brought in to replace the outstanding colliers, tells instantly on the price of the article; and, from the principles already stated, tells all the more powerfully that coal is a necessary of life. This accounts for the advantage which so many coalmasters have derived from the combinations; an advantage accruing to them necessarily from the law which regulates the fluctuation of prices—and an advantage that has come, in all probability, without foresight or contrivance on their part. The price which they obtain is the fair mar-

There is one consideration more on which the friends of the combination laws would plead for the re-enactment of them, and that is, the difficulty of legislating effectually against outrages. When once an association is formed, there are innumerable ways by which it can control workmen out of their liberty, and which are utterly beyond the correction or the cognizance of law. There is a formidable authority in the very contempt and ha-

---

ket price for the quantity of coal actually wrought; and it is a price, which, by inciting competition, and encouraging an entry upon new mines, may soon fluctuate so as to make coals as unnaturally cheap, as they are now unnaturally dear in the west of Scotland.

We insert the following, only for the sake of the fact which it unfolds, and without participation in the reflection against masters, wherewith it is accompanied.

" Sir,—A constant reader of the Free Press, respectfully recommends to the Editor, an inquiry into the present exorbitant price of coals. The honest coal-masters have added 3s. to 3s. 6d. to the waggon of 24 cwt. on the plea of giving their colliers a corresponding increase of wages. But, Mr. Editor, this is not the fact; these gentlemen having only given their workers, (unless the writer is greatly misinformed,) additional wages in the proportion of 9d. to the waggon, thus kindly affording the public an opportunity of paying to them the difference of 2s. 3d. to 2s. 9d. which they take as a *solatium*, perhaps, for their unhappy disputes with their workmen. For the perfect accuracy of this statement, the writer cannot vouch, though he derived his information from the manager of a coal work. The rise, however, is of great importance to the community, particularly to the poor, and calls loudly for the interference of the independent press. The fault lies somewhere ;—there is no deficiency in the bowels of the earth, and it is therefore an intolerable oppression that the masters or servants should have it in their power to give an adventitious value to their coals, at this inclement season of the year. Were some of the Joint Stock Companies to turn their speculating energies to coal mining, a profitable result would certainly attend their enterprising exertions. Allow me to apologize for obtruding myself on your attention, and I remain, yours, &c."

tred of a large body; and thus, by the bare existence of a combination, although no overt act can
be charged on any of its members, might all those
who are willing to work, be despoiled of their natural freedom, and brought under the power of a virtual despotism. And better, it may be thought,
that by a law against combinations there should be
a preventive security established against a very
sore oppression, against whose acts and whose
positive outbreakings no law can be devised which
might operate with efficacy as a corrective. A
law against combination, it may be contended, that
has this preventive power, even though it should
contravene the abstract principles of legislation, is
to be preferred to a law against outrages, which,
however accordant with the dictates of natural justice and morality, is utterly devoid of that corrective power which is essential to the ends of practical utility.*

---

* From the examination of Mr. Robert Hutton:—

" The law, with respect to threats, being not relaxed by the late Act, do
you attribute that increase of the system of intimidation to the change of the
law?—The law, as it stands at present, is completely nugatory with respect
to threats; it requires two witnesses to prove a threat; no man will make
a threat where there are two witnesses, and in many cases, even if only one
witness is necessary, there is an easy mode of evading the name of a threat;
A. comes to B. and says, you are a friend of C., C. had better go away, if he
does not go away, he will receive some bodily injury, but you must not mention my name in the matter, or I shall be injured; I have known a number
of instances of that kind."

From the examination of Mr. William Chippendale:—

" Has any violence, or acts of intimidation, or any ill conduct on the part

But here it is altogether forgotten, that if there
be difficulties, which we most fully admit, in de-

---

of your men taken place?—None whatever; we know this, that some men
would work if they dared."

From the examination of Robert Raven, a cooper:—

" What is the consequence to a man if he will not obey?—We say, if you
will not do so and so, we shall not work very agreeably with you.

" Do you really mean to say that is the whole penalty that a man is subject to, the not working very agreeably with the other people?—Yes.

" What do you mean by not working very agreeably?—We certainly
should distinguish ourselves from that man.

" Do you mean by that, you would not work with him?—No; we do
not mean that we should turn him out of the employ, or any thing of that
kind.

" Do you mean by that you would not work with him?—Oh! dear no.

" Then what do you mean by distinguishing yourselves from that man?—
Keeping ourselves separate from him, treating him as one who did not belong to us.

" Would you not make the thing so disagreeable to him, that he could
not possibly remain in the shop?—That is the probability I think.

" Is it not a rule in your opinion not to admit a man to work with members of the union who will not pay to this fund?—We have never, in the
employ I am in, been put to any circumstance of that kind; they always
agreed to do it; when they come in they always agree to belong to it, if
they have not before.

" You have stated that in certain cases you would make the situation of
a man so disagreeable, that he would be obliged to go; would you not do
that to a man who did not belong to the union?—He would not work so
comfortably with us as the others.

" So that, in point of fact, a man not belonging to the union would not,
to use your own expression, be very comfortable, where men belonging to
the union were acting together?—No; I think he would not feel himself
comfortable."

From the examination of Mr. Henry Heath:—

" Did the union make use of any intimidation, or any acts of violence
against them?—Only the objection before-mentioned. The Committee will
clearly understand it is a sort of moral violence, which the union men use
towards the other sailors; they only objected to sail with them, and the
non-union men being the minority, were obliged to go and join the union."

vising an effective law against the outrages of workmen, there are equal, we think greater difficulties

---

From the examination of Mr. John Oldfield :—

" What became of the other?—The other left me and remained with the
union. After that, two of the weavers who were desirous of remaining
with me, joined the union. One said, he could not possibly remain at
peace or be at all comfortable, that he was obliged to enter the union, and
if I could not allow him to continue in it, he could not help leaving me.
Another said the same, viz. that he had not entered the union, but he
should be obliged to do so for safety.

" Did he tell you why?—He told me they were so constantly wishing
him to enter, and when he went out of doors they were pointing at him and
annoying him in every possible way, so that he could not be peaceable or
comfortable in the neighbourhood, and amongst the people with whom he
usually associated. It was represented to him that it would be so beneficial
to them generally, that it was really his interest to enter the union.

" What became of the forty men?—They have remained with me. But
I found it would be really impossible for me to keep on my business if I did
not allow them to enter the union, and as I did not wish them to be longer
persecuted, I gave them permission. Having abided by me three months,
they had given sufficient proof of their willingness to oblige me if they could
do it with safety. I did not discharge any of them in consequence.

" Did any individuals in your factory receive personal violence in consequence of working with you?—I have not a factory. My work is given to
the men at their homes. They have not received personal violence, only
intimidations by gesture and threats. One of the bad effects which must
result from the union is, that it will separate the masters and work people
in a moral point of view. It will make them enemies to each other. We
had, previously to the union, been accustomed to act with a kindly feeling
towards each other."

From the examination of Mr. Chadwick :—

" Can you state any acts of violence which have produced that sort of
danger which you think prevented your obtaining men?—It is not requisite that there should be acts of violence in order to deter men, who are
not in the union, from engaging in any manufacturer's employ, because they
are marked objects of ridicule and contempt."

From the examination of Mr. Jonathan Cockerell :—

" Do you think that from the want of numbers of those who have not in devising an effective law against combinations. It is quite notorious, that, previous to the repeal of

---

been obliged to join the union, or from the apprehension of those who have joined the union?—I think from the apprehension; the men would be afraid to go on board.

" Do they apprehend personal violence?—They are subject to a degree of ridicule; they are called scab men, and pointed at and insulted.

" Have you ever seen any of this ridicule going on?—I have heard sailors express that they have been so abused and ridiculed, and called scab men, because they would not join the union."

From the examination of Mr. Henry Taylor.

" Although they have refused to work, they have not, as far as has come to your knowledge, been guilty of assaults and attacks?—No.

" But the moral effect of the union is such as to prevent any person from working?—It is."

From the examination of Mr. J. Fletcher.

" Are there not ways of insulting and annoying a man, without any offence against the law, that are well understood, and make it impossible to continue at work without acts of violence?—Certainly.

" Could you advise a perfect stranger to come from the outports and work at your yard, unless he belonged to the union; could you tell him he would be safe from annoyance?—I could not.

" In point of fact, is labour free on the river Thames? Certainly not; no man dare work on the river without he belongs to the union.

" Has it an impression on all their minds, so as to prevent their seeking work at this place?—It has. There is an instance of a ship our men finished in February; I asked them to go and do a little more work by the day, they had finished their job; not a man in the yard would touch it, they said they dare not.

" Do you think if Charles Husband had persevered in working in your yard after the meeting of the shipwrights' union, he could with safety have appeared in the open day in a lonely place?—Not without being greatly abused and insulted. The men have told me that if they did it, it would be more than their lives were worth.

" Have they received any act of violence?—They have been extremely insulted; and I was obliged to take up two union men before Mr. Ballantine, the magistrate; but it was not my wish to proceed personally against those men, because I knew they were acting under a delusion.

these laws, combinations were frequent, and fully as atrocious in their proceedings, upon the whole, as they have been since. After the repeal, there has been a most natural imagination among the workmen, which is making progress from one district of the land to the other, as if now they were on the eve of some great coming enlargement. This imagination has nearly finished its course, and has had also its correction—a far more salutary correction, from the hand of experience, than any which could possibly be administered by the hand of authority. And, meanwhile, the statute book is purged of the old unpopular aspect which formerly sat upon it. It now represents more truly the real spirit and design of Government towards the humblest peasantry of our land—a spirit of undoubted benignity and good will, if the people would only think so; and to conciliate the affection and confidence of these people is a mighty object, and an object that will at length be promoted mightily by the repeal of the combination laws.*

" What kind of insult?—It is a very easy thing to insult a workman, and to drive him almost out of his mind, without coming within the law; crying after him, ' There he goes ;' getting up when he goes into a public-house, and crying, ' Get out of his way.' Two of our men, who are at work, told me 'this morning, they must join the union, or leave the country."

* The testimonies are various, in regard to the comparative atrocity of the outrages before and since the repeal of the Combination Laws. The following are a few specimens out of the many.

It is not that we imagine of these laws against combination, that they can really keep down the

---

From the examination of Mr. Michael Farrell.

" Will you state what, in your opinion, has been the character for outrage and violence or ill humour of the strikes in Dublin since the repeal, compared with what existed in prior years?—The general spirit of combination is greater, but the number of outrages has been less.

" You mean to state that combination is more frequent, but it is more openly done, and not attended with such acts of violence as formerly?— There have not been so many acts of violence; but I consider the sudden death of Chambers, the carpenter, to be a great cause of terrifying all the other men into the measures of the body."

From the examination of Mr. W. Richmond.

" Do you think the refusal would have been attended with violence?—I should think not; there is a degree of regularity and quietness about the seamen in all their contests now, which I never saw before.

" They are less disposed to acts of violence than formerly?—Decidedly; but much more determined in their purpose.

" Do you mean to say they are more systematic in their arrangements? —Decidedly so.

" Have there been any instances of their acting with violence against their masters, or being guilty of any thing improper?—No, I am not aware of any thing of the sort, as relates to personal violence.

" In your experience, have there been any disturbances on the subject of wages between the seamen and ship-owners in the port to which you belong?—Several.

" Do you recollect any in the years 1815 and 1816?—Very well.

" Were there not very serious disputes then between the men and the owners?—Very.

" What was the nature of the disputes?—The sailors demanded an increase of wages, the same as they have demanded lately.

" Did any acts of violence then take place on the part of the men?—Certainly there were acts of violence, because I had a ship at that time confined for several weeks in the harbour, in company with many others; the ships went adrift, and they would not allow any seamen to assist them.

" Do you recollect a remonstrance being addressed to the Secretary of State at that time, stating that the property was in imminent danger, and calling for the interference of government to put down the riotous proceedings of the seamen?—Yes.

wages of workmen, or that, by so doing, they can
secure a larger profit to the capitalist than he would

" Were you one of those who signed?—I should think I would.

" Do you recollect the government issuing a proclamation in consequence
of that, and sending the military down to crush and put down this disturbance?—I recollect a large fleet of men-of-war, and the military also coming
down.

" Do you recollect any individuals who suffered personal violence, or lost
their lives on that occasion?—No, not the smallest; I do not recollect any
personal violence to any individual.

" Were there no duckings amongst each other?—I think I never saw
more decorum among men than there was at that time; quite a military organization among themselves.

" Was there any military employed?—The horse soldiers were employed.

" How long did they continue?—I suppose six or seven weeks.

" Do you recollect whether, at that time, several vessels of coals were
not despatched under the protection of soldiers?—There were some attempts made; I don't recollect how many succeeded.

" Is that the only case of serious disturbance that you recollect taking
place on the river?—No, I recollect several others previous to it.

" Any subsequent to that time?—No, that was the last. It was settled
in one hour. As soon as the military acted, the sailors never put forth a
pretence after it. All the objects they contended for they quietly lost sight
of, and resumed their ordinary duties.

" Since this association of seamen has been formed, have there been any
such acts of violence as took place during these years you have mentioned?
—No, I have remarked, in my own observation, a very considerable difference in the mode of conducting these things among the seamen.
Formerly, it was the mere angry ebullition of a parcel of school-boys.
They did a great deal of mischief, with a great deal of apparent good humour; (there are many good and valuable men among them;) and there it
ended. They were not slow in showing their indignation at that period: I
now see a marked difference, and I trace it, in my own mind, from the
mutiny at the Nore. I now hear professions of order and decorum, at the
very time they are violating the law in the strongest manner possible, by
refusing to myself and others liberty to do with our property what we
choose."

From the examination of Thomas Worsley.

" What advantage have you derived?—There has been a great deal obtain in a state of perfect freedom between the parties. The truth is, that a large profit goes to

more pleasantness between the operatives and masters since the repeal of these laws, and a better understanding than there was when they were in force.

" What was your situation before?—We viewed each other with extreme jealousy. Whenever the operatives met together, they generally met in that secret way, that the masters considered the object of their meeting was something which they did not wish to be publicly known. Their meetings were generally at that time held in secret, and that secrecy has been removed, and their meetings are now quite open."

" When was the union entered into?—Last year.

" Before or since the repeal of the combination laws?—Before the repeal."

" Has any alteration been made in the nature or constitution of the society, since the repeal of the combination laws?—No.

" Then it remains precisely as it was before, except that they now do openly what they did clandestinely?—Certainly."

From the examination of Mr. J. Fletcher.

" And is one of the regulations of the Provident Union to this effect: ' That if any member endeavours to persuade others, or form a conspiracy with them, for the purpose of destroying the said union, it is requested that all such persons, members of the union, who may be so tempted or forced, do give immediate information to the committee, who shall investigate the matter, and on proof of it to the satisfaction of the committee, as to the guilt of the conspirators, the committee shall award such punishment as they may consider just:' is that one of the regulations?—It is; and the terror of that regulation deters every man. There are hundreds of shipwrights who would willingly go to work if they dare, but it is at the peril of their lives to attempt it.

" Does not the former part of the regulations speak of a fine of one guinea, to which every member shall be subject, who shall bring forward a proposition to break up or destroy the said union?—It does.

" Do you not apprehend that the punishment spoken of in the latter part of the regulation refers to some other punishment than a pecuniary fine, or do the men apprehend it?—They not only apprehend it, 'but, if they dared to dispute the regulations, not one shipwright on the river will work with them. We had one man who held out for a considerable time, and he was almost starved. The impression on the minds of the men, which they have

augment capital, and so eventually to reduce itself.
Should manufacturers, by any artificial means, be

---

stated to me, is, that if they did any thing contrary to the rules of the committee, they can no longer be employed, (that is to say) that no member of the union shall work with them.

" Do you not believe it would be infinitely better for a man to renounce his employment on the river altogether, and seek subsistence in some other employment, than, having been a member of the union, to enter into your service, declining to comply with the regulations of the union ?—Certainly; because, while the union exists, it is utterly impossible for us to get the men to work.

" Would not a man's life be so uncomfortable as that he could not remain ?—I am sure it would; I have experienced instances of it before.

" What instances do you allude to ?—To the standing out in the year 1802, when the shipwrights stood out for six months, and kept the river in the same state.

" What took place then ?—Intimidations and violence.   One shipbuilder nearly lost his life.

" Was there any union then amongst them ?—There was a combination of the shipwrights, exactly as there is now, called the Convention.

" What other instances of violence took place then ?—Many of intimidation, and of people being ill-used : I cannot particularize them, but there were many, The shipwrights were as determined then as they are now."

From the examination of Mr. Alexander Campbell, Sheriff-Substitute of Renfrewshire.

" Will you describe the character of the Renfrewshire combinations prior to the passing of Mr. Hume's Act ?—The first that I remember, was that of the weavers in Renfrewshire; and I think the first occasion on which the magistrates had to interpose, was between the years 1810 and 1812. In point of numbers, this combination is certainly the strongest. Their organization was very perfect, and their proceedings were, at the period I have alluded to, attended with a good many petty acts of violence; but in no case was there any act of great criminality or cruelty committed by the weavers, as far as I can remember.

" What is the next case ?—The next is that of the calico printers, which was about the year 1814.

" Were they organized at all ?—They were very well organized; they had a permanent secretary, with a salary; they had district managers; and made to realize a larger profit than they would otherwise do, this at once creates and allures to their

---

they were in correspondence with similar societies in England and Ireland.

" What was the result of that?—The principal cause of the interference of the magistrate was the degree of compulsion exercised by the members of the combination towards their fellow-workmen, particularly in regulating the admission of apprentices, and levying fines, and making those who did not go into the measures of the combination feel themselves extremely uncomfortable, and in some instances suffer violence.

" How was it put down?—It was put down by the seizure of their papers in Renfrew, and some other counties, simultaneously, and by the imprisonment of some of their leaders; I rather think one of them was tried, but I really forget what was the result.

" What was the third combination?—That of the cotton-spinners, which has been by far the worst, and it was particularly troublesome from the year 1820 to 1823 inclusive.

" By what acts did this show itself?—Their proceedings were marked by very great cruelty in several instances, and by great oppression of their fellow-workmen.

" What description of cruelty?—Their mode of effecting their objects was chiefly by means of intimidation, and without that I do not see that the combination could hang together for many weeks; for when a struggle takes place between the cotton-spinners and their masters, it is necessary to the success of the workmen that they should all join together, and therefore it is quite indispensable for them (as experience has shown with us at least) to control their fellow-workmen, so as to procure that unanimity by any means. Those who do not go into their measures are termed ' knobs,' and it is quite an understood thing that these knobs are to be persecuted in various ways, and if necessary their lives are to be attempted.

" Were there any attempts at the lives of any of these individuals?— There were several such attempts; many assaults; a variety of instances of firing into the windows of houses during the night, not attended however with any casualty to human life; and there have been at least four instances of deliberate attempts at assassination; and two to burn cotton-mills.

" Are there any of these cases in which you have distinctly traced the acts of intimidation that have taken place to persons connected with the society?—That is a point that was looked upon as so extremely clear, that it never was doubted at all; but as to my own means of knowledge, independent of positive private information, on which I had reason to place per-

manufacture that additional capital, which will
bring down the profit to the rate at which it would

---

fect reliance, there were several circumstances, sufficient in my mind to indicate that these acts of extreme violence could have no origin but as connected with the measures of the combination.

"Have you the names of those who were tried?—M'Connell was one,
Cameron another, and Callaghan the third. This case of Mr. Orr was in
the end of 1820. The next case that was followed by trial and conviction
was that of William Kerr, in November 1823. Two persons of the names
of Morrison and Shirley were tried and convicted. The circumstances were
shortly these: a person of the name of Fullerton, who was a leader among
the cotton-spinners, had been apprehended on a charge of some offence, and
was dismissed by his employer. It was found difficult to supply his place
in the cotton-mill, because, in this, as in all such cases, the cotton-spinners
well know that to accept of work in place of a member of the combination,
is attended with great personal danger. But this Kerr, who was out of
work, and poor, accepted of employment in the place of Fullerton. He was
threatened, but being a man of determination, he disregarded the threats;
and this fellow, Morrison, was employed to shoot him, being an entire
stranger to the man, and, as usual in such cases, a cotton-spinner out of
work. He came from a distance for the purpose, and got another person to
point out to him the house of Kerr, and having selected his time when Kerr
was returning about eight o'clock at night from his work, the night being
then pretty dark, he concealed himself just beside the stair which the man
had to ascend, behind his house, and pointing the pistol, loaded with small
shot, through the railing of the stairs, discharged it, about a yard's distance
from the man's left side ; but the man happened to make a stumble at the
time, and in place of receiving the shot in his side, he received it in the inside of his right thigh and the inside of his right arm. This Morrison, who
committed the deed, and Shirley, who was accessary, were both convicted,
and are both now in the House of Correction in Paisley, one of them (Morrison) having received a public whipping.

"You believe him to have been employed by the committee?—I know he
was; and this same Morrison was himself one of those who employed the
three persons to assassinate Mr. Orr, and was in a public-house in Paisley
waiting the result, and was called on by the assassins after the attempt had
been made. This came out incidentally; for, upon the trial, it appeared
that these people, after having fired at Mr. Orr, had left town, and gone into
a public-house at some little distance, where their pistols having been no-
ticed by the landlord of the house, and his wife, they listened at the key-hole,

have settled in a natural state of things. That process, by which it might appear at the outset, that profits will be increased at the expense of wages, must very soon work in favour of the labourers, so that the increase shall again come back to them, and bring their wages just to what they would have been, although no disturbing force

---

and heard these people talking of shooting some person for not paying them £10. This was inexplicable to me at the time, and seemed to have no connection with the facts on the trial. On subsequent inquiry, it appeared that this was to be the reward to be paid, and that the payment had been refused, because they were not quite certain the ' job' (as such things are called) had been done.''

" Will you state those instances? There was the case of Alexander Fisher, in 1820. That man had belonged to the combination, but had been guilty of the crime of ' knobbing,' that is to say, he had accepted of work, having found that he got no support for his family, as he expected, from the combination. His house was twice fired into, and he was waylaid, and vitriol cast upon him, so as to disfigure his face in a frightful manner.

" Did that come before you officially? There was an official investigation (what we call a precognition in Scotland) taken, and a trial, but no conviction followed. It is extremely difficult to get evidence; for after nightfall it is easy for a man, without the smallest appearance of violence, to toss a quantity of vitriol into his neighbour's face as he passes, and the very circumstance of doing it prevents the unfortunate man from distinguishing his assailant. The other case was that of a man named Doran, at the end of the same year. The man was also waylaid, and burnt dreadfully in his face and breast, and his left eye was in such a state, that the poor man when examined, stated that he believed he should never recover the sight of it.''

It will be observed that all these cases are previous to the Repeal. And then follows this question :—

" Have any cases of this kind taken place at Paisley within this last year? We have had no personal violence of any description arising from combinations within this last year, except in the case of the colliers.''

The testimony of Mr. William Rose Robinson, Sheriff-Depute of Lanarkshire, goes, on the other hand, to fix a greater atrocity on the outrages which have taken place since the repeal.

had ever been brought into operation. So that though all combinations of workmen were forcibly put an end to, there would yet remain an effective security for fair and adequate wages in the competition of the capitalists. However much the interference of Government, in favour of the latter, should raise their profits in the first instance, the ultimate effect would be to allure more capital into their branches of industry than otherwise would have flowed into them; and so, by producing a larger demand for workmen, would just cause the wages to rise to the very height from which they had fallen by the adverse and unpopular law. In other words, it is not possible for any legislature, even though it would, permanently to ensure a higher profit to the masters, and that, by means of a lower wage to their workmen than what would take place on a free and natural adjustment of the matter betwixt them. It cannot, by the force of any enactment, bring up the average rate of profit in a land, by reducing the market price of labour. On the moment of this being done, there would, by the now higher profit, be the formation and the influx of more capital into all the departments where these profits were realized; and thus, by the greater competition of capital, which is tantamount to a greater demand for labour, the price or wages of this labour would be speedily brought up to the level from which it had descended.

Were there no other depressing influence then brought to bear upon wages than combination laws, these would be altogether harmless ; and the friends of the lower orders might cease from all alarm and indignation upon the subject.   But there is an evil in these laws which might well alarm the friends of loyalty.   However innocent they may be in effect, they bear towards the working classes an aspect of hostility.   The artizan or the labourer understands them in no other way than as looking adversely towards himself; and, instead of recognizing a friendly and a paternal Government, in the reigning authority of the state, he will view it as leagued with his employers in the fellowship of one common tyranny.   The only interpretation which he puts upon the enactment, is, that it is on the side of the masters and against the workmen; and it is quite fearful to contemplate the advantage which such a feeling, when widely diffused and deeply seated in the hearts of our peasantry, might give to the demagogues of our land.   There should be some very strong and imperious necessity made out ere the burden of such an odium be laid upon Government, or a task in every way so invidious be put into its hands.   It were surely better for peace and for public order, if capitalists and workmen could be left to settle their own affairs; and it is hard that the tranquillity of the state should be endangered for the sake of an interest, which the natural economics of the case seem most abundantly to have provided for.   It perhaps is all the more provoking, that for the object on account of which the interference is made, it is altogether nugatory—

that after all, neither masters are the better, nor workmen are the worse for it—that the hand which Government lifts up in this business of regulation, is a hand of entire impotency, but that, felt at the same time, by the labouring classes, as a hand of hostile and menacing demonstration, it should have the effect of alienating, from the established order of things, the largest class of society.

On the other hand, if there be an utter impotency on the part of Government to depress wages beneath the fair market price of labour, there is just as great an impotency on the part of workmen permanently to raise the wages above this level. The fair market price of labour, is that at which it would settle in *a free state of things*, on the given state of its demand and supply. Labourers, themselves, cannot force a permanent elevation of the wages above this level, but by excluding from the competition a certain number of their own body; or, in other words, by a monopoly more hurtful and oppressive still than that of any mercantile society that has ever been recorded, and which Government does a most righteous and equitable thing in preventing. Workmen cannot raise their wages above the fair market price of labour, but by the infliction of a grievous injury on certain of their own body, whom they would violently eject beyond the pale of that competition to which all are equally admissible, both by justice and by law. Government is only acting in discharge of her most beneficent functions, as the parent, and the equal protector of all, when she interposes against the restraints and outrages of labourers upon their fellows, and that with penalties just as strong and as severe as shall be adequate to put them down. But though this way of advancing the remuneration of labour cannot be permitted, there is another and a patent way by which labourers may most effectually, and, at the same time, most legitimately secure the very advancement which they are aiming at. When they succeed in raising their wages by violence, it is just by lessening the supply of labour, and this supply is lessened by the number of labourers whom they have forced away from the field of competition. The very same rise would have taken place, if, instead of that number being forced away, they simply had not been in existence; or, if the whole population of the country had just been equal to that portion of them who maintain their ground on the field of competition, after having made outcasts of the rest. Had there just been a less population by these outcasts, their object would have been carried without any assertion on their part, and simply by the operation of the demand of capitalists upon a smaller supply. It is the redundancy of their own numbers, and nothing else, which is the cause of their degradation. They charge their masters with depressing them; but the truth is, that they depress and elbow out one another. And in spite of all the ridicule, and of all the sentimental indignancy which have been heaped on the doctrine of population, it remains as unalterable as any of nature's laws, that nothing can avail for the conducting of our peasantry to a higher status, but a lessened competition for employment, and in virtue of there being somewhat fewer labourers.

This guides us to the view of another great mischief in these combination laws. The former mischief, that of creating a disaffected peasantry, is more felt by the patriot, who has conceived a strong affection for the cause of loyalty. The other great mischief to which we are now to advert, is more felt by the general philanthropist, who has conceived a strong affection for the good of the species, and more especially for the enlarged comfort and intelligence of the lower orders. He who looks to the wrong quarter for a disease, will, in all likelihood, betake himself to a wrong remedy. And this, perhaps, is the very worst consequence of combination laws. They have turned the attention of our artizans and labourers away from that only path on which they can reach a higher status in the commonwealth. They are misled as to where the disease of their economic state lies; and are, therefore, alike misled as to the application of the remedy. It were well, if they had no pretext for referring to the policy of Government, that degradation and misery which are altogether due to their own habits. They behold an adverse enactment against them in the statute book, and they look no further. They conceive this to be the only bar in the way of their elevation, and they

ply not·the expedient which is in their own hands;
and by virtue of which, they might attain an independence which Government can neither give nor
take away. They would lay upon the state the
whole burden of that responsibility, which, in fact,
lies upon themselves; and this at once makes them
resentful to their superiors, and reckless of that
alone way by which themselves can be guided onward to a more secure and permanent comfort than
they have ever yet enjoyed. It is altogether a way
of peace and of sobriety; a way that " cometh not
with observation;" and by which, without the din
or disturbance of any popular ebullitions, the solid
interest of the people will come at length to be
established on a basis that shall be impregnable.

Should the present repeal law be superseded,
not by a law that is restrictive, but by a law that
is perfective of freedom, this will conduct the people to a state of things, the best possible for enlightening them both in what that is where their
weakness, and in what that is where their strength
lieth. Let the principle, in the first place, be left
untouched of the utmost freedom to all workmen
who, either conjunctly or severally, are not willing
to work. In the second place, let this be followed
up by the principle, not yet adequately provided
for, of the utmost protection and freedom to all
workmen who, either conjunctly or severally, are
willing to work. For this purpose, let law put
forth all the preventions and all the penalties which
can be devised to secure every willing workman

from the terror or the violence of his fellows—and then the whole machinery of these combinations will proceed in that very way which is most fitted to develope, even to the popular understanding, the real cause of a people's degradation, and so the real and only corrective by which it can be efficaciously met. It will then be quite palpable, that they are the new, or unassociated workmen, who have broke up the combination—that the outstanding workmen have not been able to enforce their own terms, just because of the numbers beside themselves, who are thankful for their employment on lower terms—that their masters stood upon a vantage ground, not because of any legal power over them, but because of the natural resource which they had in the men whom they could find, or in the men who offered themselves out of the general population. For this purpose, these masters have only to enlist the willing, and do not need to compel the unwilling—or, in other words, they prevail in this struggle, just because there are so many who are willing to be thus enlisted. If, instead of finding so many, they had found that the population of the land were barely enough to satisfy the demand for labour, and to fill up its various departments in the country, then they could not have allured new workmen into their service, but by the offer of a higher remuneration than they were earning in some previous service. This would reverse the competition; and, instead of workmen pressing for admittance into employment upon a lower wage, we should behold masters detaining, by a higher wage, those whom others were endeavouring to seduce from their employment. Workmen would come at length to perceive, that the question between them and their employers all hinged on the single element of their own numbers—that if there be too many labourers, no combination can keep up their wages—or, if there be too few, no law against combinations can keep them down—and that, in short, with the command which they have over this element, they have themselves, and neither their masters nor their rulers, to blame as the authors of their own degradation.

They are not in circumstances for making this discovery, so long as the imagination lasts among them, that in every effort to better their condition they are thwarted and kept in check by the oppressive enactments of the statute book. Better far that all these enactments should be swept away, and that workmen should be let forth on the arena of a free competition with their employers. On this field, let them be made welcome to every attempt and every expedient for a rise of wages which is not criminal. They will soon arrive at a sound experience upon the subject; and at last acquiesce in the conclusion, that they have no other control over the price of labour than that general control, wherewith, by means of their moral and prudential habits, they can limit and define the number of labourers.

And certain it is that this will avail them, without the expedient of any organised association at all. For the sake of simplicity, let us confine the argument to any one branch of manufacture which we might suppose to be in the hands of a certain number of capitalists, and that it is somewhat straitened for a supply of labourers. In consequence, the commodity will be produced in somewhat less abundance than can fully meet the demand for it in the market, and its price inevitably rises. This increment of price, in the first instance, raises the profits of the masters; but its final landing-place is among the workmen, for, in the second instance, and without combinations, it will go to the raising of the wages. The rise of profits in any trade tends both to create more of capital within the trade, and to allure to it more of capital from without. In other words, master manufacturers will not long be permitted to enjoy this additional profit; for out of it there will almost instantly emerge a busier competition, either among themselves, or from new adventurers enticed to this more hopeful walk of speculation. The prosperity of any trade is ever followed up both with the means and the efforts to extend it; but this cannot be done without a call for more operatives than before. Each individual master, while the demand is brisker than the supply, and therefore profits encouraging, will try to widen and enlarge his own establishment; and, as the effect of this competition among all, a higher wage will be held out than before to labourers. Let there be an endeavour, on the part of every capitalist, to make out a full complement of workmen; and nothing more is necessary than a difficulty of doing so, from the smallness of the numbers to be had, in order to secure for these workmen a liberal remuneration. Apart from any association on the side of the operatives, their object is gained by a competition on the side of their masters. And all which they have to do, is to cultivate, each in his own family, those habits of foresight and sobriety, without which it is utterly impossible, either by device or by violence, to save them from the miseries of an over-peopled land.

It is true, that we have only reasoned on the case of one manufacture; and it is a possible thing, that any deficiency in its workmen may be recruited from the general population, either by enlisting those who are without employment, or by alluring from previous service those who are engaged in the service of other manufacturers. But the supposition of a more intelligent and better-habitted peasantry, precludes the idea of any being without employment. It would secure the state not merely of one, but of all manufacturers having barely enough of labourers to keep them a-going. It would extend the competition from masters in but one line of employment, to that of all the masters and capitalists in our land.

This of itself will elevate the condition of the working classes. Let there but be somewhat more of virtue in their conduct, and somewhat more of prudence and delay in their marriages, and there will forthwith commence that progress, by which, silently, and gradually, and indefinitely, the price of their services must rise, and themselves must ascend to a higher status in the commonwealth. And all this, without the turmoil or effervescence of combinations. These can never permanently raise the price of labour. There is one precise point at which this price settles; and this point is altogether determined by the proportion which obtains between the work to be done, and the number of workmen that are to be had for the doing of it. The effect of strikes, and associations, and long suspensions of work, followed up by hurricanes of prosperous trade, and high wages—the effect of all this may be, to produce large oscillations on each side of the average price of labour, but certainly not at all to raise the average itself. This average is fixed by the proportion before specified; and labourers have a command over this proportion, because they can command one of the terms of it. Their own number is wholly dependent on their own general character and habits; and, if they will but limit the supply of workmen, a higher recompense for work, not in virtue of any concert among themselves, but in virtue of competition

among their masters, will be the inevitable result
of it.*

---

* It has been questioned by Mr. Malthus, whether a higher standard of
enjoyment among the labouring classes would diminish the population of a
country upon the whole.   We have often thought, that it facilitated a right
apprehension of the result, to conceive of all the labourers in a land as
divided into three classes; first, the agricultural, employed in providing the
first necessaries of life—secondly, a class employed in providing the second
necessaries—and thirdly, the class employed in the preparation of luxuries, and who, on that very account, and because luxuries may either be
shifted or dispensed with, might be aptly enough termed the disposable population.

It is obvious that, if by the term "second necessaries," we include every
thing additional to food which enters into the maintenance of labourers,
then the second class, all other circumstances being equal, will increase
with every increase in the standard of enjoyment; and increasing as they
must at the expense of the disposable population, we behold, as the effect
of such a change on the habits of our peasantry, both a smaller rent to the
landlord, and fewer people employed in the service of administering to his
luxuries.

We do not take into the account at present the effect of machinery, or of
any improvement in the productive powers of labour, on the proportion of
these three classes.   This may, in the first instance, diminish the agricultural class, the same produce being raised with fewer hands than before.
It may also diminish the second class, even although there should be a
higher standard of enjoyment among the people, the same number being
able to work a much larger amount than before of all the conveniences of
life.   It is thus that the disposable population may receive accessions, with
the progress of machinery, from both these classes; and landlords, with a
larger surplus in the shape of rent of agricultural produce than before, can
enlist a larger disposable population into their services than before; and
the services of each be more effective, in virtue of the improvements in
labour which have taken place.   We should certainly incline to a higher
standard of enjoyment among labourers, even though there should, in consequence, be a positive decline of enjoyment among the proprietors of the
soil.   But it is pleasing to observe, that, by the operation of another cause,
there is room afforded, in the progress of society, for a contemporaneous
increase in the enjoyments of all.

But abstracting ourselves for the time from the consideration of this particular cause, we can perceive, first, that if an effective demand, on the part

Every thing in the state and history of the commercial world, announces how little capitalists have it in their power to sustain an extravagant rate of profit, for any length of time, at the expense of their customers or of their workmen. It is a prevalent impression among workmen, that they are too much at the mercy of capitalists. If they only knew the whole truth, they would soon perceive that capitalists are wholly at the mercy of each other; and in such a way, that without being able to help it, they are very much at the mercy of their workmen. At least, if it be not so, it is altogether the fault of the workmen themselves;

---

of labourers, for higher gratifications, take an exclusive direction towards the second necessaries of life, this will not diminish the population, and will but affect the distribution of them. The second class is extended thereby; a greater number is taken into the service of labourers, and withdrawn from the service of landlords. An addition is made to the wages of the one party; and without that addition being necessarily made (as many of Ricardo's disciples imagine) at the expense of profit, it may in fact consist partly, nay wholly, of the consequent diminution that has been made on the rent of the other party.

But should the demand of labourers for higher gratifications take the direction which it might partly do towards a more liberal use of the agricultural produce, as by the larger use of bread, or beer, or spirits, or confectionaries, or animal food, this would absolutely lessen the population, and have just the same effect ultimately on the rent of the landlord, as if the soil of which he is proprietor had been stricken with a certain degree of barrenness. There is nothing in this change of habit to lessen the agricultural population; nothing to lessen the proportion which the second class of labourers bears to the whole body, provided that each, over and above his more abundant use of agricultural produce, has just the same demand for the second necessaries of life; and so the landlord would be the alone sufferer by this change—he having both a less rent, in virtue of the greater wage now given to farm-servants, and having a greater wage to bestow for the service of each individual of the now lessened disposable population.

who, by the simple regulation of their numbers, might, not in a way of turbulence, but in a way of order and peace, become the effectual dictators in every question between them and their employers. These employers cannot, though they would, reserve in profit to themselves any part of that, which, in the state of the labour market, must go in wages to their labourers. They cannot keep up their profits beyond .a certain rate at. the expense of their workmen, and in the progress of things, too, this rate is constantly falling. For how short a time can any lucrative branch of trade be upheld in its lucrativeness! In a few months the rush of capital fills it to an overflow. Let but a stage coach upon any road, or a steam boat upon any river, have realized the smallest centage of excess above the ordinary profits of the country, and in a moment, by other coaches and other boats, the excess, or perhaps the whole profit together is annihilated. The same holds true of every other department. Each is crowded with capital—and profit, all over the land, is rapidly verging to a minimum. This is satisfactorily demonstrated by the fall in the interest of money; and perhaps a still more striking exhibition of it is the way in which capital is going about among all the schemes and possibilities of investiture that are now afloat, and absolutely begging for employment. With such a creative and accumulating force in capital, the labouring classes may be in perfect security, that any hostile combination of their masters against them must speedily be neutralised, by competition among themselves. On the other hand, would labourers but restrain their own numbers, and so guard their wages against the depressing effects of competition among the members of their own body, this would have in it all the force, without any of the ferocity or turbulence, of a most overwhelming combination. This is the high-way to their independence—a noiseless way, on which they will neither strive, nor cry, nor cause their voice to be heard upon the streets—a way on which every philanthropist would rejoice to witness their advancement, and by which, without danger or disturbance to society, they will raise the whole platform of their condition, and secure a more abundant share of the comforts and accommodations of life, than they have ever yet enjoyed.

Nevertheless, and although it is by a process altogether independent of combinations, that the state of the working population is to be elevated, yet for reasons, which have in part been already given, we should deprecate any return, however slight, to a law against combinations. The whole mischief of them will at length be wrought away in the violence of their own fermentation. It is right, too, that all the occasional violence which has attended combinations, should be repressed by the utmost force of legislation; and this is a legislation, which, however severely it may bear on the radicals or the ringleaders of a popular tumult, will at length have the full consent and acquiescence even of the popular understanding to go along with it. A government never does excite any permanent or wide-spread hostility against itself, by those laws which recommend themselves to our natural principles of equity; and it is only when the equity is not very obvious, that a sense of oppression rankles in the hearts of the people, and carries them forth to proceedings of turbulence and disorder. Now, the equity of a law of protection for all who are willing to work, is obvious. The equity of a law of compulsion against any, even although in concert and joint deliberation, who are not willing to work, is not obvious. Let the latter law, therefore, be expunged, but the former be instated in full authority, and have the weightiest sanctions to uphold it. After this, workmen might, with all safety, be left to themselves. They will soon feel their way to the evil of combinations, and make discovery, that, apart from them altogether, there is a secure and a peaceful road by which the people might help themselves onward to a state of greater sufficiency. It is a great lesson to teach them that this is the only road;—a lesson which they never can be taught, so long as law debars them from any other expedient which possesses a virtue in their imagination. It were the most precious fruit of their liberty, that this imagination should be dissipated; and that so they should be shut up by their own experience, that most authoritative of all schoolmasters, to the only remaining expedient which can avail them. It is well for them to know, that it is the weight of their own numbers, and nothing else, which degrades and depresses them; and that the cause of all their sufferings does not lie in the want of protection from the legislature, or of kindness from their masters, but in the want of prudence and economy among themselves.

And, for ourselves, we confess it to be a cheering anticipation, that the labouring classes shall, not by a midway passage of anarchy and misrule, but by a tranquil process of amelioration in their character and habits, make steady amelioration at the same time in their outward circumstances. We believe it to be in reserve for society, that, of the three component ingredients of value, the wages of labour shall at length rise to a permanently higher proportion than they now have, either to the profit of stock or the rent of land; and that thus, workmen will share more equally than they do at present, with capitalists and proprietors of the soil, in the comforts and even the elegancies of life. But this will not be the achievement of desperadoes. It will be come at through a more peaceful medium, through the medium of a growing worth and growing intelligence among the people. It will bless and beautify that coming period, when a generation, humanised by letters, and elevated by the light of Christianity, shall, in virtue of a higher taste and a larger capacity than they now possess, cease to grovel as they do at present among the sensualities of a reckless dissipation.

This dissipation stands often associated with a stout and a sullen defiance; and the two together, characterize a large class of the mechanics of our present day. But these are not the men who are to accomplish the enlargement of that order to which they belong;—at one time on the brink of starvation by their own extravagance, and then lying prostrate at the dictation of their employers; at another, in some season of fitful prosperity, made giddy with ambition, and breaking forth in the complaints and the clamours of an appetency which is never satisfied. It is not by such a process of starts and convulsions as this, that our working classes are to be borne upwards to that place of security and strength, which, nevertheless, we believe to be awaiting them. But there is no other foundation than that of their own sobriety and good principle on which it can solidly be reared. And the process in this way may be easily apprehended. In proportion as man becomes more reflective and virtuous, in that proportion does he seek for something higher than the mere gratifications of his animal nature. His desires take a wider range; and he will not be satisfied but with a wider range of enjoyment. There is a growing demand for certain objects of taste and decency; and even the mind will come to require a leisure and a literature for the indulgence of its nobler appetites, now brought into play by means of a diffused education. Altogether, under such a regimen as this, the heart of

a workman is made to aspire after greater things
than before; and in perfect keeping and harmony
with a soul, now awakened to the charms of that
philosophy which is brought down to his understanding in a mechanic school, is it that he should
hold, as indispensable to his comfort, a better style
of accommodation than his forefathers, whether in
apparel, or furniture, or lodging. And it is just
by means of a more elevated standard than before,
that marriages become later and less frequent than
before. This we deem to be the precise ligament
which binds together an improvement in the character with an improvement in the comfort of our
peasantry; and makes a taste for certain conveniences, the very stepping-stone by which a people
do arrive at them. It is enough that these conveniences should be regarded as among the essential
ingredients of maintenance; and then will a sense
of their importance come to operate with effect, as
a counteractive to the temptations of precipitate
or imprudent matrimony. The man who counts
it enough for himself and his family, that they
have rags, and potatoes, and a hovel, will rush
more improvidently, and therefore more early,
into the married state, than he who feels that,
without a better provision and a better prospect
than these, he should offend his own self-respect,
and compromise all his notions of what is decent,
or dignified, or desirable. We are aware of the
exceeding difference between one individual and
another in the same country; but this does not

prevent a certain average standard of enjoyment in each country; and thus, in respect of this average standard, may the difference be very great between one country and another. And, if we except the case of still youthful colonies, we shall be sure to find, that, corresponding to this difference in the average standard of enjoyment, is there a difference in the average period of marriage. The higher the one is, the later the other is. The greater the demand for family comforts, the smaller and the fewer are the families. The larger the ambition of labourers, the less is the number of labourers;* and sure consequence of this, the greater are the means in the hand of each for satisfying his ambition. This is one of those felicitous cases, in which the desire of good things is at length followed up by the power of obtaining them. It is thus that workmen can enforce their demand for higher wages. Those distempered outbreakings which approach to the character of rebellion, will retard instead of forwarding their cause. But nothing can arrest the march of light among the people; and when this light is conjoined with virtue, it will guide their ascending way to a vantage ground, where they will make

---

* See the last note, from which it will appear that, in as far as the higher taste of the people leads to their more abundant use of the second necessaries of life, it does not lessen the number of the people, but only affects the distribution of them. And it is only in so far as this higher taste leads to a more abundant use of agricultural produce in families, that the population is diminished thereby.

good the precise status to which their worth shall entitle them—a status for all whose comforts and accommodations, they will then be in circumstances to prefer their demand with a small and a still, but yet an irresistible voice.

It is by a tranquil process, such as this, that the general condition of our people will at length be elevated. It is by a slow, but a resistless movement, which combination cannot speed, but which will be sure to make its way, though in the absence of all combination. In none of its successive steps is there aught that can endanger the peace of society, or that should give alarm to the rulers of it. The triumph that awaits the humbler classes, will not be extorted from the higher by the outcry of popular discontent, but silently and insensibly gained from them, by the growth of popular intelligence and virtue. What is there to convulse our land, in the multiplication of schools, in the exchange which our people make of loathsome dissipation for respectable scholarship, in their habits of improving comfort and cleanliness, in their general postponement of marriages, and in the consequent result of smaller but well-conditioned families? In the whole of this beautiful progression, there is nothing to alienate, but every thing to attach the people to that established order of things under which they find that industry meets with its recompense, and that, with the labour of their own hands, they can rear their children in humble, but honest independence. Instead of so many fiery spirits, now in bitterness, under a sense of difficulties, and in the vain imagination that they are so many wrongs inflicted by the hand of an arbitrary government, casting resentment and reproach on the politics of the kingdom, we should find each in busy occupation with the management of his own thriving affairs, and recognizing, in the hopeful prosperity of his own household, the best evidence of a sound public administration. The question of wages, instead of being agitated in stormy debate between the parties, may be decided with all the quietness of a common market transaction, yet decided in favour of the workmen; and that simply because, in virtue of their now purer, and more prudential habits, they have not overdone the supply of labour. Ere this result is arrived at, there may, or there may not be frequent combinations. In themselves they are altogether useless; but let workmen be at full liberty to make the experiment. Let not government, save for the sake of justice between man and man, interpose in this controversy between them and their employers. Let not labourers be driven from their associations by the penalties of law, and they will soon be schooled out of them, by those chastisements of Nature and Necessity which follow in their train. They will, all the sooner because of this liberty, be schooled into the lesson, that wages must, by a necessity which no force or artifice of man can

overbear, be fixed by the proportion which obtains between the work to be done, and the number of workmen to be had for the doing of it—
that for this number they are themselves responsible—and that, without the education to which
all the good and the wise of the land are inviting
them, and the moral and religious culture to
which they are bound by far higher than any
earthly obligations, and the consequent elevation
which must ensue in their whole taste and standard of enjoyment—and, lastly, as the result of
all this, that, without the prospective economy
which of itself will push forward the average
date of marriages in the country, no power under
the sun can help them out of the degradation into
which nothing, on the other hand, can plunge
them, but their own recklessness and folly. Let
them look as fiercely as they may at the other
classes of society, there is most gross and grievous injustice in all their indignation. They are
only wreaking upon the innocent the mischief
which they have brought upon their own heads;
for, in truth, government and the wealthier orders of society are most innocent of it all. And
should, in the wild surges of a popular frenzy,
the institutions of this fairest and most flourishing
country in the world be ever swept away, it will
be the impartial voice of justice in all distant
ages, that, under pretence of resentment and resistance to the tyranny of the few, all the equities of human life had been most oppressively

lorded over by the iniquitous tyranny of the multitude.

In the act of dealing equally with the various classes in society, it is perhaps impossible to avoid saying what might occasionally be offensive to them all. And if, on the one hand, there are labourers who need to be rebuked out of their turbulence and unjust discontent; so, on the other hand, there are still a few of the British aristocracy who eye with jealousy and dread all the advances that are making by the people in knowledge, and even in the sufficiency and style of their enjoyments. More especially have the recent outbreakings of workmen engendered in certain quarters a dislike of Savings Banks, as the likely organs of building up such a capital for the lower orders, as might be the instrument at length of a popular despotism, at once the most fearful in itself, and the most destructive of all the great political and economic interests in our land.*

---

* From the examination of Mr. Oldfield :—

" Can you suggest any means to prevent the inconveniences you complain of ?—If the government could prevent them from accumulating funds."

From the examination of Mr. Eli Chadwick :—

" Does it occur to you to suggest any mode by which that inconvenience which you have suffered from the men could be prevented ?—I should conceive, one great means of preventing it would be, preventing their accumulation of funds; it is that which gives them the chief portion of the influence they now possess, in disturbing the manufactory in the neighbourhood."

These testimonies, however, apply to associated funds ;—and certain it is, that the accumulation of funds individually by workmen, would have an influence adverse to combinations.

We think that we can discern pretty obvious manifestations of this jealousy brought before the eye of Parliament itself. And therefore, before closing our remarks upon this whole subject, we should like, in a few sentences, to state our opinion of the result that would ensue from a habit of accumulation amongst the working classes of society.

The connection of this habit with a higher rate of wages, we have already endeavoured to explain. It is not in the foresight or the contemplation of such an ulterior effect that the habit is adopted. Each individual who does accumulate, has been led to do it from the mere impulse of a taste and an affection for a property to himself. He does not consider the effect which such a taste and habit, if they became general among workmen, would have upon society. Nevertheless, it is not the less true, though he should not perceive it, that a spirit of economy among the lower orders would land us in a more reflective, and rational, and sober peasantry; and that a certain postponement of marriages would surely accompany this growing taste for property, and for the enjoyments which property can command. The consequent rise in the price of labour, is from the quiet operation of an economic law, even the law of dependence that subsists between the price of an article and its supply; and so in the present case is the result of a somewhat diminished number of labourers.

This result is arrived at by a peaceful process,

and not by the power which a capital would give to labourers of holding out for a greater length of time in combinations. The truth is, that when once a property is built up by a man, and embodied into a given sum, and expressed by the bank credit which he holds in his hand, and made the object of his strong and distinct affection for it, he feels a pain in any violation of its entireness; and this new feeling comes into play against those combinations which impose a protracted season of idleness upon their members. Such a season, in the present state of the working classes, only brings privations upon them, which they can weather from day to day by the mere power of endurance; and far more readily, we are persuaded, than a man can suffer the careful product of the economy of many long and laborious years to be melting away before his eyes. In other words, we should hold this habit to be more a security than otherwise against combinations. By him who had won his way to the possession of a small and cherished capital, the waste of this capital would be felt as one of the sorest evils. He would bethink himself well ere he submitted to those repeated draughts upon his capital, which a suspension of labour must surely bring along with it; and so he, and such as he, would not be so prone to the rash or misguided adventure of a strike, as our present race of desperadoes.

And there is a very substantial, and, at the same time, a very pure compensation, awaiting the higher classes of society, for this encroachment, or rather for this appearance of an encroachment, that is made upon them by the increased wages of the lower. It is founded upon this: the greater amount and value of the services that will then be rendered. We are not indulging any Utopian imagination; but speaking, in fact, to the experience of practical men, when we say that there are a power and a charm in a certain generous style of remuneration, the whole benefit of which will come to be realized in that better state of things, to which we believe that society is fast tending. We are aware of the union which often obtains, in large manufacturing establishments, between the enormous wage, and the reckless, loathsome dissipation of its workmen. But, ere the higher wage that we contemplate shall obtain throughout the country at large, this recklessness must have very generally disappeared, and a sober, reflective, and well-principled character, substituted in its place. Now we pre-suppose such a character, when we prophesy a sure compensation to the higher orders, for the then more elevated status of the population beneath them; and for the experimental proof of our anticipation, we appeal to cases where servants are at once well-principled and well-paid. We are confident of being fully met by the recollection of many masters, when we affirm an overpassing worth in the labour of such servants; and that, where there are that higher tone of character, and that self-respect, and that fidelity, which can only be upheld by the well-conditionedness of a better remuneration, then the difference in the worth of the service greatly more than atones for the superior wage which has been rendered. If masters will reflect, they will generally find, that those men whom they found to be perfect treasures as servants, were never so because of the lowness of his wage, but always so because of the trustiness of their own character; and that the difference in the amount of that *materiel* which they render out in wages, is far more than made up in the larger return which comes back, because of that higher and better *morale* which pervades the workmen of their establishment. The same lesson is afforded by the reverse experience of those farmers, who employ a set of worthless, degraded, and half-paid paupers, in the business of their agriculture. They are far more unprofitable, as workmen, than the regular servants who obtain a full and respectable allowance. This points, it is obvious, to a very delightful consummation—a higher peasantry, yet a fuller tide of affluence all over the land, in which, too, the great and the noble will participate more largely than ever—the basis of the social polity more elevated, yet, at the same time, its pinnacles towering more proudly, and blazing more gorgeously than before—the labourer upholden in greater comfort, yet the landlord upholden in greater elegance and enjoyment,—the fruit of that exquisite, but substantial harmony, which obtains among all the truly desirable interests of human society.

And, upon this subject, we have often felt that
the legislature have missed an opportunity, but
which still, we fondly hope, is not irrecoverable.
They should have combined the two questions of
combination and of pauperism, and made a compromise between them. In the act of expunging
from their statute-book that law of combination
which bore an aspect of hostility to the lower orders, although it does them little harm, they were
most favourably situated for expunging from their
statute-book that law of pauperism, which bears an
aspect of friendship to the lower orders, although
most assuredly it does them no good. They should
have availed themselves of this balance between
the partialities and the prejudices of the popular
understanding. The people of England might
have acquiesced in the abolition of that law for
which they have a predilection, because feeling it
compensated by the abolition of that law for which
they had a dislike. When the burden was removed from the industry of workmen, then was
the time for attempting a removal of the burden
from the property of landlords. The thing is not
yet so definitely settled, as that it can be said to
have conclusively gone by, or as to have precluded
the adjustment of a great and comprehensive question of equity between the labourers and the landlords. When to the one there is conceded the
entire right to make the most, without the old legal obstruction, of the product of their service, to
the other let there be conceded the entire right to

make the most, and without the present legal obstruction, of the product of their soil.* It were a
fair reciprocal acquittance between the two parties—the higher and the lower classes of society
—leaving to the one an unburdened property in
their land, and to the other an unburdened property in their labour.† And even though a high
wage should be the ultimate consequence of such
an arrangement, there is no country where this

---

* We, of course, must be understood to point at the abolition of the law
of pauperism, only in the way which we have already attempted to explain, in a former volume of this work—a gradual way, by which it might
be accomplished, without violence done to any of the existing paupers, and
without disturbance to the commonwealth. It would remove the hazard
of disturbance still further, if, for the imaginary loss which the people have
suffered by one law, there could have been devised a compensation to their
prejudices and feelings, even though it were by an imaginary gain secured
for them through the abolition of another law.

† For the fancied bereavement which they sustain by the abolition of
pauperism, the people might find a *solatium* in the boon which is rendered
to them by the entire abolition of the combination laws. Or, if this opportunity be now regarded as lost, there are other boons in reserve for
them. Such is our view of the incidence and effect of taxes, that we do
not hold it possible to make them fall upon labourers; and, though ostensibly paid by them, they are really paid by the purchasers and employers
of labour. Still, a poll-tax, or a house-tax, or a tax on the necessaries
of life, have all the odium of so many felt burdens upon the poor. So
that, by a reform in the system of finance, by a transference of taxes from
the lower to the higher orders, or from the necessaries to the luxuries
of life, there might at least be the imagination of a relief to the former, without the reality of any additional burden upon the latter. This
suggests another expedient for making the removal of pauperism more
palatable to the labouring classes—even by accompanying it with the
removal of one or more of those taxes that bear on the subsistence of
their families. The gratification which they should feel in the one
measure, would neutralise the grievance which they might feel to be in
the other.

ought to be more thankfully acquiesced in by the higher ranks of society than in England. For to her, of all others, there would accrue the most abundant compensations. She, in the first place, would have a compensation in those better and more productive services that are rendered by well-paid labourers, rather than by labourers sunk as they now are, in the sloth and degradation of pauperism. And secondly, she would have still more palpable compensation, in being eventually disburdened from that enormous tax of six millions in the year for her poor, which were enough, of itself, to afford a much higher sufficiency to a perhaps somewhat reduced, but greatly more sound and serviceable population.

CHAP. XXII.

ON CERTAIN PREVALENT ERRORS AND MISCONCEP-
TIONS, WHICH ARE FOSTERED BY ECONOMIC THE-
ORIES, AND WHICH ARE FITTED TO MISLEAD THE
LEGISLATURE, IN REGARD TO LABOUR AND THE
LABOURING CLASSES.

III. IT is not alone in the minds of the common
people, that we have misunderstanding and prejudice to contend with; nor is their ignorance
the only obstruction in the way of a right adjustment between masters on the one hand, and workmen on the other. We admit, that it might go
far to effect a reconciliation between the two parties, if the latter could be rationalized into a just
discernment of all that economics which had to
do with Profit and Wages. But we are fully persuaded, that the former are nearly as destitute of
the true principle on which the question hinges,
and that, ere the reconciliation can be completed,
they have both much to learn, and much to un-
learn. We even think, that, among our most influential classes, there is a deal of false imagination as to the real economic interests of the country; and that still restrains our Legislators from
that full march of liberality, on which they have
lately broken forth, and made a progress that fills
the sanguine friends of humanity with very high

and bright anticipations. There is with all this, however, a certain remainder of fearfulness, in virtue of which they at times shrink back again, even from the proper advances which themselves had made on the career of amelioration. So that, in retracing their path, they, along with the errors into which they have fallen, do occasionally recal the real improvements upon which they had entered. We have no doubt that they are on the way of being speedily unfettered from the last drags and difficulties by which they are yet in some degree held; and that the soundest Economical System which has ever been promulgated by our philosophers in theory, will also be realized by our statesmen in practice. The tendency of our present rulers is all in this direction; although, even in spite of the great and glorious advance which they have made, it can still be perceived, that, even on the path which themselves have struck out, they walk with somewhat trembling and unconfirmed footstep. The truth seems to be, that they would proceed faster than the country will let them; and that they must for a period defer to the voice of a public, who, in light and liberality, are greatly behind themselves. We often hear of men of science, who, in their speculations, but seldom of men of office, who, in their acts or in their actings, outrun the spirit of the age. Now, this is the rare and honourable exhibition by which our rulers are at present signalized. They are fast freeing our

mercantile code of its many errors, yet still in
such a way as to evince that there is still a leaven
of the mercantile system, either in their own spirits, or in the spirits of those who have ascendancy
over them. We can imagine that we can perceive
no slight tokens of this, in their whole treatment
of the question of combinations; and if to rectify
the notions of workmen, we hold it desirable that
the light of economic science should be let down
to the very basis of society, it is not because we
conceive that to be a pure and a perfect light
which shines in its upper places. There may not
be the utter darkness of the lower region. But
there is often, at least, a glare of false speculation,
which, if it do not altogether blind, is sure to be-
wilder those who are exposed to it; so that, even
among the guides and legislators of the community, there may be notions which admit of being
rectified.

Now, one of the most inveterate of these we
hold to be that by which, not only the conduct of
Parliament, but almost our whole authorship in
political economy, is infected. If, before illus-
trating what it is by examples, we were required
briefly to express this erroneous notion in language
of the utmost generality, we should say, that it
proceeded on a preference of the means to the end.
Capital and commerce, and the various branches
of both, which are distinguished by so many interests, such as the shipping interest, and the manufacturing interest, and the trading interest;

these supply so many high-sounding terms, by which the public understanding has been juggled into a false estimate of the magnitude of things. The truth is, that this whole apparatus of commerce and of capital is but of instrumental subserviency towards an ultimate and a terminating object; and it is not surely by casting one's eye along the steps of a process, but it is by settling our regards on the result of it, that the good of the whole is to be perceived. It has all the self-evidence of a truism, and yet is strangely overlooked both in economic reasonings and in economic regulations, that the worth of that *by* which a thing is done, is all derived from the worth of that *for* which the thing is done. It is *by* several hundred ships that coals are carried from Newcastle to London— and it is *for* the comfort and utility of good fires to the families there that they are so carried ; and we affirm the latter to have the precedency, in consideration and importance, over the former. Now what we complain of is, that this is lost sight of both by philosophers and by statesmen; by the one in the construction of their theories, by the other in the business of their practical administration. The shipping interest of the Tyne is an object of greater moment and magnificence in their eyes, than the cheapness or the abundance of fuel in the metropolis. It is forgotten that the end is greater than the means; and although Smith has formally asserted that the end of all production is consumption, yet even he, in the course of his argument, seems often to have forgotten this maxim, in a certain value, *per se*, which he attaches to trade and manufactures. Now, it ought ever to be kept in mind, that trade and manufactures have all their worth and significancy as subservient to, and none whatever as apart from, the enjoyment of consumers. The worth of commerce lies wholly in the *terminus ad quem*, and not in the *iter per quod*.

Now, both by politicians and political economists, this principle is traversed. It is in the working up of the commodity, in the buying of it, and selling of it, and transporting of it, in the succession of various movements and exchanges which it is made to undergo, in that whole series of transactions through which it passes from him who first put forth his hand upon its raw material, to him who made the final purchase of it, so that it ceased to be an article of merchandise any more —it is in these various steps which properly belong to the manufacture of the commodity, or to the merchandise thereof, that the whole prosperity of our land is conceived essentially to lie. And yet they are of no farther signification, than as constituting a mere train or progression of stepping stones to the very last or concluding act of the whole process, even that by which the consumer turns his purchased commodity to use or to enjoyment. This is the *terminus ad quem*, for which it was conveyed through the busy hands of a factory, and had to travel from one shop, and from one market to another, till it reached its final destination. Without this destination, all the preceding industry which had been expended on its preparation and conveyance, is but laborious idleness. And yet this last consequence, for which the whole apparatus was set agoing, is felt to be of no consequence. They lose sight of an article of trade on the moment that it enters the house of the consumer, because then all the game of trading and trafficking with it is over. Its benefit there, is deemed of little account by those who expatiate most on the blessings of commerce. They in fact regard commerce as a thing set up for the good of producers, and not of consumers. They look to the play of its mechanism, and not to that landing place, whither its products are ultimately carried, and where the whole purpose of commerce is fulfilled, by there directly ministering to the comfort and accommodation of man. The process, and not the end of the process, is all that is in view of the disciples of the mercantile system; and even they who have obtained emancipation from many of its errors, can occasionally manifest to what amount the residuum of its spirit still adheres to them.

For by combinations, or by any other cause, let there be a suspension in some quarter of the coal trade. It is on the stoppage in some anterior part of the process, and not on the suffering that is felt at the place where the process terminates, that a genuine disciple of the mercantile system will look. And even still, what is the spectacle which on such an occasion calls forth the chief notice and sympathy of Parliament? Not the loss or inconvenience that is sustained from the higher price of coals by the families of London. But what engrosses them most, is the spectacle of commerce at a stand, of vessels laid up, of capital lying idle, of a certain portion of the national industry being suspended, and the property of merchants and owners melting away, because not alimented by the wonted returns of profit. This carries in it to their eye, a far more louring aspect on the prosperity of the country, than all the abridgment which may have taken place in the fuel, and so in the household comfort of families. This last is regarded only as a private inconvenience, but the other as a public loss. There is a strange perversion of the judgment, certainly, in thus counting the means to be more valuable than the end; and hence grieving far more because of a diminution in the work of commerce, than because of a diminution in the only thing that commerce works for. But such is the nearly universal delusion of the country—a delusion in which Parliament fully shares, as is enough manifest, in that they feel a higher price, or a greater privation of coal in London to be a bagatelle, when compared with the calamity which hangs over the shipping interest in the Tyne.

To estimate the mischiefs of this suspended trade, we observe no examinations of the inconvenience sustained by consumers, but only of the loss sustained by producers. That is the quarter where the mighty evil is apprehended to lie. The distress, or the destitution of families from the want of coal, is not inquired into. It is only the derangement that has come upon capital, and upon the plans of capitalists from the want of the coal trade. In virtue of certain interruptions which this trade has been made to suffer, there is a limited supply of coal in the metropolis. That is the essential evil—and one should think that the way to ascertain its dimensions, would have been to call witnesses from the various ranks of citizenship there, as to the amount and soreness of the consequent privation. The natural investigation would have been into the degrees of hardship and of additional expense that it laid upon the humbler classes; and, perhaps, whether it had the effect of compelling any families to apply for aid from the parish. Had the Committee on the Combination Laws taken this direction, we should have had the fathers of poor families in London, and perhaps the overseers of its parishes, or managers of its work-houses, brought under a close questionary process. It was no doubt natural to look to the seat of that which was the origin of the mischief, with a view to the application of a remedy; and this may in part explain the peculiarity to which we are now adverting. But it is by no means the whole explanation. For, in truth, upon these topics our most enlightened men are exceedingly apt to look the wrong way ; to seek for information, not from the place where commerce lands her commodities, but from the place where commerce plies her machinery for the carriage and preparation of them. Any distress in the former place is not half so formidable to their imaginations, as a derangement in the latter place. Commerce, in truth, is regarded as an end, and not as an instrument. The wants of consumers are not in all their thoughts. The great engrossment is about the producers—the stoppage that has taken place in the processes of trade and manufactures—the withdrawment or transportation of capital—the disappearance, one after another, of the branches of our national industry.

It is further instructive to perceive by what kind of mischief a committee on mercantile affairs would be most impressed, when offered to their notice on the examination of witnesses. One evil of a suspended coal trade, is the privation, or the additional expense which it would lay on private families. But let this further evil be made out, that some manufactories, such as iron works in the neighbourhood, were in danger of being suspended. This second would be felt as the heavier calamity of the two. The evil to ultimate consumers of abridging their fuel, would be regarded as nothing when compared with the evil to producers of abridging or stopping the processes of their manufactory. And yet these processes, like all others in trade, are but processes of subserviency to the wants of consumers. Trace the progress of the evil in this ramification a little farther, and its whole amount is a privation, or a higher price to families, not of the fuel which upholds the fire, but of the grate which contains it, or the fire-irons which stir it, or the pots and pans which are laid upon it. Now, a legislature would never busy itself with this last consideration. It is only when the evil is in prospect or menace, through an interruption of the works, that it appears to be of national magnitude. When the evil has reached its consummation in the inconvenience to which customers are subjected, from a more limited supply of the things which are wrought, the whole of its national importance is dissipated.

The delusion is still more glaring when the article of trade is less essential to the comfort of families. Among many others who were examined on the effects of combination, there were manufacturers of shawls. There is enough of magnitude to fill the imagination in the shipping interest. But one can scarcely uphold in his mind any associations of greatness, or of public importance, with the shawl-making interest. Still it is a branch of fancy-work; and that again a branch of the general manufactures of the country. So that the making of shawls, and the making of toilinette waistcoats, and the making even of most frivolous toys, all merge into, and serve to swell the account of what in sound, and in appearance, at least, is sufficiently imposing—the manufactur-

ing interest. At all events there are a good many
hundred workmen employed in the fabrication of
shawls; and if they choose to strike, shawls will
cease for a time to be multiplied. Now, our simple position is, that the real good of these shawls
lies in the wearing of them, and not in the weaving of them. The whole "*cui bono?*" of this
manufacture, lies in the gratification of the taste
and fancy of the wearers; and the counterpart
evil to this, from the suspension of the manufacture, is the vexation or disappointment which
they must feel in not meeting with their wonted
supply. But were either the one seen to be the
whole good, or the other seen to be the whole
evil, the legislature would most certainly never
interpose at all in the matter; and that they actually do interpose, proceeds from their imagination
of a good in this and in all other manufactures,
distinct from the subservience of their products
to the use or the enjoyment of customers. There
were something grotesque and ridiculous in an
assembly of senators, sitting in grave deliberation
on the comfort of shawls, or the tastefulness of
fancy waistcoats; and, therefore, when they do
enter upon this subject, they never bestow one
thought upon the good which the supply of these
brings to the consumers: it is altogether upon the
good which the making of these brings to the
producers. They figure some sort of inherent
virtue in trade, that is separate from and independent of the enjoyment which lies in the use of its

commodities. They have elevated commerce from the state of a handmaid, to being the very goddess of their idolatry; and would anticipate something far more tremendous to the country, from the destruction of the shawl-making interest, than a negation to the country of shawls.

But it will be said, that the worth of a manufacture is not to be measured by the mere worth of the articles which are thrown off by it. It is contended, that there is something more of importance in it than this; and really something more is necessary to be made out, in order to vindicate the high place to which it has been exalted in the imagination of many a statesman, and the system of many an economist. For ourselves, we are not aware of one other earthly contribution which a shawl-maker renders to the interest of his country, than simply his shawls; or a stocking-maker, than just stockings; or a coach-maker, than coaches. These are the respective parts which they perform; *and they are their whole parts.* More has been ascribed to them; and though neither the glory nor the strength of a nation lies in its shawls, its stockings, or its coaches; yet both its glory and its strength have been conceived, as somehow bound up with the occupations of the men who are employed in making them. It is this which constitutes another and most inveterate of our delusions, that a manufacture does more for the public and political importance of the state, than simply furnish its own commodities for the gratification and use of the individuals who compose it. A false halo has thus been thrown around commerce; and not, we believe, till it be wholly dissipated, will legislators cease to meddle with that which they had far better let alone.

And herein it is that the delusion appears to lie. It is agreed, on all hands, that a manufacture does thus much for a country. It furnishes its own products for the accommodation of those who live in it. But, over and above these products, it is further conceived, that it calls into being the returns which it obtains for them. To the articles which it works off, and by which we would. measure its whole importance to the community, there are superadded the articles which are gotten in exchange for them; and it is precisely this superaddition, which gives to manufactures all the exaggerated importance that has been ascribed to them. In rating the worth of any one manufacture, we should make account, of nothing more, than simply the goods which it issues forth upon society. But, on their way thitherward, they have to pass through a market, and undergo the operation of a sale, when a value is given for a value that has been received. Now these two values are generally blended together in the imagination of the observer, and he credits the manufacture with both; first with its own produce, and then with the price that has been given for it. It is out of this price that masters are enabled to live in splendour, and workmen to live in decent sufficiency.

A thriving village is perhaps the result of it; or, however the dependent population may be arranged, there stands visibly associated with the manufacture, a flourishing groupe of cheerful and industrious families. The legislature would, in all probability, never let itself down to a deliberation, the sole object of which, was the due and regular supply, either of ladies with shawls, or of gentlemen with toilinette waistcoats. But that is no reason why it should not bestow its most anxious care, and give all the benefit of its wisdom to a matter that seems to involve in it the employment, and, along with the employment, the subsistence of many thousand members of the British commonwealth. It is neither in the shawls, nor yet in the waistcoats, where the national importance of the question is conceived to lie; but it is in the spectacle of so many human beings, whose whole revenue and support are linked with the fabrication of them—a revenue that forms, it is imagined, an integral part of the wealth, and a support, without which we should lose an integral part of the population of the empire.

In this whole process, the distinction is lost sight of, between the two sides of every mercantile transaction, so as that the separate functions are not adverted to; first, of the manufacturer who makes the article, and, secondly, of the purchaser who uses it. There is positively nothing but the article that comes from the side of the manufacturer; and maintenance, or the power of acquiring it, comes altogether from the side of the purchaser. There might be some derangement upon the one side, in virtue of which, the article is no longer forthcoming; but this can never send across, upon the other side, a devouring blight on the maintenance that was in readiness there to be discharged, as usual, in the purchase of the article. It may so happen, that in virtue of suspended work, or of now exhausted material, the article in question has disappeared from the market, and is nowhere to be found. But the maintenance that went for the article is still in reserve, as entire in the amount, and as effective in the support and sufficiency which it can diffuse through families as before. It will neither be destroyed, nor yet will it be suffered to lie idle. It will go forth, if not in the purchase of the old article, at least of some others; the preparation of which, will draw to it as many hands as were before employed in the manufacture that now has vanished from the land. We do not deny, that a temporary distress must be felt while this change in the distribution of the people is going on. Neither do we affirm, that the very individuals who have been discarded from that branch of industry which is now at an end, will all find a ready admittance, and as liberal a recompense as before, in such other branches as are sure to spring up or be extended. But we are sure that there is nought in the destruction of any one manufacture, which can at all impair the ability of those who want to purchase its commodities, and so to effuse both among masters and workmen, all the maintenance which they ever desired from their connection with it. This maintenance will go forth upon as great a population as before, in return for some new services; not, perhaps, for shawls, but for something else in their place. And after a short season of inconveniences, and disquietudes, and boding alarms, we shall behold the spectacle of as many industrious families, as well upheld in the comforts of life as before.

There is really too much of virtue attributed to a manufacture, when it is figured, that it both gives employment to a people, and gives them maintenance also. It gives employment, but it does not give maintenance. The fruit of the employment is a marketable commodity, and the maintenance which is given in return for it, comes from some other quarter of society, than from the manufactory where the employment was carried on. Although the manufactory should come to a cessation, the same amount of subsistence for human beings will spring up in that quarter as before. Shawls will cease to be produced; but that other produce, which wont to subsist the shawl makers, will come forth as abundantly as ever. And they who have a power or a property, in the first instance, over that produce, will not cease to transfer it to others as before, merely because there are no more shawls to be purchased. They who go a-shopping will be at no loss to spend as largely as they wont; and if they cannot find shawls, they will find something else on which to expend the price of them. In so doing, they give a shift to the employments of the people. They do not support less of industry than before—they only impress a new direction upon it; so that, in place of the thousands of shawl-makers, we shall have as many thousands employed in the preparation of certain other articles of taste or convenience. With every fluctuation in the demand of customers, there will be a corresponding fluctuation in the direction of industry; but that, without ultimately affecting either the amount of work that is required, or the amount of wages which are paid for it. And, if the Legislature would only weather the period of transition, with all its uncertainties and fears, they should at length find with what safety they might abstain from all interference: sure as it is to terminate in as great an abundance as ever, discharged on as great a population.

Our Legislature would be less tremulously alive upon this subject, were the calamity of a suspended, or even an annihilated manufacture, reduced to its proper dimensions. It is only a shift, and not a substraction. It is apprehended to be the latter; and hence as prompt an alarm on the part of government, as if on the eve of having a portion of the British territory wrested away from us. Were it, on the other hand, perceived to be only the former, government would remain at quiet, amid the slight internal agitations that were

caused by the disappearance of an old manufacture, and the substitution of a new one as great
in its room. It would acquiesce in the new distribution of its family, could it only be satisfied,
that it was to remain as great and as prosperous
a family as before; and that, after the transition
had been undergone, not one fraction of its own
strength or importance had forsaken it.

These statements, though general, have a direct application upon the present question. When
a manufacture stops, an alarm is felt for the stability of the manfacturing interest; and because,
through the mistiness of those indistinct apprehensions which we have endeavoured to expose,
the importance of this interest has been most
unduly magnified, a consequent alarm is felt for
the strength and the vital prosperity of our nation. It would mitigate the alarm, could the
precise nature of the mischief be clearly understood—even that all which the nation loses, is its
wonted supply of those goods which the manufactory issued, and that, at the very worst, it has
no other character than that of an inconvenience
to families, more or less tolerable, according to
the kind of that commodity whose fabrication has
for a time been suspended. It loses for a season
the employment of the men who have struck, or
rather, the fruits of their employment. But it has
not lost the maintenance of the men. If consumers cannot obtain their wonted gratifications,
the price of them remains in their pockets; and

the maintenance which this price, in the hands of workmen and their families, would have called forth, remains in the storehouses of the nation. The country sustains no other suffering than that which we have mentioned. It is as full of power for the subsistence of men, and has within its limits the same rewards and encouragements by which to stimulate their industry, as before. If the public can afford to want the products of their industry, there are none who seriously suffer but the foolish men themselves who choose to be idle for a little, and so will not take that support and nourishment which the country has to give them, and which lies in reserve, to be discharged again upon them, when they return to their wonted occupation. And even though they should, in hard and heroic obstinacy, resolve rather to starve than to surrender, the nation will survive in as great vigour as before, the loss both of them and of their services. That aliment which they refused, will still continue to be produced and to be poured forth in as great abundance from its granaries as ever. And still, after the little hour of effervescence and of fear, which their discontents may have occasioned, will the old spectacle be restored, of an industrious population as great, and a maintenance as liberal, spread abroad among all its families.

In reference to all those manufactures where combination is practicable, Nature has given such superiority to the purchasers over the producers, that, for the protection of the former from the latter, it seems quite unnecessary for law to interfere. In agriculture, there is less danger to be apprehended of a strike among the labourers, than even of a combination among the capitalists; and it will in general be found, that, when a conspiracy among workmen for higher wages can be most easily formed and supported on the one side, then the article wrought can be most easily dispensed with on the other. It is not difficult to perceive which of the two parties has the advantage in this contest, and whether the public, on the one hand, can hold longer out with the want of the manufactured commodity, or the workmen with the want of their maintenance. There are forces in operation, and which are enough of themselves to decide this question against the labourers. It is a pity that government should step forward with a show of hostility, and anticipate the result. The terrors of a poverty that is growing apace, and looking more ghastly by every day of their perseverance in a state of idleness; at length, their own sensations of hunger, and the cries of their famishing children,—these are the guarantees of a sure and speedy termination to the warfare. The wisdom of government is forbearance. Save for the interests of obvious and substantial justice, they should leave Trade to the unfettered play of its own mechanism; and, secure in the consciousness that the basis of our nation's prosperity is more deeply founded than to be within the reach of its fluctuations, they should cease to feel as an interested party, and leave the determination of this controversy between the manufacturers and customers, to those who are immediately concerned.

On this question, then, we should feel less inclined to defer to the alarm of capitalists, than to the alarm of their customers—of those who fabricate, or who deal in any of the articles of trade, than of those who consume them. One can imagine of the operatives who make the shoes, that they might cease from work, and hold out so long as to bring a real inconvenience upon all who wear them. And the more that the article approaches to a necessary of life, the greater is the inconveniency that might be felt; as if, for example, a whole city population were subjected, from such a cause, to an artificial scarcity of coals. This alarm, on the part of the purchasers or the users of a commodity, is altogether distinct from the alarm of its manufacturers or venders, and is therefore entitled to a distinct consideration.

In reference, then, to those articles which are not of prime necessity, it will at once be perceived, how unequal the conflict is between the maker and the consumer. The former depend upon the latter for their whole income; and, so soon as by the cessation of their work any accumulated capital has been melted away, this dependence becomes urgent and immediate; and they can hold out no longer in the want of all subsistence for themselves and their families. Whereas the latter depend on the former, only for the product of their industry, which, by the supposition, not being indispensable to the support of human life, can for any indefinite season be dispensed with. The workmen, for example, of a toy manufacture, could never starve the public into a compliance with their terms, but would themselves be starved in time out of all their refractoriness, by a public resolved against the extravagance of their demands. This applies more or less to every species of work, when the thing wrought did not essentially enter into the maintenance of those who purchased it. They can keep aloof from the purchase, whenever they feel the price to be exorbitant. They who purchase have a clear superiority over those who prepare the article. The former can want the article. The latter cannot long want the employment, for their employment is to them the vehicle of all the necessaries of life which are brought to their doors.

Even in regard to many of the more necessary trades, the determination of customers not to pay more than a certain price, can far outlast the determination of the workmen not to work for less than a certain wage. Let the instance be again taken from shoes, and a competition of this kind be imagined between those who make shoes, and those who wear them; a competition, it will be observed, between the single want of one party, and that not for a first, but a second necessary of life, and all the wants of the other party for all the articles whatever of human comfort and subsistence. Even a single pair, with all its capacities of being patched and prolonged, though by household hands, for months together, could give enough of advantage in this very unequal contest; and still more, if there was aught like the possession of a decent stock: an expedient, by the way, whereby the wealthier classes might arm themselves, in all time coming, against all that appears most frightful in this bugbear of combination. By enlarging somewhat their various stocks of consumption—by means of an additional outlay on all their present stores, whether in the cellars, or the wardrobe, or the outhouses, they strengthen and prepare themselves for any future warfare of this kind. It will be found, that by this simple arrangement, an arrangement, too, which naturally follows in the train of advancing wealth, there is raised an effectual defence against that indefinite power, wherewith it may be dreaded that a growing capital would invest the working classes of our land. It would reduce itself to a contest of endurance between one species of accumulation and another; and it is not difficult to estimate with which of the parties the inducement would be strongest to terminate the contest—whether with the workmen, from whom every day of idleness would take away a portion of their general means, and so make them poorer than before, or with the customers, who, in the season of some outstanding trade, were only becoming more bare and destitute in some one article of human enjoyment. We feel, indeed, as if it were a vain expenditure of argument, to reason at all upon any such distant anticipation. But we deem it of the utmost practical importance, that legislators should feel a greater confidence than they are often inclined to do, in its own proper workings of the mechanism of human society; and that when they brood over the apprehended mischiefs of a strike among taylors, or masons, or house-carpenters, they would bethink themselves of the natural correctives which are already provided against it, in the very state and composition of the body politic. It should be enough to lull their disquietude, that it is far easier for the public at large to put up for months with such clothes, or houses, or furniture as they have, than it were for the operatives in these branches of industry, to put up for the same time with an utter suspension of all revenue.

And it is comfortable, as one goes in detail over the various articles which enter into the maintenance of a family, to perceive that those which are most indispensable are also most beyond the reach of being rendered artificially dear by means of combinations. Of those articles to the fabrication of which a long apprenticeship is necessary, and for the making of which, therefore, in the event of a strike, we cannot draw on the general population, there are many which have such a dura-

bility in themselves as will enable their possessors to stand out any season of combination that
shall be at all practicable for the workmen. This
applies particularly to furniture and houses, the
customers in which cannot be reduced to a total
destitution of them so soon as the workmen would
be reduced to a total destitution of the necessaries
of life. There are other workmanships, which,
though abandoned by the regular operatives, can
be served in such a way by domestic industry, or
by more general labourers, as must at least hasten
the breaking up of a combination. It is so with
the mending, and even making, of all sorts of apparel; and as to that most important commodity,
fuel, we have recent and most satisfactory experience, for the facility wherewith the transition
can be made, by people drawn at random from
other branches of industry to that of working in a
coal mine. And then, as to the very first of human necessaries, as to the supply of food, or agricultural produce, there is nought more palpable
than the readiness wherewith men of any, or of all
works, can be turned to field labour. There is
less, we are sure, to be apprehended from a strike
of ploughmen than of any other class of operatives
whatever. For, besides the ease wherewith they
could be replaced, there is the difficulty wherewith they could be associated for any general or
concerted plan of operation among themselves.
The same obstacles, which have been so well and
forcibly represented by Dr. Smith, against a com-

bination of farmers for a rise in the price of grain, exist in much greater strength against a combination of farm servants for a rise in the price of country labour. There could be no common understanding established among men so spread as they are over the whole surface of the land. It is among congregated, and not among widely diffused workmen, that such plans are hatched and brought into any degree of maturity; so that, save for the one purpose of interposing against crime and violence, there seems no call upon Government to meddle in the rivalry between workmen and their employers. In the case of luxuries, the public interest does not require any such interference; and, indeed, there is, in this instance, a control on the part of customers over workmen, to which the whole of the adjustment between them might very safely be left. In the most important necessaries, there are other, and still more effective securities against the damage that might be apprehended from such combinations; and the security is most complete of all in the article of food, that prime and vital necessary which is the most indispensable of all.

But there is another aspect of mischief in these combinations that is apt to alarm our legislature. In the suspension of so many works, they not only apprehend the disappearance from our land of so much industry; they further apprehend the loss or the disappearance of so much capital. The one we hold to be a bugbear, insomuch as we deem the essential evil of the stoppage to lie in the cessation, for a time, of the products of industry, and never in the cessation of a power to maintain the producers. They choose to become outcasts for a season, from the benefits of this power; and so to bring upon themselves the hardships of an increasing poverty, and, at length, the sufferings of penury and starvation. On the side of the consumers, there is an inconvenience that can be borne with. On the side of the producers, there is a hard and ever-growing necessity, that must at length compel a surrender; and when the surrender is made by a return, on their part, to their wonted employments, they will just come back again to the fountains of sustenance which they had forsaken, and find them as generous and abundant as before. To the one party there has been a stagnation of their wonted enjoyments. To the other, there has been a period of severe but salutary discipline, which we should like to see fully accomplished; and without interference, if possible, by the hand of authority. We think that labourers would come forth of the trial, wiser and better than before; and that after having made full proof of their own favourite expedient, and found its inefficacy, they would be far more effectually schooled into a state of quiescence, than by all the terrors of legislation. The petty fermentations which are now in progress over the empire, will never amount to a storm that shall overthrow the fabric of its economic prosperity; but will rather demonstrate the stability of that basis upon which it is reared. The experience that should be earned in this way, would put a most impressive mockery on the dark conjurations of many philosophers and many statesmen.

But the other we hold to be a bugbear also. We have just as little to apprehend for the destruction of a nation's capital from these combinations, as for the ultimate disappearance or diminution of a nation's industry. The one delusive fear, however, is fully as inveterate as the other; and, accordingly, in the Report by the Select Committee on the Combination Laws, we find a strongly expressed alarm, lest " capital be withdrawn, or transported ;" and so, lest " the source of every branch of our industry should gradually be cut off, and the whole labouring population of the country consigned to the distress and misery, which it is the tendency of the ill-advised combinations, in which so great a portion of it is implicated, rapidly and inevitably to produce."

This introduction of capital into the argument, suggests a new topic of alarm. It serves to complicate, and so to cast an obscurity over the whole subject. We know how closely associated fear is with indistinct vision; and in as far as the import and the precise function of capital are dimly apprehended, in so far is the mind liable to dread and to disturbance, from the imagination of any hazard to which it may be exposed. Were the darkness that hangs over this quarter of economic speculation dispersed, these spectres would fly away along with it. It is the mist that lies spread over certain departments of political science, which so magnifies the terrors of our political alarmists, and this by distorting to their vision the real shape and magnitude of things. On no subject has this been more signally manifested than on that of capital; and we even think that the views here of our most celebrated economists, have a tendency to nurture a false alarm rather than to appease it.

One thing is obvious, that after capital is formed, it is the lure of a profit which draws it to any employment; and it is the continuance of that profit which detains it there. But this profit is just an ingredient of the price that is rendered for those commodities, on the preparation of which. for the market, the capital is vested. The profit of the master is just as resolvable into an antecedent ability on the part of his customers, as are the wages of his workmen. The one channel through which the wealth of these customers found its way, carrying both to labourers their remuneration, and to capitalists their gain—this channel may be obstructed for a season; but it is one thing to shift the conveyance of wealth, and altogether another thing to annihilate it. The price that wont to be given by a family for shawls, if shawls are no longer to be had, is in reserve for some other article of expenditure; and in the purchase of that article, it will pass onward, and contribute as liberally to profit, and as liberally to wages as before. We are quite aware of the temporary inconvenience which attends every change in the direction either of capital or industry. But we are not to confound this evil with that of a total disappearance, and so a permanent diminution either of the one or other in our land. So long as the agriculture is as productive, and so the first necessaries of life are as abundant as before, capital will be as fully replaced, and labourers as abundantly recompensed as before. The fund for both is in every way as efficient—even that fund, which consisting as it does of the indispensable aliment of human life, is both that which calls a population into being, and impresses any direction that the holders of it will upon their industry. If this great primary source flow with the same copiousness, then the wealth of its holders is of the same force, both to replace stock, and to remunerate labour. The tide of it may be diverted, but neither the amount nor the strength of it is taken away; and when either the suspension of any manufacture is ended, or the shift from it to another is made out, we behold as flourishing a merchandise, both for masters and workmen, as ever.

We are aware, that what we count a delusion on the subject of capital, has been very much fostered by the speculations of Dr. Adam Smith, who every where speaks of capital as the fruit of a laborious parsimony; and who imagines, that if by any cause a portion is taken away from the trading capital of our nation, a new course of painstaking accumulation must be entered upon, till in a series of years, perhaps, we recover that fulness from which we had been reduced. Still he regards the departure of that capital, which has now to be replaced by the strenuous economy of our more industrious and sober-minded citizens, as a permanent loss to the nation; for, had it remained with us, we might still have had the benefit of those savings by which it has been made up, and so we might have had two capitals instead of one. It is this which in his eye constitutes the chief evil of our national debt, by which he conceives that so much of capital has been absorbed, and for ever lost to the nation. He calculates how much richer the country would have been, with a sum of so many millions still performing the functions of a capital; and in that capacity dispensing such an amount of revenue to its owners, and of subsistence to the people whose revenue was upheld by it. It is not to be wondered at, then, if the disciples of this great economist—the habitual and unquestioning followers in the train of such a speculation as this, should read the approaching downfal of a nation in the disappearance, by successive portions of its mercantile capital. Those enlightened ministers who proceed so fearlessly on his whole doctrine of free trade, do no more than catch the alarm of their master; when, associating with the combinations of workmen the withdrawment from the country of one branch of capital after another, they anticipate as the still gloomier consequence, " that the source of every branch of our industry will gradually be cut off; and the whole labouring population of the country be consigned to distress and misery."

We hold that there is much of exaggeration in these forebodings; but to demonstrate our views of the subject, we shall have recourse to examples. Let a capitalist, with ten thousand pounds, have his money all vested in some of the simpler manufactures, as that of bricks. We specify this, as being one of those that require almost no fixed capital, and that can chiefly be carried on by means of a circulating one. The money thus laid out is repaid to him with a profit; so that, at the end of the year, he may find himself in possession of eleven thousand pounds; of which he may appropriate one thousand as revenue to his personal or. family uses, and embark the ten thousand in his business, as before. Or, instead of this, we might conceive him, at this point, to be suddenly transformed into a spendthrift, that greatest enemy, as he is represented by Dr. Smith, of the public interest. He may be seized by a fit of extravagance, and squander the whole of his eleven thousand pounds in the course of the ensuing twelvemonth. By this proceeding, there is certainly so much of capital effaced from the country. An integral portion of that capital which was vested in the employment of brick-making, is now withdrawn from it. A fund, out of which a certain population obtained the wages of their industry, and a certain addition was made to the annual produce of the labour of the country, has now been dissipated. The prevalent conception is, that the country is thrown permanently aback by such an event; and that, though it should recover the distance which it has lost, it is by means of a force of parsimony, which, had there been no loss to repair, would have carried the country permanently forward. Now, we think it easy to demonstrate, that the deficiency could be made up in another way; and that, without any greater parsimony on the part of other brick-makers, or without any influx of capital to this manufacture from without. We hold, that ere a single year pass by, the capital embarked upon this business will regain its former extent, and so be of avail to maintain as liberally the same number of labourers, who shall work off the same produce as before.

To make this palpable, let us imagine that there has been withdrawn for a year from the business of brick-making, some sensible proportion, as one tenth of the capital that had been vested in it. There are two ways in which this deficiency may be made up; and in one or other, or both these ways, the certainty is, that it will be so made up in the course of a twelvemonth. By the disappearance of this portion of capital, there are so many men thrown loose from employment. The same master can no longer hire them; for the fund out of which he paid their wages is no longer in existence. They will, therefore, go in quest of other masters; and we may first conceive that they offer themselves to those in the same trade. This would be the natural direction for them to take; and in which case, we should behold the competition of workmen for employment from a smaller capital than can well afford to maintain them. The capital engaged in brick-making has been reduced to nine tenths of what it was; and on this diminished capital, the discarded workmen, to the amount of one tenth of the whole number, are seeking for admittance. A general reduction of wages must ensue; and, although it is not necessary to our argument, yet, in point of truth, this reduction would greatly exceed the fraction by which the capital has declined. In other words, the remaining masters would be able, and more than able, to enlist into their service the same number of labourers as were employed in the preceding year; and upon this capital, though diminished to nine tenths of what it was, the same quantity of bricks is still brought to market. But on the supply being the same, and the demand the same, (and there has nothing happened which should lessen the demand,) the price of this article will continue as before. In other words, the masters of the present year have as large an aggregate return upon their reduced capital, that the masters of the former year had upon their full capital. If ten thousand pounds be taken from one tenth of the whole capital that wont to be engaged in the business of brick-making, then the aggregate capital of the former year was an hundred thousand, and the aggregate return, by our hypothesis, of the profit, must have been an hundred and ten thousand pounds. But this return, consisting, as it does, of the whole market-price of the bricks, is just as great in the second year as the first. The same number of men is employed on reduced wages. The same quantity of bricks is wrought off, and the same prices given for them. There comes in the same sum of a hundred and ten thousand pounds as before; and the remaining capitalists of ninety thousand pounds, have not only this old capital with the old profit replaced to them; but, over and above, they have returned into their hands both the capital and profit of him who had squandered away his property, and so was forced to retire from the business. It is thus that the capital which had disappeared re-appears; and that not by any strenuousness of accumulation on the part of the remaining capitalists, but by the operation of a simple economic law. By a force, as unfailing as that of a hydrostatic pressure, the capital, in a few months, rises to its wonted level; and becomes as commensurate to the business as before. And the men, after a year of depression, are now met again by a capital as large, and may be restored to wages as large.

The capital in this case is repaired at the expense of one year's reduced wage to the labourers. The deficiency that had been created costs them a year of sufferings and privations, ere it can be made up. This is a mischief, we admit; but it is the whole mischief; and, after the straitening or the hardship of a short season, leaves no further trace behind it. It is a mistake, that the want of capital, occasioned by the extravagance of one master, must be atoned for by the parsimony of the rest. To them it is followed up by a season of prosperity; and the fruit of this prosperity is, that they become the possessors of that capital which their brother in the trade had dissipated. At all events, the capital is fully built up again; and by a process which demonstrates how little the care and the effort of a legislature are requisite to assist that law in the mechanism of trade, which ensures both its speedy and its complete restoration.

But, should this process fail, there is still another, by which a shrunk or a reduced capital is sure to be expanded to its former dimensions. The workmen who had been discarded from brick-making, in virtue of the fund which sustained them being dissipated, might not think of trying to obtain service from the remaining masters in the trade. They might seek about for other employments, and be merged into the general population. The remaining capitalists in the brick manufacture continue with their old labourers; and, having just the same number of men, and the same capital in their hands as before, they will employ them on the same wages. It is not, therefore, from the fall of wages, that they in this case will obtain any extension of their capital.; but there is another source from which they will obtain it. They can only work up the same number of bricks which they did on the preceding year; or, in other words, from the disappearance of so much capital and industry in their line of trade, there is only nine tenths of the usual quantity brought to market, upon the whole. But there is nothing in the state of things which we now suppose, that can affect the rate of demand. Purchasers will go in quest of the same quantity as before, but will only meet with nine tenths of the amount that would satisfy them. The effect of this is, a competition on the part of the customers, and a rise in the price of the article. It may not be easy to compute the proportion which the increase of price will bear to the short-coming of the supply. This will depend on the place which the article possesses in the scale of comforts or necessaries. We know that in the case of a first necessary, the rise of price would greatly exceed in proportion the deficiency of the supply; and that if grain were deficient by one tenth from its usual abundance, there might be a rise of at least one third in its usual price. Bricks would not rise in so high a proportion; but, it is likely, higher than by one tenth. But let us only assign to it the average rise of one tenth; or, in other words, that, although the supply falls short by one tenth of what it used to be, yet that, in virtue of its augmented price, the same money is expended by all the customers that there used to be. We shall still have in this second case, the aggregate return of £110,000 to the remaining brickmasters. From this source, they will have, as before, their old capital and profit replaced to them, along with the capital and its profit, which the extravagance of their now retired colleague in the business had swept off from the employ. And all this, without any extraordinary forcing upon their part. The want of capital is filled up by an influx from without, just as water flows in to fill up a vacuum. It is not they who work this effect; but the laws of the economic machine work it for them. They are the passive subjects of a prosperity which they have not caused. They have become, as before, the proprietors of that fortune which their companion had dissipated; and, just as before, in the course of a few months, their trade is reinstated in that full capital which had been previously embarked upon it. The supply of the article will again be enlarged with this enlargement of the capital; and on the price again falling to the average of profits in the country, this trade will settle down to its even and ordinary tenor.

In the first way of it, the capital is repaired at the expense of the labourers. In the second way of it, it is repaired at the expense of the consumers. Whether in either way exclusively, or (which will happen most frequently) by a mixture of them both, it will recover, and in a single year, the magnitude from which it had fallen. We deny not the evil which there is, in workmen, for even this short period, being compelled to subsist on inferior wages. Neither can we deny the evil which there is, in the country, for the same period, being compelled to put up with a scantier supply of those conveniences which are suited to it. All we affirm is, that these are the only evils; and that they are not such as entitle them to all that anxious care wherewith our legislature, in the brooding anticipation of evils still more dire and irremediable, professes to watch over the preservation and entireness of our national capital. The due increase of capital may in fact, with all safety, be confided to the force of its own native and essential buoyancy. This certainly is not a consideration for which any obvious principle, either of freedom, or of natural justice, ought to be sacrificed; and just ranks among many other of those economic interests which governments are prone to meddle with, but which they had better let alone.

These processes for the almost immediate reproduction of extinguished capital, explain what, in the eyes of Dr. Smith and others, is a seeming mystery *—the sufficiency, or rather the super-

---

* " During the course even of the most expensive wars, the frugality and good conduct of individuals seem to have been able, by saving and accumulation, to repair all the breaches which the waste and extravagance of Go-

abundance of capital, in spite of its great absorptions by the national debt. The sum of ten thousand pounds may have been withdrawn from the brick manufacture, by the owner of it becoming a subscriber to a public loan; and, although one tenth of the capital vested in this employment had been thus removed from it, there is nothing in this that will, immediately at least, lessen the demand of the country for bricks. Even when in the progress of taxation and of public debt, the revenue of private consumers comes to be shared in larger proportion by government and the creditors of the nation, the joint expenditure of all those parties among whom it is divided, will set the same amount of industry in motion, or give maintenance to as great a number of servants, as

---

vernment had made in the general capital of the society. At the conclusion of the late war, the most expensive that Great Britain ever waged, her agriculture was as flourishing, her manufactories as numerous and as fully employed, and her commerce as extensive, as they had ever been before. The capital, therefore, which supported all those different branches of industry, must have been equal to what it had ever been before. Since the peace, agriculture has been still further improved; the rents of houses have risen in every town and village of the country, a proof of the increasing wealth and revenue of the people; and the annual amount of the greater part of the old taxes, of the principal branches of the excise and customs, in particular, has been continually increasing; an equally clear proof of an increasing consumption, and, consequently, of an increasing produce, which could alone support that consumption. Great Britain seems to support with ease, a burden, which, half a century ago, nobody believed her capable of supporting. Let us not, however, upon this account, rashly suppose that she is capable of supporting any burden; nor, even be too confident that she could support, without great distress, a burden a little greater than what has already been laid upon her."—*Smith's Wealth of Nations*, Book V. chap. iii.

when more of that revenue was untouched by the impositions of the state, and permitted to remain in the hands of its original proprietors. At all events, the capital absorbed by the national debt is replaced by the same speedy operations with the capital that has been dissipated by extravagance. When a proportion of capital is thus withdrawn from any employment, either the wages of labour in that employment fall, by so many of the now disengaged workmen being unwilling to leave it, or the article which they prepare is manufactured in less quantity, and so rises in price. From one or other, or both of these sources, the capital is again dilated to its former bulk with the force and almost with the speed of elasticity, so as to be as commensurate as before to the demand which there is for its products, to the business which it is called upon to do. And, accordingly, it is quite palpable, that no sooner was capital withdrawn from the trade of the country to its funds, than its place has been filled up again; that, in spite of its immense absorption, it has never fallen behind the business of the nation, but rather overcrowded and pressed upon it; and now that the absorption has ceased, instead of a season of accumulation being needed, in order to recruit, as from a process of exhaustion, the commerce of our land through all its branches, absolutely labours under a weight of capital greater than it well can bear. We see throughout no privation of capital, but rather every symptom of a plethora. We nowhere see any employment, that wears even the remotest likelihood of a decent return, languishing, or at a stop for the want of capital; but everywhere we see capital at a loss for the want of employment. It now riots in sportive abundance among all sorts of chimerical enterprizes and wild imaginations. And this exuberance of capital, after that it had been drawn upon to the extent of nearly a thousand millions, speaks most decisively to some vast creative and multiplying power by which it is sustained.

We are aware, that this view does not harmonize, nay, that it may be in jarring contrariety with the political economy of those whose habits of thought and of speculation have been moulded by the study of the most approved writers in the science. Certain it is, that Smith seems not to have adverted to this sudden re-ascent of capital, when a portion of it has been dissipated either by the extravagance of its individual holders, or by their having become creditors, in consequence of what he would term the extravagance of the nation. And yet the way in which it regains its former magnitude, *per saltum*, and not by any slow or laborious process of accumulation, may be clearly educed from those elementary principles that have been so well illustrated by this great master. It is, in fact, the immediate consequence of that re-action which a variation of capital has upon profit. Let a part of the capital vested in any business, (the extent of which is measured by a demand exoteric to the

business itself,) be lopped away ; and then, both
from a fall of wages in that business, and from a
rise in the price of that article which it brings to
market, but whose supply is lessened for a time,
profits rise, and sink not to their former rate, till
the capital resumes the extent from which it had
been reduced. It is true that this process may
be anticipated by a rush of capital from other
quarters ; and then, instead of a sensible oscillation in one branch of trade, there will be a slight
oscillation in several, after which the old state both
of capital and profits will be restored. But it is
by an oscillation, and that a pretty quick one too,
that the re-adjustment is made. And it has this
property of an oscillation belonging to it, that, in
proportion to the wideness of the deviation which
has been made, is the regressive force that carries
capital back again to its old state of quiescence.
The more that capital is lessened in any trade,
whose commodities are as largely and effectively
demanded as before, the higher are the profits of
it raised, and a greater impulse towards a recovery
brought to bear upon it. It is thus that a nation's
capital is fitted to survive the disturbance and the
rough handling, from which many would apprehend its deadly overthrow; and that it re-attains
the bulk from which it had been at any time contracted, with almost the speed of an explosion.

In Dr. Smith's chapter on the Division of Stock,
he describes what may be termed the great economic cycle which is performed by the annual pro-

duce of the land, and labour of the country. In the course of its revolution, this produce is distributed into three parts. One part goes to repair the fixed capital. Another part goes to replace the circulating capital; and a third part enters into the stock that is reserved for immediate consumption. It is certainly possible, that during the revolution of one year, the consumption may be unduly extended, so as that too much of the produce shall go to the third part, at the expense of the other two; and so both the fixed capital may be impaired, and the circulating capital may be diminished. This distinctly took place with our brick-master, when he forsook his business, and squandered on his own personal gratifications the ten thousand pounds, wherewith he wont to pay the annual wages of those in his employ; and it would have alike taken place, had he, instead of continuing in the trade, lent the money which was vested in it to government. In either case, it is that year transferred from the circulating capital to the stock of immediate consumption; being either consumed by himself in dissipation, or consumed by the servants of the state, the fruit of whose labour does not reappear in the shape of a capital for the support of future labour, instead of being consumed by the servants of a manufactory, the product of whose labour will command a price that is to purchase and maintain their labour for the year which is to come. All this undoubtedly takes place for that year—an increase of unproductive consumption—a diminution of capital. But in the very next revolution of the cycle, there is a restorative process which brings all right again, and that, whether with the now diminished capital, there is the same work performed for less wages, or less work for the same wages. In the one case, less of the annual produce than before is consumed on the personal and household expenses of labourers. In the other case, a smaller product is served out to customers than before, in return for that price by which dealers are enabled to recruit their capital: even that product, which, turned to immediate use by its purchasers, may be regarded as entering into the stock for their consumption. It is thus, that if, on the preceding revolution, too much of the produce may have passed from capital into consumption, on the next revolution, it will, by a sure economic law, vibrate back again from consumption into capital. In other words, there is a *vis medicatrix* in the economic machine itself, that should supersede much of that anxiety which legislators have expended on it; and in virtue of which it is, that much of their vigilance, and many of their labours are uncalled for. It is a want of confidence in this, that has wholly misplaced their care, and wholly misled their policy on many questions of commercial legislation. It is true, that on most of these topics, they have now ceased to be sensitive. But they are still sensitive on the subject of capital; and, in their treatment of this very question of combinations, we can perceive the fearful imagination of certain irrevocable evils that will ensue, should either the functions of capital for a time be suspended, or a portion of capital itself be forced, in some season of difficulty and embarrassment, to take its departure away from our borders.

But before proceeding to this application, it might be right to allege something further, in illustration of our general views on the subject of capital. Although the waste created by an occasional extravagance, on the part of a few individuals, can thus easily be repaired, does it follow, that capital is indestructible by any amount or degree of extravagance whatever? Even though it has maintained itself against the most expensive wars, and borne up under the oppression of a large public debt, every shilling of which was abstracted from capital, are we thence to infer, that no process of abstraction can be set agoing, which might utterly exhaust it? Must there not be a limit to the possibility of capital thus surviving the adverse influences which are brought to bear upon it; and though, at a certain rate of bleeding, it may keep as strong and healthy as ever, may it not still be made to bleed so profusely, as gradually to consume away, and finally to expire?

But though we must admit, that there is a possible way of bringing on the decay, and at length the extinction of a nation's capital, it does not therefore follow, that there should be any practical alarm of such an event, as at all probable, or like to be realized. There is just the same possibility, and might be the same alarm, on the subject of population. A war could be imagined of utter extermination in the country, or a pestilence which might carry off the last man of its inhabitants. But history has scarcely, if ever, given authentic record of such a war, or of such a pestilence; and, in point of experience, after almost all the actual visitations of this sort, we have witnessed in a few years the population so replenished, and made up again, as to have presented no voids or vacancies, as vestiges of the many thousands that had fallen. Such is the expansive force of population, that it has now ceased to be the care of our rulers, or rather their care has of late taken the opposite direction. There is no alarm lest the numbers should not keep up to the subsistence. The anxiety is, that they shall keep within the subsistence. At all events, the old policy upon this subject has been completely superseded. It is no longer conceived of population, that it needs the fostering hand of a legislature, for the purpose either of augmenting it, or of keeping it up to that amount which the country's good shall render expedient. We do not hear, as formerly, either of checks to emigration, or of fears lest disease should waste away the inhabitants of our land.—Neither would it now be one of the arguments against a new war, that it might permanently bring down the population of our empire, and so inflict an irrecoverable damage on this great element of national prosperity and strength. We are now familiarized to other views upon this subject, and have become satisfied of the force and facility wherewith the population repairs the inroads that are made upon it. An unwonted mortality, caused by the ravages of an epidemic in one year, is followed by an unwonted number of births through two or three succeeding years. And so of the ravages in any country of our most desolating wars. And so also of the drain that is caused by a continued efflux of our people in the way of emigration. It would just create space for a larger influx in the way of births; and the influx would take place accordingly. It is conceivable, nay, possible, that there may be such an epidemic as shall wholly depopulate our land—and such a war as may turn it into a wilderness—and such an emigration as may leave it altogether empty: but practically, we do not stand in dread of any such; and so population has ceased to be one of those topics which influence the calculations or the measures of government, in the way that it used to do. It has now become one of those interests, for which those apprehensions are no longer felt, that wont to embarrass and mislead the policy of our rulers. It is found to have a *vis medicatrix* of its own, which requires no helping hand from any other quarter. There can be no question as to the individual suffering which disease, and war, and even emigration, bring in their train; but their effect on the general aggregate of a country's population is but slight even at the time, and can easily be recovered; and as it is with aggregates that a legislature have properly to do, they have begun to regard population as one of those self-regulating interests, from which it is far better that the regulations or encouragements of the state should be altogether withdrawn.

It is not so yet with capital. This is another of our economic interests, which has been the subject of kindred alarm, and we think fully as groundless as any of those which were felt aforetime on the subject of population. There is a like expansive force with both; in virtue of which, each in every given state of a country's progress, will be of that magnitude which the country can best sustain, and in all seasons will vary just at the rate which is best suited to the country's circumstances. A superabundance of food will afford room for large families by which to increase the population. A superabundance of business, created by the wants of this growing population, will afford large profits by which to increase the capital. There is no danger of either not keeping pace, and by its own proper forces, with the natural course of things; and it were just as unwise to force a capital upon a business whose profits could not afford an adequate return, as to force a population upon a country whose food could not afford an adequate subsistence. The food will certainly draw a population; and the population under a system of secure property and equitable laws, will as certainly draw a capital after it. The legislature have been led to regard the one, but not yet the other, in the light of a self-regulating interest. They are still haunted by the visions of a diminished, or of a departing capital. They do not yet apprehend, as in population, the sufficiency of those restorative forces, by which it is not only kept up to that amount which is most for the advantage of the country, but by which, like population, it tends to an overplus. The views still, in fact, of our best economic writers, have led them to regard capital more as a leader, than as a follower in the train of national prosperity—more as the creator of that prosperity, than as itself the creation of it. They do not yet perceive, when a vacancy is formed in capital, how instantly there are forces set agoing by which it can be filled up again, as surely as a vacuum in Nature by a collapse of the surrounding atmosphere. They fear, lest, with any inroad on capital, there shall be an inroad on all those economic interests which constitute the strength and fulness of a nation; and this fear still continues to embarrass a policy which has now been emancipated from the thraldom of many other fears. If this were to appear in any question at all, it was most natural that it should on a question between masters and workmen. There is no longer the apprehension now, lest our nation should suffer from the declining numbers of the latter; but there is the apprehension still, that it may suffer from the declining capital of the former. The one we hold to be as much a bugbear as the other; and in this controversy between the two parties, we should regret if government were to be misled by any bugbear, from the path of evenhanded justice between them.

They are now in full possession of the confidence, that population will soon recover itself from the horrors of war or of disease, or will maintain itself under the copious and repeated draughts of a system of emigration. But so also will capital. The armies that, in passing over the face of a territory, should destroy one third of the capital of clothiers, will leave the soil in possession of all its capabilities; and, when the population does come up again to the level of these capabilities, will leave as many men to be clothed as well as fed, and willing to offer their services, or the price of them, for their wonted supply of the second, as well as the first necessary of life. But till the capital is repaired, the supply of cloth is short, and the profit of cloth-making is high; nor will it cease to be so, till the capital be fully built up again. Ere this is accomplished, the people are worse clothed, at the same expense, than they had used to be. This is the great hardship; but it is a temporary one. This is the way in which the loss has to be borne; but after the season of endurance is over, all the vestiges of the desolation are filled up, and no longer visible. The country emerges again into its old state, and recovers not merely the symptoms, but the stamina of a state as healthy and flourishing as before.

And there is a like analogy between population and capital, in respect of the waste which the former undergoes by disease. A prevalent physical distemper might seize upon households, and carry off many families. The consequent abundance of provisions will speedily bring forward other families in their room. A prevalent moral distemper, even that of ruinous extravagance, might seize upon merchants, and sweep away many of our capitals. The consequent abundance of profits will construct other capitals, and raise up other capitalists, with a rapidity like that of magic. We question not the individual distress that is caused by the death of relatives, and the downfal of fortunes in families. But we are reasoning on the public calamity which, it is feared, might ensue from these events, in virtue either of a deficient population, or a deficient capital. The individual distress is a dire and dreadful reality. The public calamity is a mere imagination. There takes place an almost immediate adjustment to neutralise it; after which, the country is as full of people, and as full of capital, as ever.

But population has its preventive, as well as its positive checks. Instead of disease carrying off families from the stage of existence, families may be prevented from ever entering on the stage, by the celibacy of our present generation. It is true,

that, if the celibacy were universal, the present
generation would not be replaced by a succeeding one; but it is also true, that, though very
many were to refrain from marriage, this would
just make room for others to have families, who
could not otherwise have been able to rear or to
dispose of them; and with a very large proportion of celibacy, the population of the country
may still be fully kept up to its means of subsistence.   And, in like manner, there might be capitals, which come into the hands of thoughtless
and extravagant men, who dissipate them in some
rapid whirl of extravagance; and so they are
never brought upon the field of business at all.
This will just permit a freer and more prosperous
operation to the capitals that are brought forward,
and ensure to them a safety and a profit which
they could not else have realised; so as that, at
any rate, a capital is upheld, commensurate to the
need which there is for it, or to the business
which it has to do.   It is true, that, should all
the owners of capitals either withdraw or withhold them from business, and choose to waste
them utterly, capital would wholly disappear.
Still it is also true, that capital does not suffer
in extent, though there are many spendthrifts;
just as the population does not suffer in extent,
though there are many old bachelors.

Neither in population, nor yet in capital, are
the preventive checks carried so far as to supersede
the positive.   It is because of the too frequent

and too early marriages, that the field of competition for labour, and for its wages, is overcrowded; that families jostle out each other; that so many are outcasts from well-paid employment; that disease is engendered among them by spare living, and thins the overpeopled land of its numbers, by the premature deaths of infancy and childhood. To the mere student of political science, it may wear the air and the boldness of a paradox, when we affirm of capital, that too little goes into the stock for immediate consumption, and too much is adventured upon the field of commerce—that the competition for business, and for its profits, is greatly overcrowded—that traders jostle out each other, and so many become outcasts from safe or gainful merchandise—that what disease does with the redundant population, bankruptcy does with the redundant capital of our land; relieving the overdone trade of its excess, and so reducing capital within those limits beyond which it cannot find any safe or profitable occupancy. This might appear wild and extravagant to a disciple of any of our reigning schools; and yet we describe nothing but the daily and familiar experience of practical men. Should the capital of a million suffice for the trade of Britain in the one article of pepper, and half a million more, at a loss for employment, and seeking about for a proper investiture, be adventurously thrust into the business by its side, it would be absorbed in losing speculations. And so of capital in all other trades. There is a limit beyond which, for the time being, it can find no return; just as there is a limit beyond which, for the time being, the population can find no subsistence. In both cases there is a check to further extension, and in neither case does the preventive check keep capital or population within their limits, but each presses upon them, and encounters the positive check by which the one is kept even with the food, and the other with the business of the world.

Legislators have now ceased from their alarm for the emigration of people. They have truly as little reason to be alarmed for the emigration of capital. To meet the first alarm, we may quote the authority of Dr. Smith, when he says, that man, after all, is the most sluggish, and the least transportable of all commodities; so that it will be only a few out of the many who will renounce home, and all its charms, for the perils of a distant and untried land. This is very true; but another security is, that although many were to go out from amongst us, their place would speedily. be filled up again by the elastic force of population. To meet the second alarm, we may quote the authority of Ricardo, who speaks of the heavy disadvantages to which the vast majority of traders will submit in their own country, ere they can be tempted to transfer their operations to another. This also is true; but there is a farther security in the elastic force of capital,—the effect of its withdrawment from any business upon the profits of that business—the certainty wherewith, under this principle, it will speedily regain its greatness, and be as commensurate as before to the work which it had to do; so that, if we have nothing to fear from the egress of our country's population, we have just as little to fear from the egress of its capital.

At first sight, we perceive not the error which is involved in the regret of those who would calculate on a much greater population in this our day, had there been no wars in the last or in former generations, or who think that the census of our numbers would have yielded a much larger return, had the vaccine inoculation been discovered earlier. This is quite a process of reflection, that many an economist of the last century would have gone along with. And still the economist of our present century will both feel and utter a kindred regret on the subject of capital, as if there would have been more of trading capital in the land at this moment, had it not been for the expenditure of so many wars, or the extravagance of so many spendthrifts. This is precisely the regret which Dr. Smith indulges in; and it is quite evident, that he could never have anticipated such a fulness of capital, along with such a weight of public debt, as are both verified so strikingly at present. It is evident from his work, that he occasionally had bright glimpses of the true theory of population; and that had he entered on a distinct prosecution of this subject, he would soon have perceived by how speedy an operation it was, that all its gaps were repaired. There is likewise a speedy operation for filling up the gaps or deficiencies that either public or private expense effects upon capital; and we have as little reason for believing that it would have been greater now, had it not been for the dissipation of so much treasure in our wars, as that the population would have been greater now had it not been for the loss of so many lives in battle, or for the ravages of the small-pox.

From the description which Dr. Smith has given of what we have ventured to term the great eco-nomic cycle, it will be seen how much the annual produce of the land and labour can do, even in the course of one revolution. It can replenish the circulating capital of the country, and it can keep in repair all its fixed capital; and, over and above this, it supplies the whole of the immediate con-sumption. If too much have been taken in any one year into the stock for immediate consump-tion, both an encroachment may have been made on the circulating capital, and the fixed capital may have fallen thereby into a certain state of disrepair; and, altogether, the trading capital of the nation will, in some of its branches, be less effective than usual; and some commodities will become scarcer and dearer than before. We have already experienced how this causes the annual produce of next year to vibrate back again from the stock of immediate consumption into capital, so as to restore it to its old amount and efficiency. The same produce, out of which, in one revolution, all that capital which circulates is replaced, and all that capital which is fixed is upholden, can surely in one, or at most in a very few revolutions more, make up the fraction by which, through the extravagance of any one year, both those capitals have in some degree been diminished. This is done by the action of a diminished capital upon profits, which restores the capital as surely as the population is restored from any diminution which it may have sustained, by the action of that diminution upon wages.

There is much of palpable history which can only be accounted for by this regenerating power of capital, and without which principle many things can only be wondered at without being understood. Even in the hands of Smith, the buoyancy of our nation, under the weight of the national debt, was an unresolved mystery; and there is much in the state of other nations, which even our most approved systems of political economy are too meagre in experimental truth thoroughly to account for. The confident imagination of Mr. Pitt, as to the impending ruin of France, because of her commerce being in a state of stagnation, and her capital wasting away, or languishing for the want of productive employment, was the natural error of a devotee of the mercantile school, from the lessons of which we never can gather the explanation of that strong

and youthful prosperity into which she so suddenly emerged. It belongs to the same class of
phenomena, that Russia and Austria, and the
other states of the continent, recruited so speedily
from the desolations that passed over them, and
that now, as healthy in their economic condition
as ever, there is not one trace to be found in them
of the footsteps of the destroyer. These facts are
still gazed at by the politician, as so many anoma-
lies; whereas they are but the confirmations of a
general law. For let the agriculture of a country,
that has just been delivered of its ruthless invad-
ers, yield its wonted quantity of subsistence, and
the high wages that are given to its surviving
labourers will speedily bring on the families which
shall replace .its population; and the high profits
that are given to its surviving traders shall. as
speedily replace its capital; and the country, indestructible as the phœnix, shall, in a few years,
rise again out of the ruins of its overthrow, · unto
all the freshness and glory of its proudest days.

So that capital, like population, is one of those
self-regulating interests, the care of which does
not properly belong to a legislature. The fear
lest it should depart from our kingdom by successive removals, is altogether chimerical. The very
first portion that went abroad, if only large enough
for the effect, would cause a larger profit at home,
which should act first by a detaining power on the
capital that was left behind, and then, by an extending power, again to fill up the vacancy. It is

not for government to concern itself about an interest which the laws of political economy have abundantly provided for. There may be a call upon its justice, when the rights of any one order of men are encroached upon by the aggression of another, but let not this be complicated with other objects, as on the occasion before us; nor let it imagine any call upon its wisdom or its authority for the protection of an economic interest, that is abundantly safe without its interference.

If, any where, a combination could force an indefinite addition to wages, we should regard that of the sailors in the Tyne, as, perhaps, one of the most formidable; not because of its effect on the shipping interest there, but because of its effect on the supply of coals in London. One might imagine the two parties, the sailors and shipmasters, to be most obstinately at a stand; and each resolved not to comply with the terms or propositions of the other. If the trade be, in consequence, suspended, the first effect is to raise the price of coals in London, and, perhaps, to lower the price at Newcastle. The tendency of this were to enhance the profits of a voyage, so as to enable, it may be, the ship-owner both to raise the wages of the seamen, and to have additional gain for himself. It is conceivable, however, that even this temptation of a mutual advantage might not prevail upon them to come to an agreement; in which case, we should have the spectacle prolonged, both of unemployed men, and of unemployed capital. We should like

that such an experiment were permitted to have
its full swing, for it would land, we think, in an
experience more tranquillizing far, than all the terror and authority of legislation.   In the first place,
the men could not stand out indefinitely.   Their
resources must waste rapidly away; nor could all
the devices of union and committeeship ward off
the starvation which must sooner or later compel
a surrender.   But the dread seems to be, lest the
capital should moulder away, or take flight in the
mean time.   It is very true that the vessels might
fall into disrepair; and the owners, from want of
their accustomed returns, might suffer them to deteriorate.   It is also true, that some of them might
abandon this scene of idleness, and go in quest of
employment, to other, and, perhaps, to foreign
places; thereby giving plausibility to the fears
which have been expressed, of capital being lost to
our land by emigration.   But then new forces
would come into action; and, it is more than probable, that the very first movement in this direction would be of avail to break the confederacy.
All the prospects of the men would be utterly reversed, and all their calculations frustrated, when,
instead of so many ships waiting for sailors, sailors
beheld the ships moving away from the trade, one
after another, and felt themselves to be irrecover-
ably losing them.   There would be a look to them
of disaster and menace in the change which they
saw to be approaching, when, instead of more
ships than there were sailors willing to man them,

there were palpably more and more of sailors every
week, than there were remaining ships for their
accommodation. There is nought but unfaulter-
ing perseverance requisite on the part of capitalists
to dislodge men from unreasonable terms. Would
they only brave the hazards and the consequences
as much as they might, there would be less, both
of trouble to the legislature, and of danger to the
peace of society. And, after the surrender is
made in this instance, what is there so very irremediable, in the disabled and somewhat diminished
shipping of the trade, after that the trade has
again been set agoing? Should there not, for a
time, be a sufficient apparatus for the transportation of coals to London, less of coal would be
transported, and a greater price would be given
for it, till repairs were completed, and additional
vessels were procured, and the shipping were made
as commensurate to its business as before. The
capital would, almost on the instant, be got up
again, at the expense, no doubt, of the families in
London, who, for a season, would have less of
fuel, and at a heavier cost, than they had been
used to. And even, without taking into account
the rush of capital from without, to repair the deficiencies that had been incurred upon the Tyne,
we can see, how, out of the energies of the trade
itself, there would be a quick re-ascent of capital,
up to the point of its full ability for the business
which it had to perform.

We are quite sensible that matters will never

proceed so far. We have now got upon an imaginary field; but just imaginary, because combinations are not so impregnable as to permit of the supposition that alarms our legislature ever being realized. Sailors will not hold out, till ships shall either be withdrawn, or taken down in the despair of employment. Or, in other words, the process by which it is apprehended that capital and its attendant commerce are to take leave of our island, so far from taking effect to any extent, will not even be so much as entered upon. But it should complete our security, that the very beginning of such a process would prove the decisive blow which should annihilate the confederacy that caused it; and that on the trade being set up again, it would, on its own resources, make up, in a few months, all the capital which had been wasted, or removed from it. For ourselves, we do not even anticipate the commencement of the process; and though we did anticipate, we should not fear it—believing, as we do, that in its ulterior consequences, it would prove innocent of all harm to the economic welfare of our nation. These consequences, indeed, are so far ulterior, as not to have been distinctly perceived; and in virtue of the spectral dimness and magnitude wherewith they are accordingly invested, they have power to mislead the judgment, by disturbing the imagination.

Long indeed ere it come to this, in the case that we have now selected for illustration, there would certain other forces come into play, and by which the whole embarrassment might speedily be terminated. A suspension of the trade between Newcastle and London, would cause, and that almost instantly, an enormous rise in the price of coals; and, out of this, encouragement could be afforded to ships and sailors from a distance; and against this attempted monopoly in the Tyne, a force of competition could be brought from all parts of the kingdom, and nothing could prevent it but a confederacy extending over all the ports, and including all seamen; and even were such a confederacy possible, foreign vessels, and manned by foreigners, could be hired. This is the vulnerable place at which to aim, and through which it will be easy to bring down the combination. And we are aware that this also is the place where the outstanding workmen, skilled in the whole tactics and management of such a war, put forth their fiercest resistance. The violence, and the outrage, and the intimidation, are chiefly directed against the new hands that are brought to occupy the place which they have left; and could these be kept down, the victory over combinations is secured. This, then, is the great object towards which the force and the wisdom of legislation should be directed. We do not see the obvious justice of the enactment that would make simple combination amongst the labourers, who choose not to work, unlawful. But there is a justice, the most obvious and unquestionable, in the enactment, that would make every encroachment on the freedom of those labourers who are willing to work unlawful. Let such then be the enactment, and the only enactment; but armed, if necessary, with penalties greatly more formidable than any which our legislature has yet ventured upon. The whole sense and feeling of the community would bear out our rulers, when they came forward in this attitude—not as the oppressors of workmen, but as the protectors of the most needy and helpless of them all—the protectors, in truth, of the weak against the strong, of the less powerful among the labourers against the terror and tyranny of a most odious monopoly on the part of the more powerful. This is the right place for the application of law; and were law just strong enough and vigilant enough in its application here, there would just be as little need for the revival of the old common, as for the revival of the old statute law, against combinations, simply and in themselves. Our preference would certainly have been, that the common law against combinations had not been revived; but that a new and still more efficient law had been enacted for the punishment of all offences against the liberty of individual workmen. One does not altogether see the equity of a restraint upon the mere act of combination; but one immediately sees the equity of a restraint upon all sorts of violence. We believe that, upon the strength of the latter restraint alone, the triumph over all unrighteous combinations would soon have been practically carried. This we deem to be the more excellent way. By admitting a doubtful principle into any department of our public administration, we admit into it an element of weakness. On the other hand, nothing can resist the authority, all whose enactments are at one with conscience and natural morality, and when law quadrates with that sense of justice which is in every bosom. A law against all intimidation and violence, though fortified by the strongest sanctions, and most rigidly enforced in every instance of infringement, would have just been such a law. We are quite confident that, by its own single strength, it could achieve the victory over all that is really hurtful and unfair in combinations. The country never can be tranquillized under the operation of a law, although in power it is absolute, if in principle it is ambiguous. But a sure and lasting tranquillity will be the result, when the law in the statute-book, is at one with the law of the heart; and so, when, with whatever terrors it may be guarded, or with whatever severities it may be upheld, it carries the public sentiment irresistibly along with it.

We therefore persist in thinking, that all injurious combinations would have been more effectually gotten the better of, had the authority of the common law against combinations, merely as such, not been revived; and instead of making that to be an indictable offence, which does not very clearly offend against any principle of right or of equity, had the whole force of law been directed to the

one object of defending the freedom of individual
workmen, against the injustice of those popular corporations, which, because they are popular, are not
therefore the less flagrantly deformed by all that
is odious and tyrannical in the corporation spirit.
In this way the new act might have breathed but
one expression, the expression of friendship to the
unprotected, and to the unprotected among workmen, too. It would then have been in complete
harmony with the spirit of the former ones. The
object of the first was to set up, in behalf of labourers, a defensive stay against the alleged oppression of their masters. The object of the second
would have been to set up, in behalf of labourers,
a defensive stay against the actual oppression of
their own fellows in society. If the first was at all
necessary for the freedom of the working classes,
the second is indispensable for the completion of it.
To have this liberty fully made out and secured
for them, there must be a liberty to work for any,
as well as a liberty not to work at all. The one
liberty is that which masters might be tempted to
violate, and it is right, therefore, that it should
have a safeguard provided for it. The other liberty is that which fellow-servants might be tempted
to violate, and it is equally right that it should
have a safeguard provided for it. We are quite
satisfied, that the one liberty would fully neutralize
any mischief that might be dreaded from the other.
If, in consequence of all being at liberty not to
work, the artizans of any establishment should

strike their tools, and bring its industry to a stand, then, in consequence of all being also at liberty to work, a door would be opened for the competition of the whole population, and this industry be again most surely and speedily set agoing. The distinct business of law should be, to keep that door open, and the access to it safe, whether for young apprentices, or for workmen from all other places of the land. Let but competition be secure, and there is not one injurious combination that would not in time be defeated by it: and its members, in having exiled themselves to the condition of unprovided outcasts, would be sorely punished for the extravagant and unreasonable demands which they had made. Better this natural punishment, than punishment under an arbitrary law, whose principle, at best, was doubtful, and could be but dimly apprehended. Better than all the correctives of an artificial jurisprudence, are the correctives of the free and equitable system itself; and over which government presides not as the partizan of one class of society in opposition to another, but as the parent that abjured all favouritism, and stood forth the equal protector of all its families.

The intimidation of new or strange workmen by others, who, either by wealth, or by numbers, are more powerful than themselves, is not to be borne with; and no expense, whether of agency, or treasure, should be spared to put it down. We should rather that half the British navy were put into requisition, to ensure the manning of our mer-

chant vessels by the sailors who would, than that
any obstruction should remain impracticable, which
may have been thrown in their way by the sailors
who would not.　At a hundredth part, we believe,
of this, exertion, all that is needed or is desirable
in this way could be accomplished.　But still,
while the fermentation lasts, and ere that full experience, so tranquillizing to workmen themselves, is
not yet completed, it should be the distinct object
of our nation's policy, and of our nation's police, to
protect the independence of all persecuted workmen.　And, for such an object, whatever strength-
ening of the nation's police was requisite, we are
sure that the voice of the nation would go most
thoroughly along with it.　Connected with a purpose like this, a strong executive would be hailed
by all the true patriots of our land; employed as
it would be, not in fastening the chains of a universal oppression, but in unlocking these chains,
and so acting as the guarantee and the guardian of
a universal liberty.　It seems an axiom in the
rights of men, that none shall be forced to work
who is unwilling.　But it is surely an axiom as indisputable, that all shall be suffered to work who
are willing.　The line of equity between them, is,
on the one hand, to permit the combination, and,
on the other, to protect all who do not belong to
them, from the terror and the tyranny of combinations.　So long as they are not permitted, the
popular mind will continue to fester under a sense
of provocation, that will have much of the sem-

blance, and somewhat, perhaps, of the reality of justice in it. And this will be further influenced by the imaginary virtue which they will still ascribe to an expedient not yet fully tried, and from which they will conceive themselves debarred by the hand of arbitrary power. But, with the permission to them, and the protection to all others, not one shadow of complaint will be left to them. They will have leave to try their own boasted expedient, and it will be a pacific experience, both to the country and themselves: for sooner far than our fears will allow us to think, they will make full proof of its impotency. We feel persuaded, that, in a few months, this feverishness would subside, and at length give way to the sound and the settled conviction, that, after all, by the turbulence of their politics and associated plans, nothing is to be gained. And so we should look for a tranquillity more solid than our land has ever yet enjoyed, as the precious fruit of that temperate, yet firm legislation, which can at once be tolerant of combinations, yet most sternly intolerant of crimes.

CHAPTER XXIII.

ON THE EFFECT WHICH THE HIGH PRICE OF LABOUR IN A COUNTRY HAS UPON ITS FOREIGN TRADE.

THERE can be no doubt of that impartial spirit which so honourably signalizes the rulers of our country; and in virtue of which, they have the unquestionable inclination to deal fairly and equally with all. We do not think that the most enthusiastic friends of the lower orders can reproach our government with an undue bias to the other classes of society; or if ever, in arbitrating between them, there is a seeming preference of masters to servants, that they have been led to it, either by a partiality of affection towards the rich, or by any lordly indifference to the rights and interests of the poor. There is a principle of even-handed justice which runs throughout nearly all the public administrations of our land; and when at any time bewildered from this rectilinear path, it is, generally speaking, not a favouritism towards one order of the community, but a false imagination of what is best for the interests of all the orders, that leads them astray. In other words, theirs is an honest, though at times a mistaken legislation; and to this nought has contributed more than a dim-sighted political economy, a science through the opacities of which, when Parliament does attempt to flounder, it is all most purely and uprightly for the best. It is truly a cheering contemplation, to behold the effect of that light which is now breaking upon them ; and how, under its guidance, they are fast purifying our jurisprudence from the errors and the many crudities of former generations. But it will take a time ere the emancipation is completed. And meanwhile, we think, that there are certain economic dogmata, which do sway our politicians against the cause and interest of the working classes, and which dispose them to look adversely and fearfully to that higher status, towards which a virtuous and intelligent peasantry must at length make their way.

This proceeds from the association, in their minds, between a rise in the price of British labour, and a proportional fall in the extent and prosperity of British commerce. It will bring down, it is thought, our ascendancy in foreign markets; and the introduction of this new element, like the problem of the three bodies in physics, has thickened the perplexities of the whole speculation. Its general effect is, to give a hostile feeling towards a more liberal remuneration for the industry of workmen at home, lest this should proceed so far as to limit, and perhaps destroy, our merchandise abroad, and so bereave our nation of the gains of that merchandise. It is thus conceived, that the avenues may be closed of that trade which binds us to the surrounding world, and by which the whole world, it is thought, becomes tributary to the wealth and importance of our Empire. The price of labour forms one main ingredient of the price of every commodity which labour is wrought up into. Should this price then become too high at home, the price of its produce may become too high for being disposed of abroad. The article that wont to be exported, and which could be bought at such a rate here as to be sold again with advantage there, can no longer be made the subject of this profitable transaction. In other words, because of the high wages, the trade upon which they were earned comes to a cessation; and, as the fruit of our attempt to elevate the status of labourers by means of a higher recompense for their work, the fear is, that foreign trade, in the occupations of which so many of our capitalists reap their incomes, and so many of our labourers reap their livelihoods, may be wholly swept away.

The whole of our policy for centuries has been directed to the object of enabling merchants to export as cheaply as possible, so that they may undersell the competitors of all other nations, and thus obtain possession of the foreign markets. For this purpose, if taxes were imposed on any article when brought into the country, they were generally taken off, in whole or in part, when sent out of it again; or, the tax that was laid on the commodity manufactured by ourselves, and intended for consumption at home, was remitted when carried forth to be made the subject of a bargain abroad ; or every device was employed to furnish the industry of our own people with the raw material on the easiest terms, by giving every encouragement to its importation, and burdening its exportation with the heaviest duties. But when, instead of the exportation of raw material, it came to the exportation of produce that had been wrought out of it, then, in place of duties being imposed, bounties were given. And all, that the merchant might be enabled to effect a sale in foreign parts, with advantage to himself at least, and so involving, it was supposed, the utmost advantage to the country at large. Now, the whole of this policy would be traversed by the high price of British labour, affecting, as it would, the rate at which its products could be sold, just as a tax would on the high price of the raw material. It is thus that many apprehend, as the result of greater wages, the ruin of many branches of our foreign trade, and the consequent ruin of all those manufactures which this trade kept agoing. This were enough, with many a shrewd and secular politician, to condemn, as an idle romance, the whole speculation of a higher-conditioned peasantry. Their imagination is, that it would bereave us of our commerce. They could tolerate a larger payment for the services of our workmen, if it only subjected the other classes of society at home to a higher price for all manufactured commodities. This would just have the effect of admitting labourers into a more equal share of the enjoyments of life with the holders of capital and the proprietors of land. To this no objection would be felt by many who might foresee an insuperable objection in another quarter. We cannot, beyond a certain extent, subject the people abroad to this higher price for our manufactured commodities. They might find them cheaper elsewhere, and we should lose our customers. The trade, with all its beneficial ramifications, might thus be destroyed. And the feeling is, that what might else have been desirable, even a more liberal recompense for the industry of our workmen, must be deprecated and guarded against to the uttermost, when thus blended in their apprehension with the overthrow, or, at least, the derangement of a great national interest.

To meet this imagination, it may be observed, in the first place, that although our export manufacturers find their market abroad, and fetch their prices from customers there, yet, it does not necessarily follow that the wealth of these foreign purchasers is the primary fountain out of which either their own profit, or the maintenance of their workmen has flowed. The process, in the greater number of instances, is thus. The produce of our home industry is sent to some country abroad; as, for example, our hardware and haberdashery to Portugal. By this trade there are so many debtors constituted in Portugal, to so many creditors in Britain. On the other hand, there is a trade by which foreign produce is imported into our country, as of wine from Portugal, for the use of consumers at home. By this trade there are constituted so many debtors in Britain, to so many creditors in Portugal. The two trades are carried on by wholly distinct individuals, who, throughout the whole of their respective operations, may have no right, and take no cognizance of each other. The export manufacturers of Britain appear only to do with their Portuguese customers; and to these good customers they may ascribe both their own prosperity, and the livelihood of a numerous dependent population. And, conversely, the wine growers of Portugal may look only towards the British customers, with the same feeling of dependence upon their payments, and of dread lest, by any chance, trade, wherewith they link so much of their revenue, should be interrupted or put an end to. The exporters of each country look to the other, as that out of which their prosperity emanates; and the imagination is not peculiar to them, that if the channels of interchange were in any way obstructed, a large portion of the integral wealth of each would thereby disappear—even a portion, at the least competent to, and therefore commensurate with the profits of all the capitalists engaged in these trades, and the wages of all the workmen.

Now, this is a very natural, and certainly the general conception of men unpractised in economic speculation. And we are not even sure, if there be much in our most esteemed economic theories that is fitted to rectify it. It does not, however, require a very piercing or profound sight into the arcana of the subject, to prove, that however great might be the alarm of individuals concerned in this trade, did it come to a termination, there is really nothing in this event that should alarm a patriot or a statesman, either for the strength or the safety of our nation. For let us only notice how it is that the British creditors of Portugal are paid. There might be a direct remittance from the debtors in Portugal; but this is not the way of it, any more than there is a direct remittance from the consumers of wine in Britain to the growers of it in Portugal. The matter is adjusted in this way. The debtors to Portugal in Britain, are made over to the creditors of Portugal in Britain by bills of exchange. By a similar device, the debtors to Britain in Portugal are made over to the creditors of Britain in Portugal. It is thus that our export manufacturers are virtually brought into contact with the inland consumers of this country. Their orders come to them from customers abroad, but their payments come to them from consumers at home. They apparently are working in the service of those who wear British cloth, and make use of British hardware in Portugal; but effectively, they are working in the service of those who drink the wine, and eat the oranges, and use the dye-stuffs of Portugal, in Britain. The imports from Portugal are paid by exports to Portugal; and they of Britain who work up, or furnish the exports, obtain their return from them of Britain who use the imports. This is the real character of the transaction between the two countries. That part of our British population, who are engaged, whether by manufactures or by commerce, in this export trade, might have had the same maintenance from the hand of British consumers, in the direct employment of minister-ing to their enjoyment, by serving them with arti-cles of home manufacture. But the consumers happen to have a preference for certain foreign articles, and so the former are sent out in exchange for the latter; and there is the substitution of so much foreign for so much home trade. Still, it is virtually in the service of inland consumers, that these export manufacturers are employed; not in preparing the commodities which they use, but in preparing that which purchases the com-modities they use; and, in return for this service, they obtain their full maintenance, not out of a ful-ness that is in Portugal, but out of a fulness that is in the fountain-heads of their own land.

It would not be difficult to estimate the precise advantage of such a foreign trade as we are now imagining. Let the value exported in hardware be just equal to the value imported in wine, and a trade, consisting of these two processes, does not add to the population of the country, for there is no subsistence imported by it. It does not fetch a maintenance to the people who work up hardware for exportation. All that it fetches is wine, in consideration of which, a maintenance is given to these people by those who drink it, out of home resources, and home granaries. But still this foreign trade does something. It supplies the inland consumers with an article which they like, better than any other which they could procure in its place. It is altogether a mistake, that it supplies our export manufacturers with their livelihood. This is dealt out to them by the consumers of wine, and might have been dealt out to them with equal liberality, in return for any article of home industry, had there been no foreign trade, or no wine imported by it. But the foreign trade has in this instance presented another article which the consumers choose in preference, and for which they afford as good, but not a better maintenance, to as great, but not a greater population. All that this foreign trade has done, is to bring in wine to a set of home consumers, who, but for the foreign trade, would have had to be satisfied with something else. It has substituted for them one enjoyment in place of another. Their taste is better suited, in consequence, than it otherwise would have been, and this is certainly an advantage. But there is nothing more; for every thing beside which stands connected with the wine trade, is just as it would have been, although there had been no such trade. There would have been the same amount of industry, but directed to another object. There would have been the same population, but engaged in another service. There would have been the same maintenance for that population. The ability which can now uphold so many export manufacturers, who work up hardware, and get wine in return for it, lies with the purchasers of that wine at home; and should this foreign trade be destroyed, the ability is still in reserve to uphold the discarded manufacturers, equally well, in another employment. They suffer a temporary inconvenience from the change, and certain inland consumers would suffer a permanent inconvenience. But we contend that it forms the whole, and the only inconvenience which can be sustained by the destruction of this foreign trade —even that the affluent of our land are bereft of one gratification, and forced to take up with another, and to them an inferior gratification, in its room.

Could politicians be led to entertain and to adopt this view of foreign trade, they would cease to associate with its continuance, as they have hitherto done, the very existence, or, at least, the power and prosperity of our nation. But it is just with the foreign, as we have already stated it to be with the home trade. In measuring the value of each, they look to the *terminus ad quem* of neither, but merely to the processes of operation. They prize the mere working of the mechanism, more than they do its workmanship; and in reference to the goods of merchandise, are far more refreshed by the spectacle of their being made, and sorted,

and sent forth, and shipped, and conveyed, than
by the spectacle of that gratification which they
yield at their final landing-place. The good, according to their estimation, does not appear to lie
in the use of the commodities, but in the preparation of them—not in the object which set the
industry agoing, but in the bustle, and extent,
and spirit, and glowing activities of the industry
itself. The delusion is, that this industry is not
only the creator of its own produce, but is also
the creator of its own maintenance. Now, it must
be accredited only with one of these things, for it
is in no way entitled to the credit of them both.
In such a case of foreign trade as we have supposed, the maintenance lay stored with the consumers of the imported article; and in return for
it, went forth among the families of the export
manufacturers. Were the trade annihilated, the
maintenance would still find its way among the
same number of people, in return for a different
service. The whole amount of the mischief would
lie in the exchange of a better article of consumption, for a worse; or, rather, of a better liked
article for a worse. Now, the apprehension is,
that a far more tragical consequence than this
would ensue from the annihilation of our trade
with Portugal—that the operatives in this trade
would cease to work, and therefore to live; and not
merely that the customers in this trade would
cease to drink wine, or to eat oranges. The whole
regret would be, that it put a stop to the wonted

production, and not that it put a stop to the
wonted consumption; and could it only be seen
that all those who were engaged in the production,
might be turned to the service of producing something else, and be as well maintained in that service
as before, every political alarm, at least, would be
tranquillized. The change which had taken place
in the consumption, might affect the feelings of
private families, but would never call forth the
fears of our statesmen. Their big imagination of
the West India interest, would be mightily brought
down, did they perceive the whole mischief that
should ensue from its destruction, to be only of
this description, that our tea would no longer be
sweetened as it had been heretofore; or of the
East India interest, that, on its disappearance from
the land, tea itself should forthwith disappear from
our breakfast tables: or of any other trading interest whatever, that all the good of its presence
to the nation, lay in the article which it furnished,
and that all the loss of its absence, or its ruin, lay
in the loss of that gratification which was yielded
to consumers in the use of that article. The practical likelihood is, that as the ability which now
sustains all these interests, would, upon their overthrow, sustain interests of equal extent in some
other quarter, other countries abroad would be
repaired to in quest of the very same produce, so
as to uphold an equal foreign trade, and to secure
the same articles of enjoyment as before. But
even in the failure of all these resources, and though

forced by some strong political necessity to abandon the whole of our external commerce, and fall
back upon ourselves, we should only lose by this
the produce of foreign parts, and get, in its room,
the produce of that industry of our own people,
which took the direction before of export trade
and export manufactures; and they, in this new
direction of their labour, would be met by the very
wages and the very profit which they had formerly. There would neither be loss of population nor
loss of industry in consequence. But it would be
industry restricted to home products; and we cannot deny, that, in virtue of the restriction, there
would be less of enjoyment. This would undoubtedly be a loss, and the whole loss. But
other losses of a far more tremendous character
than that of enjoyment, float before the imagination
of our rulers, and lead them to associate with all
these mercantile interests, a might and a magnificence which do not really belong to them.

It is not the loss of the wine, but the loss of the
wine trade, that would so disturb our mercantile
politicians, on the cessation of all intercourse with
Portugal. But could they be made to see, that
there is really nothing in the cessation of this intercourse which can deprive us of the maintenance
we before had for our export manufacturers, and
that so, no other loss but that of the wine would
follow upon the loss of the wine trade,—then the
charm of our foreign commerce, and by which
they have been led so to exaggerate its importance,

might at length be dissipated. They would never once dream of a decay of national strength, because of the mere negation of the wine of Portugal. Neither would they dream of a decay of national strength, in the mere negation of the oranges of Portugal. It would be curious however to observe, whether they might not in all probability demur, should they be told that there is just as little danger to our national prosperity or strength, in the negation of the dye-stuffs of Portugal. This were fitted to revive the old impression of the worth of our manufactures,—an impression founded not on the value of their products, but on a value, *per se*, in their mere processes. When oranges are mentioned, this suggests the idea of mere subserviency to a consumption that might be dispensed with, and the price of it reserved for an equally large return to the export manufacturers in some other service. But when dye-stuffs are mentioned, the first and readiest suggestion is, that of their subserviency to the business of our dye-works, to the employment of producers, and not to the gratification of consumers. The illusion is prolonged by an act of mental transference from one branch of industry to another; and ere it can be dispersed, there must be another transference of our thoughts, from the work of those who put on the colours, to the enjoyment of those who are arrayed in them; and who, in paying for the enjoyment, prove that it is with these the customers, and not with those the actors of the trade, that the maintenance lies of all its dependent families. If it do not contribute to the strength or greatness of a nation, that so many of it shall drink wine or eat oranges, as little surely does it contribute to any public interest, that they should be arrayed in grey, or green, or yellow, or have any foreign tincture whatever put upon the habiliments which they wear. Yet this, in the present instance, is the whole power of our boasted commerce to aliment and uphold our nation; however inveterate the delusion may be by which it is regarded throughout all its branches, not as a handmaid to the gratifications of those who have a maintenance to bestow on others beside themselves, but as the creator of that maintenance, as the sovereign dispenser of their subsistence, and of their very being, to the families of the land.

It will probably be long ere the principle which we labour to establish, shall be fully acquiesced in; even that all which a trade furnishes to mankind is its own commodity; and that when we describe the use or the gratification of this commodity to the purchaser, we describe the whole advantage of the trade. The sugar trade emanates nothing but sugar; and the tobacco trade nothing but tobacco; and the spice trade nothing but spices. Each emanates its own article, and nothing more. It is not the emanating fountain of a maintenance to those who are engaged in it. It only draws this maintenance from a fountain-head anterior to itself, and distinct from itself. It does not even pay a tax to government. It is the price given by the consumer which achieves all, and comprehends all. The trade does nought but supply him with its own produce. The other blessings of which it is conceived to be prolific, are all due to the customer. It is he who gives both to government and to capitalists, all the revenue which they derive from the trade; and it is he who gives their subsistence to its labourers.

Were the true functions of trade precisely understood, and its importance reduced to its real and proper dimensions, it would be felt that the strength and stability even of so great a commercial nation as ours, do not rest on a basis so precarious as is commonly apprehended. It is no doubt very natural, that the people of our great manufacturing towns, should feel as if their very existence depended on the foreign countries which afforded a market to their respective commodities; that, with the American market, and the colonial market, and the other distant markets of the world, there should stand associated in their imagination, both the profits of all their trade, and the subsistence of those numerous workmen who are engaged in it; and that thus, as villages grew up to the magnitude of cities, and suburbs took from one year to another a wider circuit than before, it should be conceived that foreign trade was the instrument of all these accessions to the wealth and population of our empire. They are working for the supply of their immediate customers abroad, and are not conscious that they may, in fact, have been working all the while in the service of consumers at home ; that, when exporting muslins to the West Indies, or hard-ware to Portugal, they were, in effect, bringing home the sugar of the one country, and the wine or oranges of the other ; and that, in return for these, they drew a revenue and a maintenance from the people of their own land. It may, after all, have been the improvement of the country that surrounds them, that has given extension to our towns. Their population may have increased, just because the aliment that subsists them has increased ; and the proprietors of this aliment, now richer than before, can indulge to a greater extent in foreign luxuries than before, and so maintain a greater number of export manufacturers in the service of preparing the articles which go forth in the purchase and in exchange for these luxuries. And so, though an impassable barrier were raised between us and all foreign countries, there might remain as great a population and only a change in their employments ; the same amount of industry, and only a change in the distribution of it.

A few more explanations will complete all that we shall advance, at present, on the subject of this chapter.

For the sake of simplicity, we had conceived that the price of the wine imported from Portugal was just equal to that of the hardware exported from this country. But it is not because wine is imported here, that hardware is exported there. The people here have a taste for their wine; the people there have use for our hardware: and these two circumstances are distinct from and independent of each other. Portugal might come to stand in no need of any hardware from us, and still the squires of Britain might have such a taste for the wine of Portugal, as willingly to persist in their wonted sacrifice to obtain it. If a third country, as France, should attain to the manufacture of hardware of as good a quality and at as cheap a rate, they might dispossess our export trade from the market of Portugal. We should be undersold, and the effect would be, that while imports passed from Portugal into Britain, no exports, of British manufacture at least, would pass in return for them from Britain into Portugal.

There is one way in which this matter could be adjusted. The landed proprietors of Britain would not now support a population of export manufacturers at home, whose employment it was to work up hardware for the payment of the wine that comes from Portugal. But still resolved upon having the wine, they might, rather than want it, export directly of the produce of their estates, for the purchase of a luxury so agreeable to them. And this is just the arrangement that takes place in every country which cannot work manufactures cheap enough to pay for their imports. They pay for it by the exportation of rude produce. This would be the undoubted effect, if there were a general underselling of the British by other nations, in all foreign countries. Britain would become an exporting country; that is, would export grain in return for the products of foreign lands. That population which, in other circumstances, we could have maintained at home, would be maintained abroad. Our landed proprietors might have a command, as before, of foreign luxuries. With a produce over and above the maintenance of their own households, they could make something of it abroad, if they found no more agreeable use for it at home. If determined upon wine from Portugal, they could, by means of this spare produce, fetch it to their doors. But then we should lose our whole population of export manufacturers; and there would be the access thereby of an equal population to other countries. The manufacturers for home consumpt, might still cluster in towns as before; but then these towns should be abridged of export manufacturers; and in proportion as this underselling of Britain took place in foreign markets, in that proportion might Britain fall back towards the limits of her agrarian population.

But it is not the underselling of Britain in one, or even in several countries, which will necessarily produce this effect. Her hardware, for example, and indeed all her other manufactures, might be wholly driven from the market in Portugal, and she continue to import as much wine as before

from that country, without having a single quarter
of agricultural produce to export in return for it.
We have supposed her undersold in Portugal by
France. Let us imagine a million sterling worth
of wine imported from Portugal to Britain; and
that France now supplies the former country with
that million sterling worth of hardware, which Britain had before given in exchange for her wine.
Still it is conceivable, that though Britain is not
able to cope with France in hardware, she is more
than able to cope with her in muslin; and that
France herself is supplied from this country with a
million worth sterling of that commodity. By this
simple export of muslin, might Britain save herself from the export of grain, or of any thing else,
to Portugal. She can, in fact, pay the wine imported from Portugal, by the muslin exported to
France. She has now, it is true, no debtors in
Portugal, whom she can direct, as before, by her
bills, to make the payments due to her creditors in
Portugal. But she has debtors in France; and
these she can make over to her creditors in Portugal. By this device, which it is here unnecessary to explain with any minuteness, the receivers
of British muslin in France could pay what they
owe for it to the exporters of French hardware to
Portugal; and these hardware exporters, having
obtained their payment in this way, can leave their
debtors in Portugal to settle with the creditors of
Britain there, from whom this country received
their wine. It is thus that the wine from Portu-

gal is paid by sending out muslin to France; and it is thus that, by the indirect or circuitous route of bills of exchange, the imports from one country may be paid for, not by the exports either of produce or of manufactures to that country, but wholly by the exportation of manufactured goods to other countries.

It is thus that Britain can afford to have larger imports from particular countries, than she can pay for by the export manufactures which she gets disposed of in these countries; and that, without being reduced to the necessity of exporting agricultural produce. To save her from this necessity, it is enough that the value of her export manufactures, on the whole, is equal to the value of her imports on the whole; for then, she pays for these imports, without having to export any rude produce in return for them. In other words, she keeps all her means of subsistence to herself, and with it feeds a population at home, who by their industry provide her with all the foreign commodities that she obtains. Had it been otherwise—had she, from any cause whatever, been put to such heavy expense in the working up of her export articles, as to be undersold by competitors in foreign markets, then, if she still persisted in the use of foreign commodities, she behoved to send forth agricultural produce in return for them; and so to feed a population abroad, which she now feeds at home. Such is the precise effect of being undersold in foreign markets; an effect, however, which is not realized by our being undersold in some markets, and not in others. If we can but secure as many markets as will take off a value of manufactured goods from us, equal to that of all our imports from all places, then we shall not need to export agricultural produce for the payment of these imports. If those markets do not take off so great a value as that of all our imports, then we shall have to export agricultural produce in payment of the difference. If, on the other hand, they take off a greater value than that of all our imports, the difference is shifted to the other side, and it has to be made up by the importation of agricultural produce.

It is thus that, while the country which is undersold to a certain extent in foreign countries, becomes an exporter, the country which undersells to a certain extent becomes an importer of agricultural produce. Let any country, as Britain, be at that point of neutrality, where her export manufactures just so balanced the foreign commodities imported by her, that she had neither to export nor to import food. Then observe the effect of some sudden cheapening that took place in her working up of these export manufactures, whether by a fall in the price of labour or of raw material, by the invention of machinery, by the discovery of coal, or by any other advantage of her situation for preparing articles of commerce at an easier rate than in neighbouring countries. Let the average reduction in the expense of preparing commodities for foreign markets be twenty per cent. This, in the first instance, would add twenty per cent. to the profit of the export capitalist; and in the second instance, allure more of capital from other employments to a trade so advantageous; and, in the third, raise the profit in these other employments also, now drained to a certain extent of their capital; and, in the fourth, create among capitalists a desire to extend their trades now more profitable than before, and so a competition among them all for labourers. The effect at home would be to raise wages, and so, eventually, to increase our population by the encouragement given to earlier and more frequent marriages. It is true, that all the while we have not supposed any process going on for an addition to the food, along with this addition to the population of the country. And certainly there is nothing among the earlier steps of the process which we have now described, that should lead at once to an enlargement of the home supply of food, by any stimulus which they are fitted to give to the agriculture of our own land. On the contrary, this rise of wages should rather, in the first instance, contract our agriculture. So far from enabling the husbandman to bring more land into cultivation, it should make the cultivation of the last land taken in, or that which can barely afford a profit, and no rent, cease to be profitable. But although there is no process going on at home for the increase of food, along with the tendency which there now is, from the rise of wages, to an increase of population, there is such a process going on abroad. The export manufactures, at first twenty per cent. more profitable, are, by the rush of additional capital into the trade, wrought off in greater abundance than before. They are carried abroad in larger quantities. They become cheaper in all the foreign markets to which they previously had access. Nay, they can afford the expense of being transported to more distant markets. They can bear, perhaps, a land carriage to remote and inland districts, into which they had never penetrated before. The British merchants there supplant and undersell traders with whom they had not before come into competition. And thus, by the command of so many more outlets, and the possession of so many more markets, there may now be a much greater value of British goods sent abroad, than at the time when food did not form one of those imports by which the exports were paid. It is true, that the now additional exports could still be paid for by additional imports, not consisting of food— if we could suppose that the additional profit now made by our manufacturers, and the additional wages now given to our labourers, were all expended upon foreign luxuries—or, in other words, that no sooner did the means of purchasing a certain style and amount of enjoyment come into their possession, than they instantly fixed upon this higher standard of enjoyment, and expended accordingly. This is not likely. Capitalists, instead of spending all their augmented . profits, would, for the pleasure of accumulation, extend their business the more, and so add to the manufactured products for exportation. Workmen, instead of spending all their augmented wages, so as to marry as late as before, would, for the pleasure of a domestic life, marry, on the average, somewhat sooner, and with greater frequency, and so add to the population of the land. This increase of population would increase the price of food, would make it bear the expense of being transported from distant countries, would, in fact, call for the additional import of food wherewith to balance the additional exports that were now sent forth, in consequence of their being more cheaply manufactured than before. Thus it is, that those facilities or advantages for industry, which enable one nation to bring manufactured commodities cheaper to market than its neighbours, may at length cause that nation to be an importer of food; and so land it in an excess of population beyond what it can maintain out of its own agricultural produce—a superinduced population, dependent on foreign supplies for subsistence, and so forming an excrescence upon that natural population, which can be fed and sustained from the natural resources of their own land.

There is a limit, however, to this excess of population; and that, in virtue of causes which act so speedily and powerfully, as, in most instances, to prevent its going very far beyond the extent of the natural population. Ere we arrive at this, we do not need to wait till the world is saturated with British manufactures; for, long before the completion of such an object, these manufactures must, in spite of all our peculiar advantages, be at length wrought at such an expense, that the world will, after being supplied with them to a certain yearly extent, cease to look after them. It does not follow, although manufacturers, at the outset of the process which we have now imagined, could afford their commodities at 20 per cent. cheaper than before, they will be able to afford it long. In the train of consequences that flow out of such a state, there is a rise in the price of food, and, connected with this, a rise in the price of labour. The very fact of grain being imported to help out the subsistence of a nation, implies a dearer subsistence in that nation than in others. Two grains of the same quality do not fetch two prices when brought to market; and so the home and foreign grain will be equally dear. In other words, the population at home are fed at a greater expense than the population abroad; at an expense greater by the price of the carriage of grain from foreign countries. This will so far countervail the original advantages wherewith the British manufacturer set out, and by which he was enabled to undersell the manufacturers of other nations by more than 20 per cent. He might not now be able to undersell them by more than 10 per cent., and

that in the more accessible markets. The more
remote markets, which the original superiority of
twenty per cent. could have found him access to,
might now, with this reduction, be shut against
him. He might have been able to carry his
goods with advantage to remote and inland districts, had he retained his original superiority; but
not with this superiority impaired by the rise of
provisions, and consequently of wages, at home.
This supplies a limit to the demand for British
manufactures; and, what gives a surer necessity
to the limit, it should be recollected, that, in
proportion as we extend our supplies of grain
from abroad, it must be brought home at a heavier
expense to us. We must fetch it from more distant or dearer countries than at the first; or that
country, whose coast, or the side of whose navi-
gable rivers, could satisfy our moderate demand,
might, when that demand increased, have to draw
the produce from its upland districts, and so expose us to a great addition of expense for carriage. It is out of these two causes,—first, from
the expense attendant on the carriage of British
manufactures; and that an expense constantly increasing in their progress towards the more inaccessible parts of the world,—and, secondly, and
chiefly, from the expense attendant on the carriage of agricultural produce to Britain; and this
too, an expense constantly increasing, in proportion as we extend our demand, and have to draw
for it from more inaccessible parts than before;—

it is from the operation of these two causes, that a certain limit is formed, beyond which, the exportation of British manufactures can no longer proceed with advantage to the capitalist. He finds that, even with all his original advantages, there are countries so impracticable, that he could not introduce his goods amongst them, but at an expense which would subject him to be undersold. But he farther finds, that these original advantages are counterpoised by the now higher price of subsistence, and so the now higher price of labour. There is thus a point of equilibrium between the natural advantages of a country for the industry of its people, and the high price at which a people, when these advantages have accumulated beyond the extent of their natural population, are consequently maintained,—a point beyond which a greater amount of manufactures will not be exported, and a greater amount of agricultural produce will not be imported,—the point, in fact, at which the accretion ceases of families subsisted from abroad, and when the country labours under all that weight of superinduced population which it can bear.

There is perhaps no country in the world, where the industry of man is made so effective, both by natural and political advantages, as Britain. Its unbounded supply of coal, its machinery, its extent of coast, its roads and inland navigation, enable it, beyond most other nations, to bring its manufactured goods cheaply into market. It was therefore to be expected, that it should be a country which imports grain, and it does so accordingly. It would have been interesting to notice, how far all these advantages carried its population beyond their natural limit, or at what point it would have ceased to import agricultural produce. From this we are in a certain measure precluded, by the operation of our corn laws. It is only under a system of free importation, that we could have known how far a country, with our peculiar advantages, would have extended its population beyond their natural limits. We do not think, that even with full scope and encouragement, and the removal of all prohibitions, the excess would have proceeded beyond a small fraction of the natural population, and neither do we think it desirable that it should. In years of scarcity, when all the restrictions on importation are taken off, the greatest annual importation ever known, amounted to about one-tenth of the whole consumption of the island; and the actual importation, on the average of several years previous to 1800, only supplied eleven days consumption, or one thirty-third of the whole. It would, we have no doubt, be greater than this, were the corn trade thrown completely open; our export manufacturers, on the one hand, being enabled thereby to work off their goods at a cheaper rate, from the somewhat reduced price of corn, and so to obtain a more extended possession of the markets abroad; and foreign countries, on the other, finding it cheaper, in consequence of our signal

helps and facilities for all sorts of industry, to purchase our manufactures, though wrought by a
population whom they feed at a distance, than if
they were wrought by a population whom they
feed at their own door. This, however, from the
causes already explained, would have its limit;
nor do we think it either likely or desirable, that
this exterior limit should go very greatly beyond
that of the natural population.

When there is not enough of imports to pay for
the exports, the exchange is in favour of the exporting country. But that state of exchange
which is in favour of a country, is against its export manufacturers; and may at length be so
much against them, that the trade shall cease to
yield a remunerating profit. This affords another
view of the limit, beyond which they cannot carry
their operations. Did they continue to export
more, even though with as little expense at home,
and as great a price abroad, yet to realize that
price, it must come to them through the medium
of an exchange, which their own augmented transactions have made more unfavourable to themselves. It is quite evident that a free corn trade
would enlarge this limit. It would add to the
value of our imports, by allowing a free admission
to this import commodity. The exchange would
not be so much in favour of the country, and less
against the export manufacturers than before;
and they might work up commodities, and send
them forth to a greater extent, ere they touched

that limit where the exchange became so unfavourable, that the profit of the trade yielded a bare remuneration for the capital invested in it.

Ricardo, in his chapter on foreign trade, states with truth, although not with sufficient explicitness, that the improvement of a manufacture in any country tends to increase the quantity of commodities, at the same time that it raises general prices in the country, where the improvement takes place. He here makes an important correction, on a position of Dr. Smith's, when, by a conclusive, but greatly too concise process of reasoning for general readers, he establishes the rise that takes place in the general money prices of a country, when the commodities of some one or more manufactures can, by the abridgment of labour, be wrought up at less expense than before. This effect must be farther aggravated by our corn laws, seeing that export commodities, which might have been paid by corn, will, in defect of a sufficient value of other imports, have to be paid for by gold and silver. Hence a still larger accumulation of the precious metals in our country, and an increase beyond what would otherwise have place in the money price of all its commodities. Were corn permitted a free entry from foreign parts, this accumulation would be reduced, and a general cheapening of all things would be the consequence. The produce of British industry would become cheaper than it is now; and there is no doubt that the abolition of our corn laws would give an im-

pulse and an extension to our export manufactures. We should, after this abolition, have a
larger importation of agricultural produce than we
have at present, and, corresponding to this, a larger
excess of superinduced over our natural population.

Now, the undoubted effect of lower wages at
home, were to increase our exports, and so to enlarge this superinduced population. It would just
land us in a greater number of people, over and
above those who are subsisted by our own agricultural produce. It would stretch the population,
by a certain degree, beyond the limits of the natural population, and land us in some fractional
excess of families, for whose maintenance we
should have to depend on supplies from abroad.
The good of this, to say the least of it, is very ambiguous. It might be deemed by some an accession to our empire; but certainly it is not such an
accession as would be afforded by an enlargement
of our borders, by such a circumambient belt of
territory reclaimed from the sea, as should feed
the whole of these additional inhabitants. There
would accrue thereby an additional population to
the country; but, in computing the additional
wealth, you would only have the wages of so many
more labourers, and the profits of so many more
capitalists, without the rent of so many more landlords. This last ingredient only belongs to that
wealth which is connected with the natural population; for the surplus population may be said to

labour in the service of landlords in other countries, whose rent or revenue it is that forms the
main, if not the only fund, out of which the public expenses of a state are defrayed. When to this
is added the precariousness to which a nation is
exposed, when thus dependent for food upon distant countries, it will be felt to be not a clearly
desirable thing that her commerce should be very
greatly extended beyond the basis of her own agriculture, or that, having much of subsistence to
import from abroad, there should be a much larger
population residing within her borders than can be
fed from the produce of her soil.

And the particular views of many statesmen are
in full coincidence with these doctrines of theory.
Our corn laws, at least, indicate that the extension of our people beyond the produce of our own
land, had not been felt by them as an object of
very urgent importance. The taxes which still
continue on the several necessaries of life form
another obstacle to this extension, as serving to
raise the price of British labour, and so to lessen
the power of British merchants to undersell the
merchants of other countries. In both these ways,
the tendency to a surplus population in Britain
has been considerably restrained; and yet, notwithstanding, a certain surplus population has
been actually formed. Even with the corn laws,
then, and with our present taxes on various of the
secondary accommodations of life, a higher wage
could be afforded to our labourers; and on the

abolition of these laws and taxes, a much higher wage could be afforded ere the natural population would be trenched upon, or ere we should become the exporters of agricultural produce. In other words, there is no country whose clear and substantial interests would be less endangered by a high standard of enjoyment among our workmen, and a consequent high remuneration for their work, than those of Britain. Such are her natural advantages, that even with a great comparative dearness of labour, she could maintain that superiority, or rather that equality in foreign markets, which is really all that is desirable. So that without, let or hinderance from any apprehension in this quarter, she may give herself indefinitely up to the pure and patriotic task, of raising the condition, by raising the character of her peasantry.

We are abundantly sensible, that the argument of this chapter is altogether superfluous to those, who, with Ricardo and his followers, maintain the doctrine, that profits fall just to the extent that wages rise. It were out of place, to offer here any estimate of this doctrine; nor is it necessary for any present or practical object of ours, seeing that the economists of this school can have no such alarm, as it is the purpose of our foregoing observations to dissipate. They, on the contrary, must regard the high price of British labour as forming, not a prohibition, but a passport for British commodities into foreign markets. The truth is, that, according to this view, any rise in the ele-

ment of labour must be more than compensated
from the element of a reduced profit; for this last
will tell, on each successive transfer of the commodity from one dealer to another; so that, on the
last sale which it undergoes in the market, it will
turn out to be all the cheaper for the work of preparing it having become dearer than before. We
repeat, that we do not now mean to appreciate this
doctrine; but hold it satisfactory, that the disciples
of a fashionable and rising school must be all on
the generous side in the question of wages. In
their apprehension, a liberal remuneration for the
work of British hands must extend the sale of British manufactures. We can scarcely persuade ourselves of such a result; and we count it enough of
vindication for the cause, that, with a far more liberal remuneration than labourers at present enjoy, there might still be such an export of manufactures as would save the exportation of food,
and so maintain the entireness of our natural population.

CHAPTER XXIV.

ON MECHANIC SCHOOLS, AND ON POLITICAL ECONOMY AS A BRANCH OF POPULAR EDUCATION.

THE mechanic schools which are now spreading so widely and so rapidly over the face of our land, must be regarded as a mighty contribution to those other causes, which are all working together for the elevation of the popular mind. But it should not be forgotten, that the scientific education which they provide for *those who choose it*, forms only one of these causes, and that ere we can prevail upon all, or even upon the majority in the working classes of society so to choose, there must have been anterior causes, both of a preparatory and of a pervading nature, in previous operation. We can scarcely expect any demand for a higher scholarship from those who have not been furnished, in some tolerable degree, with elementary learning; and we might farther affirm, with all safety, that the most willing attendants on the ministrations of a Sabbath, are also the most willing attendants on the ministrations of a week-day instructor. However little it may have been reflected upon, it is not the less true, that there obtains a very close affinity between a taste for science, and a taste for sacredness. They are both of them refined abstractions from the grossness of the familiar and ordinary world; and the mind which relishes either has achieved a certain victory of the spiritual or the intellectual, over the animal part of our nature. The two resemble in this, that they make man a more reflective and a less sensual being, than before; and, altogether, impress a higher cast of respectability on all his habits, and on all his ways. It does occasionally happen, that, on entering the house of a mechanic, the eye is pleased with the agreeable spectacle of a well-stored book-case. It is generally the unfailing index of a well-conditioned family; and this, whether it be loaded with the puritanic theology of our forefathers, or with the popular science of the present day. Now, we are sure that this never can, from an occasional, become a common or a frequent exhibition, but by a process through which our peasantry must ascend to a higher style of outward comfort, as well as to a higher state of mental cultivation. We, therefore, hail the scientific education of the people, as being a most powerful auxiliary towards a translation so desirable; and we are sure, on the other hand, that the cause of mechanic schools will be most powerfully aided, by a greater efficiency being given, both to the methods of common and of Christian education, in parishes. How this can best be accomplished in cities of overgrown population, we have already, with all amplitude, endeavoured to explain; and we barely refer to former chapters of this work, for our description of those processes, by which we conceive that the lessons both of religion and of ordinary scholarship, may most effectually be served out to plebeian families.*

We have also, in part, to make the same reference, that a complete view may be afforded of the estimate in which we hold the salutary operation of mechanic schools, on the circumstances of our general population.† We have already made application to this subject of the very obvious truth, that a process of political economy may take effect upon men, who do not understand the steps or *rationale* of the process. It is not necessary, for example, that the philosophy of Malthus should be studied by our common people, ere they shall come under the operation of that moral and preventive check, through which we are taught, by his philosophy, that labourers might attain to a greater comfort and sufficiency than they are now in the possession of. It is not necessary, for this purpose, to read lectures, or to circulate tracts among them, which shall expound the theory of population, in order that they may realize the benefits which would ensue from a right practical application of this theory. The same object is accomplished by the ordinary and general pro-

---

* See more particularly the 4th Chapter in the First Volume of this work, and a pamphlet which I had occasion to publish some years ago, entitled, " Considerations on the System of Parochial Schools in Scotland, and on the advantages of establishing them in large towns."

† See the first chapter of this work.

cesses, whether of spiritual or of scholastic culture. A lettered and religious population will exemplify the truth of this system, though ignorant of all its doctrines, and therefore totally unacted upon by its authority. Such people have, generally speaking, a self-respect and a self-command —a taste for decent accommodations—a habit of enjoyment, and, therefore, a habit of expense, which demands a higher wage than what can afford the mere homely subsistence of an Irish family. And we have already explained how it is that the demand becomes effective—just by the habit of later and less frequent marriages—a habit to which, without the bidding of any theory, they are naturally led by their own sense of what that is, which makes the adequate and the respectable provision for a distinct family establishment. This stands very palpably out, in the custom, at one time nearly universal, of our Scottish peasantry, when, after the virtuous attachment had been formed, and the matrimonial promises had been exchanged, even years of delay were incurred, ere the matrimonial state was entered upon. These years formed an interval of economy and exertion with each of the parties, whose aim it was to provide respectably in furniture, and in all sorts of *plenishing*, for their future household. Here the connection is quite distinct, between a higher standard of enjoyment, and a later period of marriages. And it was certainly then by another tuition than that of any

economic theory, that a habit in every way so
wholesome found its establishment among our
population. And the exposition of such a theory
to the understanding of the people, is just as
little needed now, for the purpose either of re-
storing or of raising this practical habit amongst
them. The thing is brought about, not by means
of imparting a skill or an intelligence in political economy, but simply by those influences
which give a higher tone to the character; and
of which influences, education may certainly be
regarded as one of the most powerful.

It is thus that mechanics' schools, even though
the lessons of economic science should for ever
be excluded from them, are fitted to work the
greatest of economic improvements in the condition of the people. It is enough that they call
forth the aspirations of that higher nature, which
has so long been overborne by the urgency of
their animal wants, and the unchastened violence
of their mere animal propensities. Political, it is
true, may, like physical science, be addressed to
them as an object of liberal curiosity, and simply
by the excitement and the exercise which it gives
to the mental faculties, it may sublimate the whole
man to a more intellectual region than the one he
usually breathes in. But either astronomy or
chemistry could subserve the same end; and
therefore we repeat, that, though in deference to
a general, but ill-founded alarm, the education of
workmen in political economy should be kept out

of these schools, another education can be devised which shall be fully as effectual for the accomplishment of the most desirable processes in political economy. They might be made to exemplify the principles in which they are not enlightened; and, without being taught the bearing which a higher taste and style of enjoyment have upon the circumstances of our peasantry, they can be led to imbibe this taste, and so to realize all its eventual benefits. For this purpose, it is not one, but many kinds of scholarship, that are effectual. Whatever may stimulate the powers of the understanding; or may regale the appetite for speculation, by even that glimmering and imperfect light which is made to play, in a mechanic school, among the mysteries of nature; or may unveil, though but partially, the great characteristics of wisdom and goodness that lie so profusely scattered over the face of visible things; or may both exalt and give a wider compass to the imagination; or may awaken a sense that before was dormant, to the beauties of the divine workmanship, and to the charms of that argument, or of that eloquence, by which they are expounded;—each, and all of these, might be pressed into the service of forming to ourselves a loftier population. Every hour that a workman can reclaim from the mere drudgeries of bone and muscle, will send him back to his workshop and his home a more erect and high-minded individual than before. With his growing affinity to the upper classes of life in mental cultivation, there will spring up an affinity of taste and habit, and a growing desire of enlargement from those various necessities by which the condition of a labourer may now be straitened and degraded. There will be an aspiration after greater things; and the more that he is fitted by education for intercourse with his superiors in rank, the more will he be assimilated to them in a taste for the comforts and the decencies of life. In the very converse that he holds with the lecturer, who one day expounds to him the truths of science, and another day examines and takes account of his proficiency, there is a charm that not only helps to conciliate him to better society, but that also familiarizes him in some measure to the tone of it. This might only proceed a certain way; and yet, however little that way is, it must be obvious, that such a man will not so aptly, or so heedlessly, rush into marriage with no other prospect before him than a potatoe diet for his constant regimen, and one closely huddled apartment for his home. Now, this is all that we want, to relieve the labour-market of the glut which oppresses it, and so to secure a higher wage for our labourers. Towards this result, the mechanic schools lend a most important contribution; and they will speed a most desirable process in political economy, even though they should never initiate so much as one disciple into the principles of the science.

Still, however, we hold it desirable that this

science should be admitted, with others, into our schemes of popular education; and that for the purpose of averting the very mischief which many have dreaded, and which they apprehend still from the introduction of it. To this they have been led, by the very title of our science giving rise to a fancied alliance in their mind with politics; and, in virtue of which, they would liken a lecturer upon this subject, in a school of arts, to a demagogue in the midst of his radical auditory. Now the truth is, that the economical science which enables its disciples to assign the causes of wealth, is as distinct from politics, as is the arithmetical science which enables its disciples to compute the amount of it; and there is just as much reason to fear an approaching democracy, because the people are now taught to calculate prices, as there will be when people are taught soundly to estimate and to reason upon the fluctuation of prices. We do not happen to participate in the alarm even of those who should, above all things, deprecate, from our mechanic institutions, what might strictly and properly be termed the science of politics, believing, as we do, that all truth is innocent, and that the greatest safety lies in its widest circulation. But we confess a more especial affection for the truths and the doctrines of political economy; and, so far from dreading, do greatly desiderate the introduction of its lessons into all those seminaries which have been instituted for the behoof of our common people. It is ut-

terly a mistake that it cannot be taught there,
without the hazard of exciting a dangerous fermentation. Instead of this, we are not aware of a
likelier instrument than a judicious course of economical doctrine, for tranquillizing the popular
mind, and removing from it all those delusions
which are the main causes of popular disaffection
and discontent. We are fully persuaded, that the
understanding of the leading principles of economical science, is attainable by the great body of
the people; and that when actually attained, it
will prove not a stimulant, but a sedative to all
sorts of turbulence and disorder; more particularly that it will soften, and at length do away
those unhappy and malignant prejudices which
alienate, from each other, the various orders of
the community, and spread abroad this salutary
conviction, that neither government, nor the higher
classes of the state, have any share in those economical distresses to which every trading and manufacturing nation is exposed; but that, in fact, the
high road to the secure and permanent prosperity
of labourers, is through the medium of their own
sobriety, and intelligence, and virtue.

But, in confirmation of this our sentiment, we
must go somewhat into detail; and, in so doing,
shall have to describe the rapid sketch of what we
deem to be a right course of popular economics.

It, in the first place, can be made abundantly
obvious to the general understanding, that the
price of an article has a certain and necessary de-

pendence on the two elements of demand and supply; and so, on the one hand, that the buyers can promote their interest of lessening its price, by lessening their demand; and that the sellers can promote their interest of raising its price, by lessening the supply. The principle is too elementary to be dwelt upon here at any length, yet, nevertheless, might, with its many instances and illustrations, be made the subject of a most pleasing and popular lecture; and might, when once in thorough possession of the mechanic scholars, be subsequently turned into the instrument of many precious applications. It might be made, in fact, to neutralize, or to sweep away the most inflammatory of those topics wherewith the radical orator seeks to irritate the passions, and to enlist upon his side, the violence of the multitude—that multitude, of whom it has been well said by Talleyrand, that we have nothing to fear, if we but treat them with frankness; and over whom, so soon as we carry their reason and their sense of justice along with us, we are sure to gain a resistless ascendancy.

On the strength of this single doctrine, it will not be difficult to convince them, first, that in the scarcity of any article, when the supply is small, they are not properly the sellers, but the buyers who make the price. It is the competition of those who are in want of the commodity, and fear that they cannot get enough—it is this which is the efficient cause of its dearness. In the higglings of a market, it is often the seller who names the price, and hence the popular imagination that he makes it. But substantially the juster view of the case is, that the buyer offers the price. The dealer, in fact, would have sold it at a lower price to one customer, had not another customer, more urgent than he, been willing to give a higher price for it, rather than want it altogether. The odium of the high price is cast upon the merchant, whereas, at each given state of the supply, it may be regarded as wholly the creation of the purchasers. He no doubt takes the highest price that he can get; but this is only saying that he takes the highest price which any buyer is willing to give, rather than suffer the inconvenience of wanting it. In other words, it goes to him who is most eager to obtain it; and, had it gone to another, or which is the same thing, had it sold at a rate beneath that market price to which it would be brought by the free and natural competition, it would have been an act of favouritism to one, but at the expense to another, of a sorer and heavier disappointment. The vender, in closing with the highest prices for his article, just sends it to those places where there is the most intense feeling of its necessity. The interest of the dealer is at one with the interest of the public; for, in taking the highest offer, he is just sending his commodity to the quarter where it is most needed and desired. It is thus that the streams of commerce are made to flow towards the places of greatest vacancy; and any violence by which this process is thwarted, for the relief of suffering and destitution in one place, must be at the expense, in another place, of a suffering still more intense, of a destitution still more grievous.

It is by a train of simple argumentations like these, that Smith's great lessons upon the corn trade might be still further extended and brought home to the popular understanding. They are all of them eminently fitted to allay the passion and prejudice of the working classes. They are not the farmers, or the middlemen, who make the high prices in a year of scarcity. They are the purchasers, each intent upon his own share, and each labouring to outbid his fellows. This may not be ostensibly, but it can be easily demonstrated, even to the satisfaction of the most plebeian student, that this is virtually the process. It is not the growers, or carriers of the corn, who fix its price. They are the consumers of the corn: and to force the sale of it at a lower price than that at which the free operation of the market would settle it, is just to wrest the food of our land from those whose necessity is most urgent, and shift its direction to those whose necessity is less so. There cannot be a doubt that there would be more of acrimony and bad blood excited by such a restraining policy, than when the trade is left to its own spontaneousness. This surely is a lesson fitted to pacify, and not to exasperate. To expound a doctrine like this, is not to scatter mischief among the people. It would act, in truth, as an emollient upon their

feelings. And whether it be the reasoning and reflective process, which, in a mechanic school, they
might be made to undergo, or this conclusion of
a sound political economy to which it carried them,
there is not only wisdom, but the meekness of wisdom in them both.

But a still more important application of the
elementary doctrine on the subject of prices, is,
that when instead of a scarcity, there is the over-
abundance of any article, the low price to which
it falls, may be regarded more properly as the
deed of the sellers, than that of the buyers. All
the keenness of the competition, is transferred, in
such a state of the market, from the latter to the
former. The anxiety is now on the side, not
of the customers to obtain goods, but of the
traders to dispose of them. For this purpose,
each tries to undersell his neighbour; and as in
the first process, we saw that they were the consumers who made the ascent from one step to
another, in the lifting up of price, so in the second
process, we see that they are the venders who
make the descent in the letting of it down. In a
season of dearness, you cannot blame the merchant for taking the highest price which men will
consent to give ; and if blame in the matter attaches
to any, it must be to the other party who offers
it. In a season of cheapness, you cannot blame
the purchaser for taking the article at the lowest
terms on which he finds the seller willing to part
with it. It is not his doing, but the doing of him

who holds the commodity. It is thus that we cannot carry the pupils of this science, a very little way into the interior mechanism of trade, without reversing to their eye the first aspects of things; and we are persuaded, that in these very first, and in all their future advances in this philosophy, it will be found, at every step which is correctly taken, that the alliance is most intimate between the spread of philosophy in a nation, and the stability of its peace.

The exemplification of this last doctrine, in which the attendants of a mechanic school have the greatest interest, is that which regards the price of labour. It is not a tangible commodity, but liable to the same laws of variation in price, with every other commodity which is brought to market, or which can be made in any way the subject of a bargain. It is exposed to the fluctuations of a greater or a less demand, and it might be furnished at a greater or less rate of supply. The labourers of our land are the sellers of this article; and it is virtually they who fix and determine the price of it. The buyers are those who employ them; and they are not to blame because of the miserable price which they give for labour, for this is the price at which the other party have offered it. The true cause, at any time, of a depression in the wages, or the price of labour, is not that masters have resolutely determined to give no more, but that servants have agreed to take so little. The infuriated operatives, instead of looking to capitalists as the cause of their distress, should look at one another. They would have greatly more reason, at a time of well-paid labour, to look to capitalists as the cause of their high wages, than to look to them as the cause of their low wages, at a time of ill-paid labour. In the one season, it is the overbidding of each other for labour, by the masters, which is the efficient cause of its high price. In the other season, it is the underselling of each other, by the labourers, which is the efficient cause of its low price. Whatever be the external complexion, this is the substantial character of these transactions; and this might easily be made to appear to the disciples of a popular economic course, among the foremost revelations of the science. It is a science, through the arcana of which, the ordinary attendants on a school of arts are abundantly capable of being led, and we should confidently look for patience, and peace, and charity, as the practical fruits of it.

A master may require one additional workman, but may have no use whatever for two. Two, however, may offer themselves, whereof the first is willing to serve him for two shillings a-day, and the second, rather than be without employment, would thankfully agree for one shilling and six-pence. It is not the master's fault that he has hired in a labourer at this lower wage. It is the doing of the labourer himself, and not his doing. He would, in fact, have inflicted a sorer disappointment, by accepting the proposal of the first, and rejecting that of the second, than by closing as he has done, with the inferior offer. He would, at least, have withheld the employment from him who stood most urgently in need of it. He would have refused admittance to the man who, by the very terms of his proposal, made demonstration before him of the most abject necessity. There is odium cast upon the masters, in every season of depressed wages; but the truth is, that, did they reverse their proceedings, and acquiesce in the higher demand, while they rejected the lower offer, they might inflict a suffering still more grievous, and perhaps incur an odium still more implacable. It is felt as all the greater hardship, when one man's solicitation for work has been declined by the master, though upon more favourable terms, while another, upon terms less favourable for the master, has been preferred before him. It is not, in fact, the hard-hearted tyranny of masters which has brought down the wages of workmen. It is the imploring cry of the most helpless among themselves, craving a participation with their fellows, and offering to be satisfied with a smaller share, rather than be outcasts altogether. The lowness of the wage is, in fact, all resolvable into the excess of their own numbers. And, in every season of ill-paid work, the true character of the transaction between masters and workmen, is not that masters refuse to give a greater wage, but that workmen consent to take a less one.

There could, after this, be explained the cause

of those periodic depressions which take place in the wages of manufacturing labour, and the way of averting it—even, as we have already stated, by an accumulated capital in the hands of workmen. And, even although the economical lecturer could point out no remedy for this state of things, there would be a salutary and pacific influence in his demonstration of the causes which produced it. It is well when workmen are convinced, that the low price of labour is not what they at first sight imagine, the doing of their proud oppressors; but the fruit of a necessity over which masters have no control. If wages were at the fiat of their employers, why are they ever permitted to rise at all, and often to treble at one time their amount at another? But these tides of fluctuation, at one time adverse, and at another favourable for one or other of the parties, are set agoing by different forces altogether from the arbitrary will of capitalists; and it must serve to disarm the hostility of the humbler, for the higher classes, when they are made to understand that the ebbs and flows of a labourer's prosperity, depend upon the laws of a mechanism, for which their masters are as little responsible, as they are for the laws of the planetary system.

But what should make an acquaintance with political economy so valuable to the working classes, is, that a remedy can be pointed out. The low price of labour is as much the doing of the labourers themselves, as the low price of a commodity is the doing of the dealers, who, in the case of an excessive supply, undersell each other. Their only relief is in the limitation of the supply; and there is positively no other permanent or effectual relief for the low wages of labour. All that combination can effect in this way, is but partial and temporary; and it is only by a lessening of the proportion between the number of labourers, and the demand for labour, that the working classes will ever find themselves on a stable and secure vantage-ground. They have no command over the second term of this proportion. They cannot increase the demand for labour. But they have a full command over the first. They can restrain the supply of labourers. A general conviction of this amongst our work-people would go far to tranquillize them. It would wean them, at least, from all vain and hopeless experiments. Even though they should despair of any immediate result from that expedient which is alone effectual; yet it is well for them to know that it is the only expedient, and that there is no other. It may at least keep them from idly or mischievously rambling in pursuit of other expedients; and, far better corrective to that general restlessness of our mechanics and labourers, which of late has so alarmed us, than the force either of our statute or common law against combinations, would be the spread of an enlightened conviction among them of their total inefficacy.

But though no immediate effect on the wages of labour could accrue from any change in the habit of labourers, yet the effect would be far

speedier than is generally counted upon. And
this were one of the most important lessons that
could be urged or expounded among the disciples
of a mechanic school. It were not at all difficult
to manifest to their understandings, that a very
slight excess in the number of labourers, creates
a very great reduction in the price of labour;
and so conversely, that it may only require the lopping away of a very small excess to elevate, from a
state of very sunken debasement, the condition of
an overpeopled land. It would serve to remove
from their minds the despair of any quick or great
amelioration; when made to perceive on how minute a difference in the number of labourers, there
turns a most momentous difference in the remuneration which is given to them. And if, in any
manufacture, as in that of weaving for example,
there should be a small overplus of hands, and so
a great depression of wages, it is not by the instant and forcible exclusion of this overplus that
the relief is arrived at. It may be obtained by a
more quiet and gradual, but withal a very speedy
operation. Simply, let the egress at the one end,
of individuals from the general body of weavers,
by old age or death, not be so fully replaced as
heretofore by the ingress of apprentices or new
hands at the other. Let there be somewhat of a
slackening in the annual supply; and this, in a
few years, will lighten the competition for work,
by at least some small yet sensible fraction of the
sum total of operatives; a fraction which, though
minute in itself, would be mighty in its conse-

quences, and would tell with effect on the general circumstances of the whole body. This were the treatment by which the workmen, however low they may have fallen in any branch of trade, might be restored to a state of sufficiency and respect; and there is no other treatment by which we ever can accomplish any great or general ascent in the circumstances of a whole population. It is not by a sudden excision of the overplus that relief is arrived at. Even though a single year of emigration should take off the whole redundancy, a very slight increase of the births would speedily fill up again the room which had been left; and a land will always be peopled up to the degree at which its inhabitants hold existence to be tolerable. It were better that they aimed at something higher and more dignified than a barely tolerable existence; and so, that the population were kept considerably within the limits of its utmost possible extension. But this can only be done by the taste and habits of the people themselves; by a rise in their standard of enjoyment; by a consequent shifting forward in the average period of their marriages, and so a lighter progeny wherewith to burden and oppress the coming generation. And to accomplish a desirable change, so very great a stride, as some may apprehend, would not be indispensable, and far less any thing like a revolution in the customs of society. That very gradual refinement of soul, which might be achieved among the people by their now improving education; that small, though perhaps nearly insensible effect which this is calculated to have on the time of their entering upon families; and hence the almost imperceptibly fewer births that will take place in the country;—these are the sure, though simple means of that enlargement which we believe to be awaiting the peasantry of our land. A very small oscillation in the number of workmen, will produce a very great oscillation in their wages; and so when their translation is effected into a state of comfort and sufficiency which they have never yet experienced, this change, momentous as it is, will proceed in a way so gentle and so noiseless, that it may truly be said of it, " it cometh not with observation."

Now all this might be set forth with enough of clear and commanding evidence for the understandings of the common people. With all the incredulity which they feel about the philosophy of Malthus, they recognize the whole truth and application of it in particular trades; and when they combine, as they have often done, to limit and restrain the admission of apprentices into their own craft, they are just lending their testimony to the obnoxious theory of population. A smaller general population will supply fewer apprentices; and this favourite object of theirs, and which they have tried to effectuate by forcible exclusions, can be rightly arrived at in no other way, than by that which the philosophy of Malthus has expounded. And here may be exposed with effect, the odious and unjust character of many of their combinations—in that, by dictating the number of appren-

tices, they are acting in the unfair and illiberal
spirit of monopoly. They are quite vehement
against the alleged tyranny of masters; yet, in
this instance, they may well be charged with having become the tyrants and the oppressors themselves. They would enact corporation laws in
their own favour; and, under the pretext of obtaining security against the aggression of their
hostile employers, they would, in fact, by the restrictions which they propose upon the employment, commit an act of most glaring hostility
against the families of all other workmen save
their own. It is thus that each distinct trade
would form itself into its own little oligarchy;
and in no possible way could a system be devised
more fatal to real liberty, and more full of annoyance to the general population. We are confident, that a lecturer of any talent at all might,
upon this subject, carry the most crowded am-
phitheatre of plebeian scholars along with him.
He might, in the first instance, gain their compliance with the whole of Smith's argument on
the subject of free trade. He might enlist them
on the side of competition, and make them par-
take in his own indignation against the hatefulness
of monopoly. He might thus prepare his way
for entering upon the subject of combinations;
and, however fair or innocent he might allow
them to be in themselves, yet, on the strength of
such principles as he had just expounded, he
might feel himself on high vantage ground for
disarming them of all their evil, by denouncing

whatever is wrong or mischievous in their practices. All the terror, and outrage, and forcible exclusion, which they have at any time directed, whether against new apprentices or workmen— the enormity of these he could make quite palpable to the popular understanding; and would, I am persuaded, be borne along on the tide of popular sympathy, when, in the midst of his applauding hearers, he lifted, against dictation in all its forms, the honest remonstrances of justice and liberty; and advocated the general rights of the population, whether against the now exploded oppressions of the statute-book, or the still sorer oppression of upstart and recently organized bodies among themselves. It is not through bearing down the passions by the force of law, but through forming and enlightening the principles of the commonalty by the force of instruction, that the present fermentations are to be allayed. And we despair not of the day when the science of political economy, instead of being dreaded as the instrument of a dangerous excitation, will be found, like all other truth, to be of powerful efficiency in stilling the violence of the people.

On this branch of the subject, there is one invaluable result, that might be obtained from the demonstrations of a lecturer; and that is, a conviction, on the part of his hearers, that pauperism was in truth their worst enemy, though their enemy in disguise, and that it had a most depressing effect on the wages of labour, and the real comfort of the labourers.

After having discussed the causes which influence wages, the explanation of those causes which
influence profits, would lead to another, and a
most interesting branch of a popular course.
And here it must be obvious, how easy it were,
on the strength of a few plain and intelligible
simplicities, to infuse, even into the hearts of
workmen, a spirit of candour and of conciliation
towards their employers.   More particularly,
could they be made to apprehend, how impossible it is, in a state of freedom, for profits to subsist, during any length of time, at a higher rate
than they ought to do.   When profits are high,
capital accumulates; and when capital is accumulated, profits fall.   Again, when, in virtuè of
some accidental influence, profits are very unequal, so as to be unreasonably high in one trade,
there is, in a state of liberty, a rush of capital
from all other trades, so as to bring all down to a
general level.   In this increase of capital, and
competition of capitalists, labourers will at length
be made to perceive that their security lies; and
that, if they will only so far respect themselves,
as that their high standard of enjoyment shall
have the influence already explained, in restraining the increase of population, a high wage for
work will be the inevitable consequence; and
such a wage, as is alike independent, either of
illegal enactments, or of illegal combinations.   It
would have been greatly more satisfying to us,
had the legislature not felt it necessary to assume
even the semblance of hostility to the working

classes. Certain it is, that no real hostility is felt; and that, even if it were, it would be wholly ineffectual. It could not depress the wages of labour a single farthing beneath the rate at which it would have settled, in virtue of those economic laws over which the government of a country has no control. Even though it were death by the law, for one labourer so much as to talk of wages to another; and though a universal espionage were to make the law as operative as it is barbarous; yet this could not bear down the elevating power upon wages, which lies in an accumulating capital upon the one hand, when it meets, upon the other, with a population restrained within right limits, by the prudential and moral habits of the individuals who compose it. The law against combinations is a *telum imbelle*, if its object be to depress wages; and it is only desirable, that workmen should be so far enlightened as to perceive this. Then would they leave it to repose in its own inefficiency; and, instead of going forth to the battle, either against their rulers or their employers, they would learn, that the sure road to victory was, for each quietly to betake himself to the virtues and the frugalities of private life.

It is thus that, without any effort, certainly without any combined effort, and without even their looking for it, there may, purely by a change of general habit, on the part of our workmen, be a gradual, but sure elevation, in the price of their labour. Capitalists cannot, though

they would, long realize an extravagant profit at
the expense of wages. The same competition
among labourers which brings down wages, operates also among capitalists, to bring down profit.
What labourers have to do, is, to slacken the former competition, by keeping down the supply of
labourers, and leave the latter competition to operate. Let them but restrain the increase of population, and then make their harvest of the increase of capital. Masters, however willing, have
it not in their power to realize, for any time, an
excess of profits to the prejudice of the servants;
for excess of profit gives rise to the exuberance of
capital, and so to a keener competition for more
labourers. Other capitalists will plant themselves
in their neighbourhood, and, either by outbid-
ding, wrest from them their workmen, or force
them to give a higher wage than before. There
is no organization of labourers required to bring
about this result—nothing, in fact, but that higher
style of comfort and decency, which it is the
effect both of Christian and common education to
spread over the land. The foolish but impotent
outbreakings of the last year will end in no permanent result whatever. A busy process of moral
and mental culture, would, in a very few years,
tell, and permanently tell, on the condition of our
general peasantry. The market is overstocked
with capital. Let not the advantages of this to the
working classes be neutralized, by the market being
also overstocked with labour. Then, instead of
men seeking after masters, we shall have masters

seeking after men. Instead of workmen underselling their labour, we shall have capitalists over-bidding for it. For this blissful consummation, workmen do not need to step abroad and form themselves into grotesque committees, and frame laborious articles, and make their cunning inventions of sign and countersign. They will gain nothing by all this, so long as they suffer themselves to be oppressed by the weight of their own numbers. It is this, and not the tyranny of their masters, which oppresses them. Let them but relieve themselves of this, and they will carry their point without all that curious machinery of councils, and correspondence, and deputations, in which heretofore they have vainly imagined that their strength lay. They would not need, in fact, to call upon masters; for masters, overcharged with capital, and desirous of extending their works beyond the supply of workmen, would call upon them. Instead of turbulently meeting in the hall, or in the field, each might stay quietly at home, and at his own business; and the day of a coming enlargement to our labourers will not come one whit later, though they should leave the expedient of a combination for ever untried. There is no other way in which the tables can be turned between them and their masters; so that instead of workmen begging from capitalists for their employment, capitalists shall go a begging among workmen for their services. This we should rejoice in, as a consummation devoutly to be wished. It were a great economic revolution brought about

by the peaceful operation of moral instruments.
Labourers would share more equally with land-
holders and traders than before; insomuch, as
wages would bear a higher proportion, both to rent
and to profit. The social fabric would still have
its orders, and its gradations, and its blazing pinnacles. But it would present a more elevated basis. At least the ground floor would be higher,
while, in the augmented worth and respectability
of the people, it would have a far deeper and
surer foundation.

One great object of a wisely conducted economic school, whose presiding spirit would be that of
loyalty to the state, and love to the population,
were to labour well the proposition, that it is not
in the power of master manufacturers to realize,
for any length of time, any undue advantage over
their workmen. And here it might be well to expound the relation which there is between the profit of capital, and the interest of money, after which
the fall of interest might be alleged as affording
patent exhibition of the universal decline that has
taken place in profits. This would lead to some
other cause for any depression in the wages of
operatives, than the extravagant gains of their employers; and would enable even the homeliest of
the disciples to perceive, that they are deprived of
the advantage which they might have gotten from
the competition of a now greatly increased capital,
just because it was outdone by the stronger competition of a still more greatly increased population.
In other words, that it was an advantage of which

the population had deprived themselves. At all events, the capitalists are quite innocent. They cannot help themselves as the labourers can. It is well for the spread of peace and charity among the working classes, that they should be delivered from the false imagination that their masters are their oppressors. And it is further well for the spread among them of virtuous, and temperate, and elevated habits, that they should be thoroughly possessed with the true doctrine of wages; that they are themselves their own deadliest oppressors; and that, without the co-operation of their own moral endeavours, no benevolence on the part of the affluent, and no paternal kindness or care on the part of their rulers, can raise them from the degradation into which a reckless or unprincipled peasantry shall have fallen.

It is needless, at present, to inquire how much farther mechanics could be raised, in the scale of doctrine and information, on the subject of economical science. This would better be ascertained afterwards. But we are thoroughly persuaded, that the few elementary truths, along with their obvious and popular applications which we have now specified, could not only be received by the popular understanding, but would go far to dissipate all those crudities of imagination which excite the fiercest passions of the vulgar, and are, in fact, the chief elements of every popular effervescence. To make the multitude rational, we have only to treat them as if they were fit subjects for being discoursed with rationally. Now this, in reference to the great topics of misunderstanding between them and their employers, has scarcely ever yet been done; and the experiment remains to be made, of holding conference with the people on the great principles of that economic relation in which they stand to the other orders of society. We anticipate nothing from such a process, but a milder and a more manageable community; and feel confident, that the frankest explanations of the mechanic teacher would be received by his scholars in the spirit of kindness. He may be in no dread of the utmost explicitness, or lest those truths which bear severely either upon the sordidness or the violence of the people, should fall unwelcomely upon their ears. They will bear to be told both of the worthlessness of pauperism, and the gross injustice of those workmen who would infringe on the liberty of their fellows. Even those truths which go to vindicate their masters, and which look hardly or reproachfully upon the operatives, ought, in no way, to be withheld from them. We affirm, that reason will make any thing palatable to the lower orders; and, if only permitted to lift her voice in some cool place, as in the class-room of a school of arts, she will attain as firm authority over the popular mind, as she wields now within the walls of parliament. And political economy, the introduction of which into our popular courses has been so much deprecated, will be found to have pre-eminence over the other sciences, in acting as a sedative, and not as a stimulant to all sorts of turbulence and disorder. It will afford another example of the affinity which subsists between the cause of popular education, and that of public tranquillity. Of all the branches of that education, there is none which will contribute more to the quiescence of the multitude, than the one for whose admittance into our mechanic schools we are now pleading. They will learn from it, what be the difficulties by which the condition of the working classes is straitened, and how impossible it is to obtain enlargement therefrom, while they labour under a redundancy of numbers. It will at least help to appease their discontent, when given to understand, that with this redundancy, any solid or stable amelioration of their circumstances is impracticable; and that, without this redundancy, the amelioration would follow of itself, and that, to bring this about, the countenance of legislators, and the combination of labourers, were alike unnecessary. The lessons of such an institution would be all on the side of sobriety and good order. They would at length see, that for the sufficiency of their own state themselves were alone responsible, and after bidding adieu to all their restlessness, they would be finally shut up to that way of peace and of prudence, by which, and by no other, they can reach a secure independence.

FINIS.

Printed by W. Collins & Co
Glasgow.

CPSIA information can be obtained
at www.ICGtesting.com
Printed in the USA
LVOW12s0045040418

572228LV00001B/23/P